W9-BOK-413

DAVID FELLMAN
Vilas Professor of Political Science
University of Wisconsin
ADVISORY EDITOR TO DODD, MEAD & COMPANY

The Democratic Community

GOVERNMENTAL PRACTICES AND PURPOSES

The Democratic Community

GOVERNMENTAL PRACTICES AND PURPOSES

Robert Y. Fluno
WHITMAN COLLEGE

Dodd, Mead & Company
NEW YORK 1971 TORONTO

WITHDRAWN
Theodore Lownik Library
Illinois Benedictine College
Lisle, Illinois 60532

JC
423
.F67

Copyright © 1971 by Dodd, Mead & Company, Inc.
All rights reserved

No part of this book may be reproduced in any form
without permission in writing from the publisher
ISBN 0-396-06295-4
Library of Congress Catalog Card Number: 74-140060

Printed in the United States of America

EDITOR'S INTRODUCTION

THE world over, and throughout history, the concept of democracy has held a commanding position among the seminal political theories with which man has been concerned. Even the exponents and practitioners of the crudest sort of anti-democratic systems of thought and government have found it desirable to ape the language and forms of democracy. After all, the notion that government rests upon the consent of the governed is a powerful one which has a continuous history from the time of the ancient Greeks to our own day. But perhaps what is most significant about democracy, both as a system of government and as a body of political theory, is that it is not a simple, straight-forward concept which can be conveniently described in terms of a few simple generalities. On the contrary, it is a richly complex concept, full of elusive subtleties which defy categorical constructions.

I think this book responds to the need for a treatment of democracy which explores its myriad ramifications by doing full justice to its place in the actual world of human affairs. I am confident that Professor Fluno has made a substantial contribution to the literature of democratic thought. Surely those who read this book with the close attention it both deserves and requires will learn much about a complicated body of fundamental ideas which has always been cherished by civilized men everywhere who believe that the best of all governments is self-government, but who understand that such government is neither easily understood nor practiced.

DAVID FELLMAN

PREFACE

THE condition of widespread affluence and the fantastic acceleration of other kinds of social change are too fresh in our communal experience to have, as yet, become the product of thorough analysis. But even as we talk about these phenomena, their effects surround all of us. And, to complicate matters for the democrat, they do so before we have eliminated certain more ancient confusions concerning the nature of democracy. Ever since the world became infatuated with democratic rhetoric there has been a tendency to inflate the language of democracy, to commit the typically American sin of the oversell—a democratic habit only slightly less treacherous than Hitler's Big Lie. When long-term confusions concerning the practical processes and the ambitious goals of democracy are joined with the more recent inflation in expected gratifications, when personal expectations move from materialistic desires to difficult social and cultural goals, we begin to hear of demands for instant solutions to complex domestic and world problems. Democratic government is expected here and now to eliminate the evils of the ghettos or immediately to untangle an incredibly complex overinvolvement in Asia. At the same time there is a totally confusing demand for a different kind of democracy, somehow more participatory than anything in our past experience. When a materialistic kind of instant gratification seems no longer to gratify, as our younger generation has wisely come to discover, there is a danger that it will be supplanted by a similar kind of overexpectation directed toward the political order and that our traditional descriptions of democracy will exaggerate these demands with frightening consequences in political disillusionment.

It may be fruitful, as we meet the great challenges of our day, to have reexamined democracy in terms of the earth-bound realities of its actual operating processes, while, in the same breath, stressing the quite proper ambition of all democrats to achieve the high aims of individual freedom and communal participation. Such broad goals deserve to retain their glamour and will do so if we admit their inherent ambiguity, viewing them somewhat in the manner that we have learned to view love—as something our inability to describe does not tarnish. The broad democratic objectives will not result in disillusionment if we anchor them in down-to-earth kinds of social processes that are not, taken alone, glamorous in their appeal. It is important to bring about a deflation in our expectations concerning the processes of democracy without simultaneously deflating the appeal that the highest democratic goals have long had for the minds of men. Such, very briefly then, are the motivations behind the words to follow.

Since the thoughts in this book arise out of a quarter-century as a student whose official vocation has been that of a teacher, the author's indebtedness extends to innumerable authors, to dozens of colleagues, and to hundreds of challenging students. Although I have avoided extensive quotations and references to the work of contemporary political scientists as well as to analysts from other disciplines, I hope that this will not be taken to mean that I feel no sense of indebtedness. Even though I part company with a few of them, I am appreciative of their help. Some, but not all, of the persons to whom I owe such debts will find their names in the bibliographic notes.

I am especially indebted to my friends and colleagues engaged in the governance of Whitman College. They have provided material help in leaves of absence and in grants for specific expenses. More importantly, the college has provided an atmosphere free from pressure to publish but conducive to the kind of freedom of thought the contemporary tendency toward specialization so often frustrates. I am specifically obligated to those of my colleagues who have provided indispensable critiques of the manuscript, particularly to Professors David Fellman, Harry Lazer, and Alan Wolfe. I appreciate the intelligent editorial assistance of the staff of Dodd, Mead & Company. I also owe individual debts of gratitude to a group of helpful women who have assisted in compiling reference materials and in transforming a disorderly manuscript into workable form: Jeanne Alkins, Evanne Elliott, Diane Pancoast, and Edna Soper.

Above and beyond all other acknowledgments, however, is the appreciation due my wife. She has been my most important critic. But at the same time, she has provided the essential inspiration to undertake a task which has sometimes stretched my skills to the utmost. There is no way to verbalize such an obligation.

ROBERT Y. FLUNO

CONTENTS

The Democratic Community

GOVERNMENTAL PRACTICES AND PURPOSES

CHAPTER 1

Toward Freedom and Community

AMONG all of God's creatures, only man is known to laugh at himself. Perhaps this is because he is the only one who needs to do so. Only he has the capacity to heighten himself with a mysterious substance called dignity; hence, when he falls from these self-made heights, only he can look quite so foolish. This dual capacity for foolishness and dignity, for stupidity and wisdom, is a product of human freedom. Individual man has the capacity, at least in limited extent, to create himself in his own image. He has a peculiar ability to achieve something known as freedom, about which the philosophers have speculated endlessly. The central concern of this book is with freedom socialized, with the fact that men are able to collectivize the activities through which they either make fools of themselves or rise to new heights of dignity. The topic of these pages is communal liberty, something called democracy.

It is well, when entering a discussion of democracy, to emphasize that man's liberty to choose is both a freedom to improve himself and to make what, in retrospect, may turn out to be foolish mistakes. Democracy does not turn Plato upside down; it does not make every man a philosopher-king. Utopian democrats merely weaken the case for democracy when, in their overly earnest way, they can picture it only in a remote, perfected form.[1] It may be that

1. The concept of utopian democrat used in these pages is similar to Joseph Schumpeter's concept of "classical democracy" in *Capitalism, Socialism, and Democracy*, revised ed. (New York: Harper, 1947).

perfected democracy would be the ultimate in social organization, but that ultimate will always be quite distant from ordinary life. Freedom and perfection are by no means synonymous, and thus democracy, as freedom socialized, will always be a bit less orderly than the logicians of this world would like. Once we admit to the somewhat untidy character of practical democracy, we will be less likely to demand a beautifully constructed model or a single theory of definition. We cannot refuse to analyze it in the abstract, but we can attempt to bring our discussion as close as possible to the real world of imperfect men and clumsy institutions.

THE AMBIGUOUS SOCIETY

A century and a half ago, the democrat was a bit too radical for polite society. Even those communities which were well on the road to fitting the description did not have the courage to call themselves democracies. The tables have since turned. The word "democracy" has gained such a favorable connotation that even patently autocratic societies have appropriated it. The concept has come to signify the widespread aspiration of modern man toward freedom and his vague awareness that liberty can be achieved through communal participation. But the growing popularity of the idea has not made our understanding of the particularities of democracy that much clearer. This lack of clarity may, in fact, be inherent in the democratic purpose. The search for the kind of maximization of freedom that is compatible with an orderly community is, after all, by no means identical with a search for strictly efficient, meticulous orderliness; these two goals may, in fact, turn out to be mutually inconsistent.

A typical statesman in a democracy is called a politician—a creature who often seems muddled, inconsistent, and on occasion corruptible. He is as often swayed by warm human emotions as by cool reasoning. This imperfection in democratic leadership is not without parallels in the social pattern itself. The free community takes on some of the highly personal coloration of its typical leaders. Democracy is an inherently frustrating kind of experience for any man who values order above all, for someone who seeks a totally coordinated, highly logical kind of community, or for the person who finds the inconsistencies and vagaries of human conduct intolerable. The democrat views the renowned dilemma of freedom and order peculiarly. After denying that they are unalterably opposed, he comes down on the side of liberty. Orderliness becomes a secondary virtue, even though, paradoxically, democratic communities often appear more stable than regimes that put more stress on order than on freedom.

As the democrat sees it (following an ancient metaphor), the autocratic regime sails along in a majestically ordered fashion until it suddenly hits a rock and sinks without a trace. But a democracy looks more like a ship always in need of bailing: it floats much longer but not because it is consistently better commanded. There is both order and confusion in the democratic pattern, an order that arises out of a well-institutionalized process of participation and out of the constitutional habit of following the rules of the game. But the more one looks at various democratic regimes in the nations of the world, the more slippery and amorphous become the essential elements in their numerous schemes to achieve an orderly kind of freedom and communal participation. Searching for the heart of the democratic scheme must be not only comparative but also a matter of personalized experience. There are types of knowledge that frustrate the encyclopedist as well as the computer programmer. There are features of human life that, like the wind, exist only in action, refusing to stand still long enough for us to analyze them. Under such circumstances it is important to distinguish description from understanding—two objectives that are not always totally identical. If we could possibly do so, we should, as George Orwell suggests, "let the meaning choose the word" rather than the other way about. In our present inquiry, we are already presented with a word, one given us by the Greeks. We can reserve final judgment on its meaning, however, until all the experiential and comparative facts are in our hands—a condition that will undoubtedly never be met.

Many undoubtedly know what it means to be in love, even though they would find it difficult to verbalize it. It is erroneous to assume that difficulty of precise description must in all cases indicate a failure of understanding. Many men and women who live in such nations as Canada, the United States, or Sweden undoubtedly know what is meant by democracy. They live with its processes. They feel its freedoms, an experience that may serve to make description all the more difficult. If the citizen of one of those nations describes the "people's democracies" of Eastern Europe as fake, however, he undoubtedly knows what he is talking about, even though he could not provide a neat set of distinguishing criteria. Love, art, freedom, creativity, maturity—all such things are ambiguous; democracy differs only in that the experience is peculiarly communal. It, too, is a big word, too thoroughly packed with meaning to permit total clarification.

Leaving men free means leaving them less determined, less predictable, less ordered. This indeterminacy is at the heart of democracy. Even though, as other social systems, it seeks order, the democratic community tries to maximize the permissible flexibility for each individual, and, consequently, it increases the fluid nature of the whole collectivity. An unlettered man once said that "democracy has a kind of looseness to it." The dominant element of democracy may well be precisely that looseness. The fact that the exact quality of a social pattern defies precise description may in itself say worlds about its nature. But the purpose here is to tell something *about* democracy, not merely to admit that it is ultimately indescribable. The existence of ambiguity in the democratic experience means that authors must continue writing new approaches, since none among them is likely to earn a final copyright on the one perfected version.

It is easier to see the pitfalls confronting those who go exploring for the meaning of democracy than to construct a positive method for its examination. How, for example, can democracy be seen as a specific human experience without the analysis becoming tied to a particular culture? The answer is simple: it is frankly not possible to free any such an inquiry from all cultural myopia. It may be best to admit such limitations and to remain aware of the consequences. All existing democracies are culture bound, tied to a particular social setting, to the history of the nation they represent. Democracy is more than a mystical abstraction or a utopian ideal, and, as a human experience, it cannot avoid being a *particular* experience. Even the peculiarities of language affect our perspective. The English language gives different shades of meaning to social expressions than Italian, Danish, Bengali, or Swahili. Languages reflect historical development. The English words liberalism, equality, and law have different meanings in the Anglo-American context than their supposed equivalents in other tongues. The language of democracy remains, in many respects, colloquial.

Definition, since the time of Socrates, has been assumed to be the beginning of wisdom. An argumentation that does not start out with definitions begins, allegedly, in a state of original sin. Yet it is particularly clear that in the disputable zones of politics and religion precision can both serve the cause of orderliness and act as an inhibition. It is essential to use the language clearly without thereby binding it in tight knots that cramp our imagination—for the greater glory of well-sterilized logic. Sensing this danger, a wise theologian postpones his definition of God until he has covered his subject, and even then, he may not reach the point of genuine definition, preferring to leave us to suffer with both old and new doubts. Such a theological treatment would hardly seem fair play for the examiner of democracy; he is obliged to provide some kind of clarification from the start, at least to provide a kind of predefinition.

If the definition of democracy remains, at the start, purely preliminary, the reader preserves his inalienable right to discover his own meaning out of the analysis that follows. To move toward a hesitant beginning for this book on the democratic experience, let it then be noted that talk about democracy relates to a social practice in which individual freedom is combined with community participation. The democratic pattern arises out of the age-old dialectic between the dual goals of freedom and order. The democrat thinks of participation as at least part of the solution to this dilemma of dual goals without going so far as to say, with Cicero, that "freedom *is* participation in power." Participation can make order more palatable to the freedom-lover because he is (or should be) aware that he has some small part in determining the nature of that order. If the definitional process begins in the observation that citizens of a democracy seek a balance of communal activity and personal liberty, the democratic goal seems reasonable even though difficult of perfection. Although nearly all human associations undoubtedly achieve some degree of both participation and freedom, democracy is that kind of community purposely working toward an optimum combination of these elements as valued objectives.

One of the ways, then, in which democracy as we know it today differs from older, nondemocratic societies is in its conscious concern for the maximization of freedom through collective action. A democracy is a community that tries, and tries hard, to increase liberty without sacrificing order. In American constitutional language, the democrat asserts that, forming "a more perfect Union" is entirely consistent with securing "the Blessings of Liberty to ourselves and our Posterity." But the precise pattern by which the difficult goal of liberty through community is to be achieved must, of necessity, be evolutionary. It must, consequently, be tied closely to a particular culture. Paradoxically, part of the success of Anglo-American democracy is due to the fact that its various Founding Fathers were not yet conscious democrats. When the American founders sat together to create a written constitution, their attitude was not entirely different from that of the kings of England who strengthened Parliament because "it worked," because it served their purposes. American constitution-writers and leaders of constitution-developing parliaments were themselves free men even if everyone else in their society was not; they were accustomed to defining their own goals and to seeking practical means for their fulfillment. Most of them were, at least politically, self-made men. But none were anarchists. It would not occur to them to separate liberty from orderliness; they were community men as well as individualists. Without much awareness of the philosophical conundrums of freedom *versus* order, these predemocrats saw no reason why expanding freedom should be inconsistent with social stability. But modern democrats, attempting to discover what that something called democracy has gradually come to mean, convert this vague objective into a more conscious purpose.

Later generations may have spoiled democracy by talking too much about it. The American Founding Fathers, whether or not they can now be called democrats, had no model or definition of democracy in front of them. They were, however, close to the free life of the American frontier, and they were familiar with the great liberal revolutions that had been taking place in England. Colonial history and their British background had taught them the virtues of parliamentary government. A backward glance toward the origins of democracy demonstrates that it need not arise out of an explicit, well-ordered political theory. It becomes immediately apparent that creating a free-participating community is very much a practical matter. But practical men can be goal oriented. The pragmatic aspect of democratic development does not preclude the existence of goals.

One preliminary way of looking at the broad meaning of democracy is to view democracy in terms of its purpose, particularly the goal of freedom-in-community, with order achieved through participation. Quite obviously, purpose alone is insufficient: the democrat may share some ultimate aims with the Communist who advocates a dictatorship of the proletariat. Although a democracy can be distinguished through its primary objective, it must also be evaluated in terms of present practices. The democratic purpose must be pursued in good faith; it must be demonstrated through tangible present effort. A democracy need not have achieved its ultimate intent, but that goal must at least be in a state of becoming: it must be progressively developing a more generous degree of human freedom and more effective mechanisms of popular participation. It must, as of this moment, display features that distinguish it from other kinds of historical and contemporary communities. There must be concrete evidence that the liberating goal is substantially meaningful and not merely campaign oratory. The Founding Fathers of both American and British democracy were practical men dealing with real rather than with philosophical problems. It should not, therefore, be difficult for citizens of either nation to deal with the ambiguities of the democratic experience or with the seeming illogic of living in a democracy and hoping for its fulfillment.

THE MEANING OF LIBERTY

James Thurber tells the story of an incorrigible young moth, who, in adolescent revolt, refused to fly around ordinary street lamps. Despite parental scoldings, he persisted in what became a lifelong crusade to reach a particularly enticing star. While brothers and sisters burned their lives away one by one, dashing against scorchingly hot light bulbs nearby, he lived to a ripe old age, endlessly reaching for the unreachable star hundreds of light-years away. Like a band of gallant moths, the single, most obvious element that unites democrats and democratic communities is the direction of their ambition. The star that guides them is the distant goal of human liberty. The attempt of such men and such societies to maximize freedom consistently with communal order may be no more likely to succeed than was the endless flight of Thurber's intrepid moth, but the result of the trying brings intermediate gains well worth achieving. The fainthearted may give up the quest, particularly after they discover that the best minds of the ages—men such as Hobbes, Locke, and Rousseau—could not find the exact formula. But, like the persistent moth, it is the essence of the democratic character to continue striving.

Even though the grand solution to the dilemma of balancing freedom with social discipline may never be found, incremental solutions may arise out of a profound faith in the possibility of liberty. It seems certain that communities that share a general belief in the possible consistency of freedom and order will come closer, through a kind of self-fulfilling prophecy, to attainment of that goal than those that give up the task as hopeless. But this credence given to the feasibility of the democratic goal is faith in the basic content of the democratic idea, not in the particulars of the democratic form as found in any of the various modern nations. The general objective of achieving freedom consistent with the necessities of social order has its own theoretical difficulties, but they are of a different order than the problems of providing particular procedures for its achievement in a given community.

Form and content in the democratic experience are, by no means, in opposition. "Form," as the artist, Ben Shahn, puts it, "renders content available to others, giving it permanence, willing it to the race." The democratic *form* gives particularity in terms of process and structure, making the democratic idea a tangible reality for each nation, even when that reality varies widely from nation to nation. The *content* of democracy (ambiguously concerned with human liberty) gives it an attractive meaning, one that men all over the world wish to take for their own. Even though, in politics as well as in art, it is easier for the critics to talk about forms, the collective authors of the great piece of art we call democracy created it out of concern both for form and for content. Most of the discussion to follow inevitably deals with forms. The processes of democratic politics and the structure of governmental and social order serve to institutionalize, to make lasting, the basic effort to achieve the content of the democratic goal. Even though the greater part of this book will be devoted to *form,* there is clearly a need to bring about some clarification of the *content* of the democratic idea, particularly that something called human liberty.

Discussion of the nature of freedom can be long-winded. One writer has recently attempted to gather, catalog, and analyze all significant ideas about man's freedom. This effort forced its author,

Mortimer Adler, to issue some fourteen hundred closely packed pages quoting something like two hundred writers.[2] After placing Adler's two volumes alongside the large library previously existing on the subject, the student who faces the prospect of formulating his own conception of the term will start out with considerable fear and trembling. Trepidation is increased when it is realized that, despite all the profound tomes of the philosophers, liberty is still an experience that also comes to ordinary men. It may well be, in fact, that it is better grasped by those who feel it than by those concerned with its abstraction. But, whatever the hazards, no discussion of democracy is quite complete without some examination of the central purpose of that pattern of social life.

Let it be assumed, to begin with, that to be free means to be human in the fullest sense of the term. It means to be able to make complete use of one's humanity, to be able to utilize one's human capacities to the limit. Liberty is thus conceived in terms of opportunity. To be free means to have the chance to choose what one wishes to make of life and to be able to work toward that self-determined personal objective. Without picking any quarrels by placing this concept in relation to the thousand and one meanings others have given the term, this at least provides a beginning, a focal point around which to build more discussion.

Man is, among a hundred other things, a goal-creating animal. He is, as the philosophers might prefer to put it, a normative creature. At the same time, he is a frustrated creature. His ability is frequently inadequate for his goals. A man's external surroundings, his heredity, and his past all serve to inhibit his opportunities. To be a human being, according to the psychologist Alfred Adler, results in quite normal incapacities, leading each individual to a feeling of inferiority that consistently "presses toward its own conquest." Everyone knows such a feeling. No man is immune from self-unassurance. This feeling comes partly from the facts of life; everyone is, in fact, inferior in some respect or another. But inferiorities

2. Mortimer Adler, *The Idea of Freedom,* 2 vols. (Garden City, N.Y.: Doubleday, 1958, 1961).

lead to fears and to the irrationality that accompanies fear. Man can overcome some of these more irrational feelings of inferiority in the processes of growing up, in becoming a man, in putting away childish aspirations and childish fears. He can become a more complete human being by making his own way in life on the basis of self-realized limitations and self-defined goals. But this means making choices. He must learn to choose, and to choose with knowledge, if he is to become a mature man, and, by the same process, he must become free to make choices that are genuinely his own. This concept of liberty is consistent with that expressed by the anthropologist Malinowski, who sees freedom in terms of those conditions essential for "the formulation of a purpose, its translation into effective action through organized intermediaries, and the full enjoyment of the results." [3]

As the Christian tradition asserts, man has his purpose handed down for him by God. Even so, the democrat, mild heretic that he is, refuses to allow any mere man to tell him what God may have had in mind. While believing that, through communal participation, men can get collective goals for themselves, the democrat generally prefers to stress the individual nature of goal-setting. Without denying that there may be higher goals for all humankind, the democrat believes that every mere mortal must find his own primary expression in purposes that are self-determined. It may well be that each man or woman can only build his individual idea of purpose out of the given, existing universe, but he can still compose that objective in his own peculiar way. Even though the single human creature seems but an insignificant being, standing within a large environment of mothers and mothers-in-law, heroes and tyrants, hydrogen bombs and race problems, there remains room for personal choice. There remains scope for individual discretion in reacting to the complex world. The essence of the democratic idea is in that individual choice. It focuses, in the words of Paul Tillich, on personal "deliberation, decision, and responsibility."

3. Bronislaw Malinowski, *Freedom and Civilization* (London: Allen & Unwin, 1947), p. 25.

"We are," says Bergson, "what we do." We create ourselves through choice and by acting on that choice. Liberty is meaningful to those who believe in the possibility of self-creation. The process of self-building takes place even when men are unaware that every choice they make has a part in developing a personal meaning. Sometimes these choices that define personality-shaping goals are created hit and miss, by little, supposedly insignificant, decisions. The schoolchild who fails to complete his day's assignment takes a certain role, consciously or unconsciously making a choice that relates to broad ideals for himself, even though he might be totally unconvinced if this were pointed out. If he decides to be a scholar, to go beyond the required assignment, he makes another small choice that helps mold a set of ideals. Such acts, small ones and large ones, simultaneously express a personality and develop it. In choosing, each man builds a past that can either haunt his future or push him on to greater glories.

Freedom for children and for unthinking adults may sometimes mean the ability "to get what I want." But in getting there is also becoming. Freedom for the adult—for the mature individual we should all hope to become before we die—is the ability not to get anything so much as it is to be what we admire. To be free means to have the opportunity to create a self in a pattern particularly personal to me. Others may inhibit my efforts, influence my conception of the choices before me, and help mold the pattern of my self-perception, but, if I am free, no one can dictate the shape of the self I create. Our leeway for self-creativity is always affected by our world, and it narrows down day by day as we grope along from childhood, through adolescence and adulthood, until all choice is gone at the point of death. The society that does the most to encourage an originality in the self-creative process of all individuals has the greatest right to call itself a true democracy. Although few communities have a right to be boastful at the moment, it is reassuring to know that some are at least trying.

The modern social scientist is, quite typically, afraid of ghosts. He does not like aspects of man and his community that float eerily about like emanations from the spirit world. He abhors ambiguities. He feels an obligation to make his analysis as concrete as he can. This is sometimes no easy task. The very nature of freedom, as has already been stated, is to leave men less defined, their options more open, making them less predictable and less amenable to analytical dissection than if they were not free. Freedom is almost the opposite of definition. But it is necessary at least to make the effort. How can the concept of freedom be made more behavioral and thus more acceptable to modern social scientists? Perhaps the solution will come through a tangential approach that uses other concepts that relate to human fulfillment and hence to liberty.

One way to bring the concept of liberty a half inch closer to the standards of behavioral language is to search for words meaningful to a psychologist. If it is the goal of freedom to enable one to grow up, not in absurdity, but with creativity and originality, perhaps the meaning can be brought down-to-earth by use of the concept of maturity. Synonyms for maturity used by psychologists are similar to the conception of liberty expressed here: self-realization, self-actualization, environmental mastery, personal integration—all of these near synonyms appear as elements in the concept of freedom. The man who is truly grown up, who comes close to fitting the description of maturity, has no great desire to repeat his youth. He finds that his freedom has grown with self-understanding. He has, if he is lucky enough to have cast aside most of his childish ways, achieved a state of mental well-being to which such terms as "maturity" and "personal liberty" are reasonably applied. For those psychologists who use the word, maturity is a kind of conceptual model or ideal type. They do not expect to come across any truly mature man any more than the philosopher expects to meet one who is truly free. But the model can be approximated: a man can be imagined who has sufficient realistic self-understanding to permit him to work effectively toward a self-established goal. It is possible to conceive of a person who knows who he has been and what his world is like, so that he can see his own limits and his own potentialities and can act on the basis of them. Such a man can advance toward becoming what he wants to be; he can move toward both freedom and maturity.

The day-old child has all of his options (and frustrations) ahead of him. He is, for the moment, also totally dependent, totally lacking in autonomy. If, eight or nine decades later, his choices over the years have been wise ones, he will have a feeling of autonomy—a feeling that he has been his own man, a feeling of self-created fulfillment. Yet his options for future development will be almost nil. Which is the real state of freedom? Perhaps neither. Freedom is not a static condition at either end of the human progression. It is a process, the process of maturing under conditions suitable for self-creation. The infant is unfree in the sense that he lacks autonomy. The aged man is unfree in terms of available options. But if the man near death has enjoyed a certain kind of life, one that has permitted self-directed fulfillment, his life, as it moved along, must have gone through a dynamic process that may properly be called freedom. Neither the state of having all options ahead nor that of having all options worked out is precisely describable as freedom, but the in-between process of self-directed maturation is close to what we mean by liberty.

The free man wants to grow up, to become a man. He possesses what the psychologist would call growth motivation. He wishes, again in language familiar to the psychologist, to move steadily from the total dependency of the infant toward a maximization of autonomy. He wants to pick and choose as much as possible among environmental factors, determining those to which he will adjust and those he will attempt to utilize or develop in a manner of his own liking. He hopes to solve, in his own way, the problems created by his past and by his present environment. For this he needs self-perception and social understanding. To be able to achieve a situation in which he can work, play, and love with a self-satisfying fullness, he will sometimes adapt to his world, sometimes declare his independence of it, and sometimes try to change it. The man who is living a free kind of life is capable of dealing with his environment. sometimes bending to it and sometimes mastering it, but always in control of his own responses, so that the resultant personality is very much his own invention.

What, after all of this, do men want from democracy? It is unfair to presume to speak for all democrats without asking them personally, but this author would guess that the ultimate search is for organized ways to permit men and women—all men and all women—to join forces for the maximization of self-knowing, self-creating maturity. It appears to be the democratic assumption that men working together can help each other to uncover that golden urn at the end of the rainbow and, in it, to find the formula for self-fulfillment. The goal is so incredibly difficult that it calls for full communal participation to make it even a partly meaningful objective. The democrat does not wish to emulate Robinson Crusoe's kind of freedom. The autonomy of a desert island has too few options even if it is free from social interferences. Men normally seek the wider range of choices offered by a socially rich community. The great spirits of the ages—Socrates, Saint Francis, or Gandhi—were not hermits but men in the midst of society. They achieved fulfillment in relation to a collectivity of fellow men. Democracy, as perceived here, constitutes an attempt to find the institutional means of allowing all men to become great spirits in their own small way. The staggering nature of such an objective is obvious, but merely making the effort moves men toward a higher level of humanity.

THE LIBERAL TRADITION

A community, acting in some ways like an individual man, will develop a character of its own—more ambiguous and more treacherous to describe—but not necessarily less important. If, despite the nonscientific nature of such a concept, we admit the existence of such character, we will note that its nature will be a reflection of its urges. The cluster of ideas a community expresses and the very language it develops will reflect the direction of goals toward which leading members of the society aim. In those communities that have, for a long time, been making a determined effort to deserve the appellation of democracy, there will be a gradual development of words and ideas recognizing, identifying, and praising the slow progress toward freedom. There will have arisen a whole cluster of philosophies, myths, and traditions that help to distinguish it as a society that is in the process of becoming a democracy. We can consider this cluster of ideas as an ideology, but what name tag should be attached? With what ism should it be labeled? We could hardly call it democratism, a name both unfamiliar and clumsy. The word that sticks, despite the infinite confusion it creates, despite endless uses and misuses, is liberalism. The basic liberal philosophy is well suited to democracy. Its linguistic roots emphasize the idea of *libertas.* Except for this fundamental belief in human liberty, the liberal (and thus the democrat) is supposedly flexible and nondoctrinaire. The democrat may, if anything, hesitate to pin any label at all on his breast. The wise man objects to being branded, reserving his strategic pliability and avoiding the confusions that the clumsy language of isms can create. But communities of men are different. They need to communicate an ideology in order to achieve some level of agreement on social purposes. When a group adopts a doctrinal symbol, it helps it to rally supporters and to distinguish allies from enemies.

The liberal brand name, in its traditional conception, says enough about the thinking of democrats without saying too much, without outlining a precise dogma. Since the liberal tradition is nondoctrinaire and nondogmatic, it needs, beyond the core idea that man's actions must spring out of as well as create his personality, to lay down few specific edicts. It commands the society to find ways to encourage the individual to take full advantage of the potentialities of liberty; that having been said, there is little that could be called an authorized creed. The democrat as a liberal begins by confounding his dogmatist friend with the paradoxical idea that the only faith worth defending is that achieved through doubting. The liberal approaches ideas, new and old, with a skeptical scrutiny. Only after such a doubt-oriented beginning can he offer full support for any program. Since freedom is built on such questioning, the liberal is forced to defend the right of others to doubt, to question, and to talk about such questions. He must, if he is to operate on the basis of faith through doubt, fight for the right of others to express their own particular doubts. Only in the company of other men can such a process for reaching decisions on policies and principles be effective. Although the goal of liberalism centers on the single individual as an ultimate aim, it cannot be meaningful as a solo performance. Liberalism, like liberty itself, is not a doctrine for hermits. It is concerned with practical freedom, a mutual product developed within the framework of community.

The chief concern of the liberal is with man's bonds. He wishes to find ways and means to loosen whatever restrictions are preventing the individual from reaching the outer boundaries of his particular talents. Admitting the existence of limits on individual self-responsibility and rationality, the liberal persists in trying to create the kind of social setting in which every collective resource is turned toward making personal choice more possible and more effective. But such broad objectives do not suffice; from that initial point on, when faced with day-to-day policy choices, the concept of liberalism runs into definitional difficulties. There is no sure way to eliminate misuse of the label because no liberal can be content with generalities. He must favor or oppose specific policies concerning which others, who may not be at all liberal-minded, will also be taking sides. He cannot preserve the virginal purity of the liberal tag. There is no academy that fixes the meaning of political language, no bureau of standards to weigh the specific applications of isms against particular sets of beliefs. The most damaging confusion is that which associates liberalism with tight-lipped moralizers, doctrinaire reformers, dour-faced pessimists, and dogmatic Socialists. The root of this widespread mix-up lies in the popular tendency to use liberalism as synonymous with progressivism, as a dogma diametrically opposed to conservatism. Despite this very damaging delusion, the concept of liberalism is too valuable to discard. It is necessary, instead, to digress for the moment in order to discuss some of its causes.

The liberal-conservative dichotomy is both perplexing and widely followed. When it is used (and most of us do use it), we are forced to ignore the existence of many strange comrades who gather together under the liberal umbrella. Consider three of the Liberal parties of recent history: those in New York state, in Italy, and in Britain. The reform-minded Democrats of New York, the Italian business-oriented "free-enterprise" party, and the independent-minded British middle party may all be liberal in some ultimate concern with the goals of freedom, but they can also be quite conservative on particular issues of the day. They totally confound the idea of a natural liberal-progressive alliance. The laissez-faire economic liberalism of a century ago was, later, to become the proud cause of many extreme conservatives in the United States. The difficulty becomes doubly compounded if we consider those historians who view liberalism as the very heart of the western democratic tradition; when, in the words of Frederick Watkins, it is known as "the secular form of Western civilization." It is strange to picture liberalism as both simultaneously traditional and radical; obviously, there is a linguistic mix-up.

It is particularly odd that such nations as the United States and Great Britain, so deeply rooted in the liberal tradition, should be the very ones in which liberalism is often alleged to be opposed to conservatism. The supporter of democracy is forced to be both liberal in his orientation toward freedom and conservative in opposing any new restrictions on liberty. Any liberal with a modicum of intelligence has to be aware that the strength of Anglo-Saxon liberty rests upon its long heritage of respect for personal dignity and human freedom. Even though he may frequently wish to strengthen that tradition with new measures and with adaptations to new problems, he is likewise often impelled to defend the tradition against vigorous foes. When he is acting in the role of defender of the tradition, it is proper to call him conservative. When, however, he is working out innovations to advance the freedom quotient, he may properly be called progressive or even radical. The liberal reaction to the innovative ideas of Communists and Fascists is a recent example of liberalism in conservative dress. As common as the habit is, it tangles our thinking to assume that the liberal idea is intrinsically tied either to conservatism or to progressivism.

There are numerous explanations for the tendency to see an antipathy between liberalism and conservatism. One inescapable cause of this tendency is found in the simple fact that many of the nineteenth-century conservatives were antilibertarian. But more importantly, there is a certain logic in the association of the two concepts: the conservative commonly stresses community tradition, and this may often be opposed to individual experimentation. The conservative can be individualist in his attitudes, but quite often he has stressed community values. Such values need not be anti-individualist or antilibertarian, but they sometimes are. Another cause for confusion lies in a historical assumption, namely that democracy in its western form was the product of radicalism. History is filled with the names of radical democrats and populists. The existence of a few firebrands such as John Lilburne and Thomas Paine does not, however, prove the point. Nor does the existence of scattered revolutionary moments through the long evolution of democracy prove that it arose out of political violence. Revolutions helped to feed the ideological fires of democracy; yet the central development of democratic institutions appears to have been evolutionary. The Puritan Revolution of the 1640s started in religious ferment and ended in a disappointing dictatorship. The final overturn of the Stuarts in 1688 was basically a restoring of the Restoration of 1660, which James II had misinterpreted as an invitation to absolutism. The American War of Independence resulted chiefly from the American desire to share in the benefits of the Settlement after 1688: its original aim was to achieve for itself the kind of balanced government for which Britain was already becoming famous. The French Revolution was at one stage led by radical democrats; the final result was, however, anything but democratic. The French kept repeating the effort, but the various revolutionary attempts left matters no more settled than before, raising as many problems as they solved. The French attempt at democracy by revolution ended merely in ensuring that the Anglo-Saxon evolutionary pattern would continue to be the primary model of western democracy.

Although a brief summary of centuries of history is unsafe, it is reasonable to assert that the American pattern of democracy originated out of a particular set of political institutions in medieval England. The Angevin kings of England, sometimes out of strength and sometimes out of weakness, found it convenient to accept political institutions that eventually provided a foundation for democracy. King John was forced to swallow the doctrines of Magna Carta, which, from the standpoint of the nobility, constituted an attempt to maintain feudal rights but later provided a base for liberating concepts. Henry II played a key role in developing a legal system that, in contrast to the Roman law then popular on the Continent, was constructed on the Germanic concept that law belonged vaguely to the whole community, that it was something separate from the men who governed. The early strength of the English monarchy made it unnecessary for the kings to adopt a legal system supporting absolutist pretensions. The common law system provided a base for the later concept of constitutionalism—the idea that law has superiority over government—a concept of vital importance to the development of the parliamentary pattern of politics.

Even more importantly, the elected assembly, which eventually turned out to be the central instrument of the democratic process, was used by the Angevin monarchs because they found advantage in having representatives from the shires and boroughs included in meetings of the king's council. The weakness of Henry III and the rebellious actions of men like Simon de Montfort converted these meetings into parliaments. Later, stronger kings learned that such representative gatherings had several virtues. They were useful in raising revenue, in informing the king of attitudes of the publics with which they had to deal, and in carrying the king's edicts back to the provinces. The kings may also have learned, as historians later noted, that the peculiar form of English parliaments helped to unify the nation behind the royal foreign policy. The Tudors, at the pinnacle of monarchical power in Britain, used the parliamentary institution in issues of church-state relations, in matters relating to the royal succession, and in battles with Spain. They found there was no substitute for a cooperative parliament in getting the job done. Numerous men had a part in building the British legislative assembly, and many of them were opponents of royal policy; yet it could be said that the greatest builder of parliamentary power was Henry VIII. He found, quite pragmatically, that a representative assembly provided exactly the tool he needed to bring the power and lands of the church within national control. He and his daughter, Elizabeth, were capable of converting this instrumentality to their own purposes; they were so capable that they built its power beyond reversal. When their Stuart successors tried to operate without parliamentary support, they found themselves incapacitated. In the end, Charles I and James II had to be forcibly shown that the instrument was no longer a tool of kings but a national power in its own right, an independent source of policy, sometimes even a kingmaker and kingbreaker.

No one could be so foolish as to label Angevin or Tudor monarchs or their parliaments democratic. Even the Restoration of 1660 and the clarification of its principles in 1688 were not, by any normal definition, democratic. They resulted, as has already been indicated, in the concept of balanced government that captivated constitution-writers in America and elsewhere; yet few of the Founding Fathers would have called themselves democrats. Modern democracy evolved out of undemocratic, conservative concepts of medieval representation and out of the discovery of the merits of an assembly as an instrument of national autocracy. The last British monarch that was at all strong in his own right was George III, and it is notable that he found his strength within Parliament, using tools of corruption and manipulation, not, like his Tudor forebearers, as a lordly force sitting above it. In the eighteenth century Parliament grew into a force more powerful than the king but not into an instrumentality of democracy. The nineteenth-century Reform Bills finally converted this medieval institution into a democratic device, but again, the process was seldom dramatic and was never violent.

Democracy, in its modern western version, is deeply rooted in the British example. The British model was the result of long ages of development. Only in the past hundred years or so can it be called democratic, and only in the more recent past was there any conscious effort to achieve government based on popular consent. The democratic tradition had liberal elements: it gradually moved from vague origins in medieval law and forms of representation toward greater and greater freedom and participation. But it has also been conservative: it built in incremental fashion, step by step on past traditions, attempting to adapt ancient institutions to contemporary needs. The moments of radicalism in the history of Anglo-American democracy are few and far between. A strong tradition of personal liberty and popular participation was gradually built out of ancient institutions and ideas. This tradition provides the central theme for the liberal-democratic idea as it exists today.

THE FEASIBILITY OF FREEDOM

"The communal life of human beings," according to Sigmund Freud, rests on a "two-fold foundation: the compulsion to work . . . and the power of love." [4] He looks upon the first as an economic drive, based on "external necessity." He finds the second motive neatly founded on the sexual urge. Whether his ideas concerning the roots of these civilizing forces are right or wrong, there is much to be said for the argument that the more advanced cultures have built upon these impulses. When the work drive is thought of in terms of creativity and love is conceived as the basis of socialization of the personality, it becomes apparent that much of human progress arises out of the two motives. These are incentives common to all highly developed cultures. What, then, does freedom add? A tangential answer is, perhaps, that it adds that particular ingredient which has permitted the West to move ahead so dramatically in the technological realm. It may be difficult to prove em-

4. Sigmund Freud, *Civilization and Its Discontents,* trans. James Strachey (New York: Harcourt, Brace, 1958), p. 209.

pirically, but it is reasonable to argue that the work motive cannot be converted into the highest form of creativity without maximum freedom and that the love impulse cannot be transformed into the highest form of socialization without the kind of voluntary participation implied in the whole democratic concept. The gift, then, of the liberal tradition is to add an individualistic and participatory element that will convert the work and the love impulses into more dynamic civilizing forces.

If it is a happy truth that democracy makes possible a more sophisticated, higher kind of civilization than other systems, then all nations should seek to become democracies. But there is another side to the issue. Some kinds of civilizations appear to encourage the development of democratic practices, whereas others discourage it. What causes the disparity? The easy answer may not be the right one. It does not follow that whatever exists today in the West is better, in libertarian terms, than what exists in Africa and Asia, even though conditions in the past—the Greek idea of the community, medieval forms of government, and Renaissance ideas of the free spirit—have contributed to the present extent of western democracy. Past progress does not prove that the future path of democratic civilization in the West will by any means be smooth. Whatever questions one may ask about the potential for democracy in non-western areas can also be matched with questions about the future of democracy in the West. For example, what does the uncontrollable increase in complexity of the modern industrial community do to meaningful popular participation? Can the mechanics of popular participation, based on the medieval idea of the representative assembly, serve a nation as large and complex and with such diverse political issues as the United States of America?

There are hundreds of questions that need to be answered before a prognosis could be made about the future health of western democracies. But the mere fact that some of them have come so far and, more importantly, that some of them have created a strong tradition of freedom, makes it unsurprising that the Anglo-Saxon nations are not the usual focus for the question: will democracy succeed? Not all European nations have yet demonstrated that they possess such a democratic tradition, despite their sharing some of the same heritage, and the question becomes even more difficult in relation to non-European communities. The world is taking a direction that makes it more and more necessary for western democrats to look abroad, concerning themselves with political structures in areas that, a few years back, were viewed with no social concern. The time has passed when westerners can think of far-off communities as primitive curiosities or as places for exotic travel. Isolation is no longer possible for those of us "living off the fat of the land" in what we boastfully consider to be the freedom-oriented English-speaking nations. Even when they have rising doubts about their own political health, it has become immediately urgent for Americans, Australians, Netherlanders, Norwegians, and others with democratic traditions to concern themselves with social structures in parts of the world that were, not long ago, simply places for exploration and exploitation. It is doubtful that democracy can succeed indefinitely while isolated within the boundaries of a small bloc of nations. Democracies, despite their own difficulties at home, are forced to become engaged with the future development of the democratic life in those areas of the world that have not yet established the tradition of freedom and participation.

Discussion of democracy in the pages to follow will necessarily be much concerned with institutional arrangements that are believed to facilitate freedom and participation: electoral schemes, party- and pressure-group systems, and governmental structures. Most of the discussion will build out of the kinds of social patterns found in English-speaking nations because they are so central to the western democratic tradition. But this approach necessitates a special degree of caution against defining democracy in terms of particular institutions developed in a particular historical setting. Although particulars are essential and even though the Anglo-Saxon nations have provided excellent models, it is necessary also to keep in mind a view of democracy that is broader and not as culture bound. If we remember that the development of a free society can be viewed as a vague cultural pattern evolving toward certain broad goals, we will be on safer ground when discussing the spread of democracy to nonwestern areas. This ambiguous approach should eliminate all talk about exporting democracy. Even among western nations, the experience in imitating British institutions has not been altogether a happy one. When nations with strikingly different cultural backgrounds make the same attempt, it is to be expected that success will be even less impressive. Lessons in how to maximize freedom through social participation can surely be learned one place and applied elsewhere. Yet the major object should be to discover and adopt the principles lying behind existing democratic institutions—adapting these to circumstances elsewhere—rather than slavishly imitating structures and processes. The American relation to the British model is a case in point. Far more than some Americans would like to admit, the American system arose out of home-country ideas. But the specific institutions, as anyone can plainly see, are far from similar. The American Founding Fathers recognized that they faced different problems, and they attempted to solve them pragmatically under obviously different circumstances.

It is reasonable to assume that environmental conditions can be hostile or friendly to the development of institutions directed toward the democratic goal. Factors in the economy, in social organization, and in personal attitudes of the population will determine whether or not a freedom-oriented society can develop. Social institutions well suited to such environmental circumstances cannot be prescribed in the way a physician presents instructions to his patient. Westerners would be wise to avoid the physician role. They cannot, with their better luck, act like fountains of wisdom lecturing on prerequisite conditions for democracy when their own house is seldom more than half in order. The listing of preconditions becomes particularly absurd when we move away from the assumption that democracy is a particular set of institutions toward the more ambiguous idea that it is a community in a state of becoming free. Once such ambiguity is admitted, there is no reason for precluding strange political institutions with which western democrats are unfamiliar. Had there been English students of democracy in 1789 who understood what is now meant by cabinet government, they would, if institutional-minded, probably have opposed the presidential idea. But if they had been concerned only with a more ambiguous set of democratic objectives, they would have cheered on the experimenters in America.

Quite possibly one of the best places to look for clues about the relation between environmental conditions and the efficacy of the democratic idea will be through study of the evolution of existing democracies. But there will still be no recipes; history provides no magic elixirs, no prefabricated formulas for development of a free society. The nature of the democratic experience may, perhaps, best be analyzed through historical methods, but history has the misfortune of being unique to its setting. It will offer a variety of clues to the puzzle of democratic development but no set answers. Even if this essay were a historical survey rather than an analytical one, all we could expect to learn would be how present democracies have, in fact, evolved. There could still be no perfected guide lines for future efforts to achieve the same objective. Students of non-western political development would do well to be aware of western history, but they would also be wise not to look for specific historical prescriptions.

It is safe to say that the easier experience in developing a democracy in Britain, compared with the difficult experience in France, resulted from the smoother rise of national monarchy in England and the less traumatic nature of efforts to institute representative institutions. As has already been indicated, evolution provides a more hospitable background for democratic processes than revolution does. The absence of the medieval remnants that help explain British democracy was undoubtedly influential in producing the quite different forms democracy took when it evolved in the former British colonies in America. The United States became a more unified federal democracy than its Canadian neighbor because, among other reasons, Canadian independence was not achieved through a dramatic and unifying war against their British kinfolk. The late and militaristic arrival of national unity in Germany, the persistence of medieval sectionalism in Italy, the isolation of Britain from the Continent, the availability of untapped resources in America—all such factors must be accounted for in explaining the peculiar forms of democracy in those nations today. The development of different religions, mythologies, and customs in the Orient will affect whatever peculiar paths nations in that part of the world take on the road to democracy. The results of a cultural mix of western and eastern ideas following centuries of colonialism will affect the democratic pattern that may someday emerge in the various post-colonial nations. The evolution of central Africa toward democracy will surely be altered by the existence of tribalism and by the superficial nature of western colonization.

Complex differences in culture and political history between modern democracies are common knowledge, yet much of the point is missed: the historical approach demonstrates the absurdity of establishing any set of criteria by which we may objectively determine the future of democracy in any locale. History makes it clear that the democratic idea, like other ideas, will take divergent forms in various environments. We should be particularly careful not to assume that, although economic abundance contributed to the development of American and British democracy, although medieval representation provided certain representative governmental forms, and although the existence of a frontier in non-European Anglo-Saxon nations provided growing room, any of these conditions are democratic prerequisites. Historical causes should not be converted into laws of social development—not until we have a thousand or more years of history behind us.

Some prerequisites may arise from the broad definition of democracy. It is probable, for example, that a democratic nation cannot exist without a degree of psychological security inasmuch as fear is generally observed as antithetical to the central goal of freedom. But psychological security is not the same as economic security. No one has yet convincingly proven that only a middle-class society can be democratic. It may be that a middle-class society has common, not quite diagnosed, roots with democracy, but we must be cautious in asserting that western experience provides a foolproof model. We would be wise to recall that such schizophrenic societies as ancient Athens and the antebellum American south managed to obtain a degree of democracy while also retaining the institution of slavery. Perhaps such caste and slave cultures will aways be basically unstable when they attempt also to be democracies; yet we need to explore such problems rather than taking anything for granted in the process of listing the necessary conditions for the existence of democracy.

CHAPTER 2

The Governing of Free Men

SUCCESSFUL democracies, if there are any, are, like good marriages, made in heaven. But, just as a happy marriage is an intensely human affair with the hand of God not very noticeable, a functioning democracy is very much a human creation. Like both Mother Goose and the Bible, its authors are many and anonymous, so that the individual genius of no single maker dominates the whole piece. The humanity of the creators shows through, although the individual founders are largely lost to history. These innumerable architects of the democratic pattern of life have sometimes been visionaries; yet unlike the more utopian Socialists, the dreams have usually been down-to-earth. Theirs are daytime visions, sturdily constructed on foundations that accept the evolutionary process of history. They have generally built on what is already in existence, making few sudden breaks with traditions of the past. Democracy is not, for most of us, so much a plan of reform created by the imaginativeness of particular men, as a historic response to ancient hopes for liberty consistent with order. Democratic theorists appeared after democratization had begun. They represent an intellectualization, an attempt to synthesize and comprehend man's increasing freedom, to foresee its future, not an effort to plan a new, ideal world.

The fact that democracy is a creature of history rather than an invention of individuals has not stopped all men from writing about democracy in utopian fashion. There are, even today, writers who conceive of democracy as a condition in which men and women rule themselves, even if the authors add the word, "indirectly." They set up a model that, in some manner or other, provides a mystical unity called the people or the majority, which governs the community. But, despite such theorists, democracy continues to develop in a thoroughly pragmatic manner. Even though there are great names in democratic political philosophy, the problems of freedom in the real world of organized society are too complex for any father figure. No democratic thinker has a position equivalent to that of Karl Marx. This is because the idea of democracy has seldom centered on a hypothetical society. It is more frequently a historic concept, describing (and perhaps idealizing) a stage in man's social development. Although Socialists have often been intensely conscious of history, they have frequently chosen to battle with it. Angry at how history has treated mankind, they seek a logical end to it in a perfected society. Although the democrat is also future-minded, he is usually less concerned with the exact shape of history's ultimate end. On the assumption that men can be much more self-determined than at present but in awareness that freedom is a highly ambiguous goal, the democrat can urge history on, but he cannot describe the precise nature of the end toward which it is working.

If the student of democracy wishes to help history along, he will discover that he needs to know all that is knowable concerning man's social life. He may not achieve that overwhelming goal, but if he is to avoid being a mere dreamer, he must have a basic understanding of the governance of man. He must look for those central facts about governing which ought to be self-evident but are all too frequently overlooked. Some of these basic propositions concerning man and his governance will provide the subject matter for this chapter.

THE GOVERNING FUNCTION

"Government is at best but an expedient," says Henry David Thoreau. But whether the friends of Thoreau have liked it or not, they have been forced to live with government. Sometimes they can evade it, and sometimes they can change it by taking an active role in its reform, but they can seldom divorce themselves entirely from its powers and functions. Abstract thinkers can imagine society without government, but, even after minds as great as Hobbes, Locke, and Rousseau have experimented with such visions as a method of political analysis, the idea seems no less fantastic. Life without government now seems not only "solitary, poor, nasty, brutish, and short" but totally impossible. Even before formalized, bureaucratized government was invented, our primitive ancestors had some equivalent. Man's heterogeneity is not a novel, modern development. Because nature neglected somehow to implant within the human mechanism the kind of automatic social instincts that permit ants and bees to manage complex societies, because human individuals rely only in a very limited degree on biological impulses to guide their social conduct, each such creature develops a unique means of reacting to his fellows. Human relations have thus always been both highly unpredictable and infinite in variety. The existence of all these individualized creatures acting on each other in a variety of ways creates both dynamic kinds of social conflict and dynamic efforts at cooperation. Increasingly sophisticated devices of organization are demanded as the community becomes larger, more complex in function, and more expert in its modes of communication. Government is, above all, a contrivance to answer these needs. It is the primary device for the achievement of that kind of social structure human necessities demand, permitting men to live together in large, complex collectivities.

If we look at the functions of government in a slightly more specific sense, it is clear that government must, first of all, keep us from tearing ourselves to bits when social conflict reaches the point of maximum frustration. Before it can concern itself with providing the conditions for cooperative conduct it must act as a policeman to eliminate war within the community. It must do what the League of Nations and the United Nations have not yet proven capable of doing: it must maintain the peace. But in order to maintain a condition in which conflict does not reach the violent stage, government must do something more constructive. It cannot wait until internal, domestic war is about to break out. It must attempt to settle disputes as they arise and to eliminate the problems that lead to an overly intense state of strife. Government must, to put it briefly, mediate and arbitrate in social conflict as well as bring it to a halt. It needs to act as a judge, not only in courtrooms but also through such agencies as the Interstate Commerce Commission, settling disputes at an early stage so that it does not have to use all of its energies as a policeman, removing blazing pistols from the hands of angry men and women. This mediation function is an exceedingly broad one—much broader than that performed by modern law courts. It is a matter of problem-solving. Groups and individuals learn that they can bring their troubles to various officers of government and expect action, not always the action they ask for, but some attempt at solution. When this mediation function is operating smoothly, social conflicts are in a constant state of being settled, even if perfect settlement is not quickly achieved. There is then neither the need nor the impulse to take up arms. Certain types of conflict will be most easily settled through the ancient method used by the courts, but many of the newer and more difficult conflicts will be settled in the political arena through legislatures, executives, bureaucrats, parties, and pressure groups. A major part of the machinery of any effective government must, in any case, be available for this prime conflict-settlement function.

Government, by the very logic of its definition, must thus perform certain basic conflict functions: it mediates to prevent disputes from ever reaching an explosive stage in the first place, and it acts as a superpower to prevent the strife that does break out from turning into warlike violence. But in this world of nation-states it has another function related to human conflict—that of acting for the community in its relations with societies bound together under other governments. In certain ways these two conflict functions appear as opposites. While with one hand it is occupied internally, controlling disputes among subordinate individuals and subnational groups, acting as a judicious, pacifying superpower, the other hand is busily engaged in a different sort of conflict and cooperation—that concerned with relations between nation-states. In this other role it has become one of the contending elements in battle rather than a force above other forces. It turns from mediator to contender, from peacemaker to troublemaker, using its sources of power not as judge and policeman but as antagonist in diplomacy and as combatant in war. If a government is strong and self-confident, it can permit wide diversity within the nation; it has the means of settling an internal conflict that gets out of hand. But in its external relations, a strong government traditionally demands maximum unity in its own community in order to assume the role of agent of a nation, speaking with one voice and acting militarily with unanimity of purpose. Thus, although both of its conflict functions require the concentration of superior strength in governmental hands, the external function is less tolerant of the kind of freedom inherent in the democratic idea.

All of these conflict-related functions of government are inherent in the very concept of governance. When it does not perform them —when it abdicates its role as agent of a sovereign nation or when anarchy replaces domestic order—government in the functional sense ceases to exist. Officeholders may cling to their titles during a state of anarchy, but, if government is defined as the activity of governing, it can exist only if it governs sufficiently to maintain order internally and to deal with other governments abroad. Although these conflict functions are essential in the very idea of government, they do not nevertheless constitute the totality of its functions. Certain less inherent tasks are normally added. Having attained sufficient power to perform the mediation and preservation-of-peace functions at home and the foreign-relation functions abroad, governments universally perform other services for the community. They care for the sick, educate the young, build highways and airports, bring balance to the economy, bring improvements to agriculture, and make factories safe places to work. Having accumulated the very great power required to perform their essential conflict roles—power with dangers to be remembered later—they go on to use this power to make a richer and happier life for at least some of their citizens. Although a government could logically be imagined that performed none of these service functions, no government could be politically strong if it did not meet the demands for services its power makes it capable of. It would weaken its ability to perform its conflict functions if it resisted all pleas of its citizenry to provide help not efficiently attainable through private means.

There is, it needs to be said, a close relation between these various functions. Despite its thousands of parts and its many definable functions, government retains a certain unity. It is still one despite its plurality. President Johnson discovered this intertwining of functions when his deep involvement in Southeast Asia led much of the public to forget his domestic accomplishments. It spoiled his hopes for further innovations on the home front. Somewhat similarly, President Nixon's sudden intervention in Cambodia appeared to alter the whole base of support he needed for his domestic policy. When, for another example, government is giving rather than fighting, when its function is service rather than regulation, social conflicts may develop that require mediating and peacekeeping activities. A kind of battle royal often develops when government is giving privileges. An agency such as the Federal Communications Commission, in its free grant of fabulously profitable television-channel allocations, both gives and regulates as it determines which of the intensely anxious applicants will receive the prized license. The Department of Agriculture acts as both an economic regulator and a giver of beneficences when it pays the farmer for controlling the production of his crops. Government is still governing when it gives; it is regulating when it issues franchises; it changes its own community when it engages in foreign entanglements.

The democrat must understand the basic functions of government before he can turn his efforts toward making that government more compatible with human freedom. Despite occasional revivals of anarchist thinking and even a few episodes of nihilist bomb-throwing, there is now a general acceptance of the necessity of government. This is helpful for the democrat. It makes it possible for him to make a serious approach to the problems of freedom and order. It does not, however, solve those problems for him. Nor does acceptance of the ordering function of government tell us how much freedom is practical for individual men. There have been enough cruel autocracies in the history of mankind to demonstrate how small a share of freedom and how minimal a benefit of order large sectors of society may be given by their governors. The democrat learns to have respect for social order because man's capacity for freedom can apparently be increased by the proper kind of organization. He is not allowed the luxury of impatience with the idea of government itself. What he must do, having accepted government, is to make it more efficient in a peculiar sense—not in its control over people as much as in its effectiveness as a device of human self-fulfillment. His task is to make social discipline serve the cause of freedom. It is difficult to think of a task more challenging or more beset with contradictions, paradoxes, and endless conundrums. The goal of the democrat is more exacting than that of the anarchist because he resists the temptations to brush aside casually the more troublesome obstacles to human freedom. It is more difficult than that of the autocrat who simply surrenders freedom whenever social order is challenged by it. The democrat aims for the highest level of social existence: that in which neither orderliness nor liberty are sacrificed to one another. Knowing that the prime agent of communal organization is government, the democrat focuses on this problem rather than walking away from it. It is not surprising, therefore, that discussion of democracy deals largely with governmental processes.

Government has, in these pages, been defined primarily in terms of its functions.[1] In terms of the offices and men who perform the governing function, it can also be defined as a group. And, more importantly for the discussion of democracy, it is definable in terms

1. I make no use of the concept of the state in these pages. Sometimes that concept is used as synonymous with government, but for others it may have an international law significance or may be used to indicate the entire political community. There seems no necessity of confusing matters with such a term in this essay.

of its basic tool—power. Government remains the most important of groups because it maintains a superiority, sometimes amounting almost to a monopoly, of certain kinds of social power. Most notably, it tends to monopolize the major instruments of the harsher kinds of power, which are supported by sanctions of violence and brutal coercion: imprisonment, death, warfare, physical punishment. Although democrats wish to keep both this and the milder kinds of governmental power within bounds, they realize that government, by the logic of its function, assumes the existence of power. The democrat can shift his government away from its more brutal instruments toward that kind of power which is founded on man's reason, on his social habits, and on his consent. He can, by developing participatory processes, ensure that the governed have some say in how the governors use power bestowed upon them. He can tame governmental power, broaden the process of decision-making that determines its use, and make it serve the interests of liberty, but he cannot expect to discard it. The democrat cannot eliminate government as a problem for human freedom. He can, nevertheless, bend every effort to the solution of the fundamental problem of making order and liberty more compatible.

DECISION-MAKING AND LEADERSHIP

Any one of us can be stricken by the hand of fate. But it is not such unpredictable acts of the gods that determine who we are or what we are to become. Each human animal assumes a personality, becoming a social as well as a biological being, through innumerable acts of choosing. Only at moments of decision does man experience freedom; only then does he become truly human. A community is, in this respect, like an individual: it, too, becomes a distinguishable being; it, too, assumes a kind of collective personality through the making of choices. In the discussion of collective decision-making, however, we come very quickly to a question that never concerns us in dealing with choices made by an individual for his own purposes: who makes the decision and what relation has he to his community? The question of decision-making then becomes entangled with that of leadership, and, for a democracy, the form leadership takes must, quite obviously, be a fundamental issue.

Democrats have often become confused about the role of leadership because they have erroneously assumed that democracy, being opposed to autocracy, is therefore against leadership itself. Democracy is, in fact, definable as a peculiar system of leadership. It must attempt, not to eliminate its leaders, but to create a particular form of social direction that is compatible with the democratic purpose. The democrat has, however, good reason for apprehension. Ancient Greek thinkers were among the first to be aware of the ease with which a democracy can slide from freedom into tyranny. The history of democracies supports this anxiety, providing a multitude of examples of demagogues and conquering heroes on white horses. A democracy must create its own peculiar form of communal direction; it must guarantee that its leadership is selected by a process entailing wide community participation. It must also take precautions against any perversion of leadership that might destroy democracy itself, a problem to be discussed later (in Chapter 7). Discussion of democracy must, at a very early point, concern itself with the nature of leadership and, before that, with the nature of decision-making in a collectivity.

The function of leadership at a moment of drama or of confrontation between societies, as with the Bay of Pigs invasion or the Cuban missile crisis during the 1960s, will differ quite notably from that in some perplexing social circumstance such as the tiresome farm problem or the undramatic struggle against inflation. Leadership differs from situation to situation in so many subtle ways that it would be ridiculous to attempt cataloguing all the different kinds of decisional circumstances, even those for a single office such as that of the president of the United States. But it is possible to mention one differentiation that will begin to indicate the complexity of the problem and perhaps help to clarify the function of democratic leadership. This distinction is one between a precise policy choice in which a community takes a *decisional* type of direction and, at the other end of the spectrum, the community takes a more obscure kind of direction, appearing in the shape of a *trend*. Starting at this latter, most ambiguous extreme, it might be useful to choose an example of *trend direction* so amorphous as hardly to be classifiable as social policy at all—the choice by western nations of capitalism. Millions of small choices, most so minor as to escape the chronicles of history, pushed western European communities on a capitalist course. Leadership was of the pluralistic kind, comprising innumerable actions of men and women, few having sufficient drama to gain wide public attention. The "choice" of a certain kind of capitalism was surely a crucial one for each nation; yet there are no founding fathers for schoolchildren to revere and no dates for them to memorize. Men sometimes assume, in such a situation, that history itself is somehow the actor. This, however, requires us to overlook the role of worldly bankers in Florence, of industrious merchants of Amsterdam, and of venturesome enterpreneurs in London and Boston. Fashionable Marxist language disguises such ambiguous social choices with a new kind of fatalism, giving credit to broad "revolutionary forces," which, although not unreal, tend to hide the fact that whole communities made decisions through the specific choices of innumerable men and women over many generations.

It may now be useful to come down to earth slightly, taking a set of examples that are more relevant to a modern democracy. The gradual establishment of a racial policy in the United States in the late nineteenth century and the slow reversal of that policy in the mid-twentieth century may be more meaningful illustrations of ambiguous social choice-making. As is now widely known, the white-supremacy policy that developed as a substitute for slavery after the Reconstruction era established a paradoxical caste culture within the midst of a nation relatively devoid of class consciousness. Politically, it resulted in something called the Solid South, an atrophied state of party politics, a no-party system that, from the national perspective, looked confusingly like a one-party system. It should, for our purposes, be emphasized that at no time did anyone issue a decree establishing a Jim Crow culture or give a clear command to isolate the Negro politically. Many men made choices that brought a policy into being, and others, including presidents and courts, were carried along; but no one can be named as decision-maker. In the more recent past there occurred a remarkably spontaneous movement to reverse this policy. But again, although the reversal has been dramatic, no one can point to a single date or to the action of a single man or even to that of a single group of men who made the crucial decision. A small band of impatient college students in North Carolina and Mrs. Rosa Parks, a tired housewife standing in a Montgomery, Alabama, bus—these "small but courageous" people were as much the heroes of the day as were Martin Luther King or the justices of the Supreme Court. The enormously significant policies determined in each of these instances, the battle to reverse the original repressive policy, have overshadowed all the men who had any role in it. Little people and small choices can sometimes stand a nation on its head just as effectively as can a great president in a decision consciously undertaken at one dramatic moment.

A democracy, because it stresses community participation and because it maximizes freedom of decision, encourages minor leadership. *Trend-direction* kinds of choices will occur in any society. While a democrat considers it a sign of health that minor leadership plays a significant role in decision-making, the dictator worries about matters getting out of hand. The democratic leader is expected to be pleased when his community seems capable of making decisions for itself through the numerous subleaders and subgroups that make up a pluralistic society. Democracy encourages small decisions and numerous decision-makers by giving men freedom and by making it possible for such subleaders to rise into positions of top leadership with a little bit of luck and some serious effort. It is a serious mistake, when thinking of leadership in a democratic community, to conceive only those circumstances requiring energetic leadership, to be concerned solely with names in the headlines. Much of the policy process of the nation will be the product of free and responsible men and women scattered throughout the society. Their choices are seldom the kind that attract swarms of newsmen and television cameras, but democracy is secure only to the extent that this broad, secondary leadership echelon is functioning in a healthy fashion.

The idea of a spectrum of types of social policy with *trend direction* at one end and *decisional direction* at the other is, of course, a crude one. Not only are there infinite shades of differentiation on the long continuum between the polar extremes, but any one social choice may itself involve numerous kinds of decisions and trends. The decision of the United States to drop a new kind of bomb on Hiroshima on a specific day in 1945 would surely seem to fall within the category of decisional direction. There was a choice between carefully weighed alternatives. The choice was made by specific men whose names will enter the history books. It was made within a specific time period at a specific place, with close communication between a handful of participants. Yet there is also a larger story. Years of decision-making by atomic scientists, military men, and political leaders finally led to the single decisive event at Hiroshima. As Robert Jungk has put it, "the sum of a thousand individual acts of an intensely conscientious character led eventually to an act of collective abandonment of conscience, horrifying in its magnitude."[2]

Even the most precise decision is seldom as simple as it seems. We might find it easier to design neat mechanisms for democratic accountability if we could count on decision-making as always constituting a distinct choice between definite alternatives at a given time and place by specifically named men. The fact of the matter is, however, that this is rarely the nature of any decisions and is practically never the situation when the issues are of major social consequence. Democrats cannot afford the pleasures of oversimplification. Only through the assumption that decision-making and its control is a fantastically complex process can the democrat be

2. Robert Jungk, *Brighter than a Thousand Suns,* trans. James Cleugh (New York: Harcourt, Brace, 1958), p. 209.

aware that his plans for popular participation must include not only formal devices of accountability but the construction of an entire leadership process that inbreeds a sense of social responsibility. When devices of democratic control are being discussed (as they will be in Chapter 6), it is important to remember that there exists an entire echelon of people making small decisions that lead to big ones such as the Hiroshima bomb, the Bay of Pigs fiasco, or the passage of civil-rights legislation.

It is undoubtedly inevitable that discussion of policy-making will err by overstressing the more specific, the more easily documented kind of events. The student of democratic government should make some effort to offset this tendency when analyzing the workings of the system. He should remind himself of other elements in the story. The fact, for example, that Harry Truman, a crucial decision-maker in the case of the 1945 bomb, was an elected official facing another election in three years, is an essential part of that story. But it may be of equal importance to remember the kind of society from which he arose, the kinds of schools he attended, the kind of family in which he was reared, and the kind of reading material he chose for his spare moments. Democracy must operate through the indoctrination of all persons who might conceivably enter the leadership echelon, as well as through laws and election processes. This demands nothing less than the education of a whole race of people, since democracy insists on giving all of its citizenry something akin to equality of opportunity to enter the realms of political power.

THE MEANING OF LEADERSHIP

"So still he seems to dwell nowhere at all; so empty no one can seek him out." The truly enlightened ruler, according to Han Fei Tzu, writing in China some twenty-two centuries ago, "reposes in nonaction above, and below his ministers tremble with fear." [3]

3. Han Fei Tzu, *Basic Writings*, trans. Burton Watson (New York: Columbia University Press, 1964), p. 17.

Even Machiavelli, at the beginning of the modern era, would have found these words quite strange as advice to the prince. To the citizen of a modern democracy it sounds like sheer nonsense. The ruler was advised to "be empty, still, and idle, and from your place of darkness observe the defects of others. See but do not appear to see; listen but do not seem to listen, know but do not let it be known that you know." There is not a trace of the modern concept of leadership in the remarks of this ancient sage. They idealize the complete autocrat in a static, bureaucratized society. There is no hint that the ruler should display creative imaginativeness or use the tools of persuasion. But the precise idea of leadership that is common to English-speaking readers is, even now, less common than it might seem. Some other languages do not possess a word for the exact equivalent of it. They lack any term that distinguishes the persuasive kind of control from the more general idea of "rule," with its implications of command and obedience.

In a dictionary of English synonyms, the verb "to lead" is placed in conjunction with such words as "guide" and "steer." We need to look in another part of the book to find the listing of "govern" and "rule." There is, however, a difference between leadership and guidance; the former "stresses the idea of going in advance," showing the way, and keeping "those that follow in order and under control." The leader possesses attributes of power not inherent in the actions of the guide; yet there is, in both cases, an implication of voluntariness. Leadership is a particularly valuable concept for democracy because it provides an idea of social control that does not deprive the follower of all freedom of choice. It emphasizes that the human animal can be made to follow his supposed superior as a result of something quite unlike the habit of a trained dog answering his master's whistle or the coercion that pulls the puppy along on his leash.

The leader achieves his objective, and the follower feels that his action has been, at least partly, a matter of his own choosing. But the concept of leadership, signifying as it does that people will be drawn along, seems also to infer that the leader has a direction he wishes the group to follow. Leadership implies a kind of creativity. While the leader will frequently act as a synthesizer for ideas arising from a number of sources in the community and is seldom the originator of brand new ideas, he must be an innovator in the respect that he awakens his followers to the possibility of fresh direction. The Oriental despot, sitting silently with an inscrutable expression, can clearly have no desire that the community "go" anywhere beyond the track of established custom. Today we would not call him a leader of men because it is the leader's function to develop and clarify objectives and to appeal to the community to follow his direction in goals that may partly have arisen out of their own vague desires. The leader differentiates himself from the community by being ahead of it, but, at the same time, he remains close enough to it to possess an almost instinctive knowledge of those goals the collectivity would express if it had the single voice to do so. He stands slightly removed from the community, and this remoteness is based supposedly on a superior capacity to define the collective aims of the community and to suggest concrete action.

In American society of the 1960s the assassination within five years of two highly articulate young men with what was called political style and of the one man who seemed most capable of harnessing the bursting energy of the newly awakened Negro population created a large dent, which is evidence of the rarity of leadership even in a nation as rich in manpower as the United States. It is possible that none of these three men would have turned out to be heroes had they lived long enough to become bogged down in the intricacies of carrying out policies about which they talked; yet, whatever the eventual merits of the Kennedy brothers or of Martin Luther King, the trauma of their deaths illustrates the emphasis a democratic community places on supposedly creative leadership. Much is expected of the leader. He must have his roots firmly planted in the customs and attitudes of his nation; he must build on history while pushing forward in new directions. He is expected to do the impossible—to fly like an eagle with his ear to the ground. Even in a dream, this is a vision difficult to contemplate, but it may help to illustrate why, except for those with early deaths, history is so devoid of names of many men to whom all would agree to assign the title, "true leader."

The leadership function is also integrative. The leader must have followers or else he has no claim to the title, and he must, by the very act of leading, bind the people into a group behind his unfurled banner. There are several aspects of such integration. Much of it is accomplished by a means that is not normally called creative, by bureaucratization—the creation of orderly machinery of control. But it is also accomplished by the assumption on the part of the leader of what might be called representational qualities: the leader comes to symbolize the community, acting as spokesman for its desires and fears. From within the society the leader becomes something of a father figure; from without he becomes its agent. In more primitive groups this paternal relation is taken more literally and felt more deeply as a psychological truth. Even in sophisticated modern communities, however, a certain dignity is expected of the leader because he is in the position of father among his fellow citizens and because this is the way outsiders may be expected to view him. The leader expresses the collective direction of his community, showing the way both by persuasion and by the image he creates at home and abroad by word and deed. This is why a man such as Lyndon Johnson, one of the most effective men to sit in the White House, was something less than a total success. He did not present the image that many of his followers demanded of their spokesman. A president who presented nothing but image, with no capacity to get the job done, would be far worse. However, the symbolic aspect of leadership is no less important simply because it can conceivably be based upon fakery.

The historically significant leader takes his community somewhere. The fundamental meaning of leadership is found, however, in the act itself more than in its results. The act of leadership is that of persuasion and of guiding a group in a collective direction, regardless of the content of that direction. The leadership function brings men and women along; it takes them in some social direction, not on the basis of coercive commands, but on the basis of an educative process. This is why leadership is so important to democracies. No society rests purely on coercive devices of governance, not even an oriental despotism; nor does any society rely entirely on persuasion for its rulership. A democracy, however, tries to replace coercion with persuasion whenever it can; it emphatically prefers leadership over command. Democrats prefer teachers to policemen as instruments of social integration. Contemporary, postdemocratic autocrats are quite aware of the value of propaganda as a source of political power, but they view educative devices as morally interchangeable with coercive devices. They sometimes find that schools are more effective than prisons in capturing the minds of men, but either one will do. A democrat, by contrast, will even forgo some community objectives, such as national conformity of opinion, if it appears that these cannot be achieved through voluntary followership.

Democracies need to find ways to formalize the features that distinguish them from autocracies. They need, for example, to institutionalize the concept of leadership as it has been explained here, to work it into the processes of governance. The central mechanism for accomplishing this formalization is the voting process. In addition to its obvious and overwhelming value as an expression of community opinion—the kind of expression the leader needs and seeks if he is to succeed in his role—voting provides a major symbol of the dependence of democracies on persuasive implements as contrasted with the coercive apparatus typical of a command situation. The importance of voting becomes more than procedural and more than symbolic; it is also psychological. Before the election comes the campaign, an activity forcing those men who wish to assume the highest centers of power to humble themselves by asking a mass of voters to select them in preference to their competitors. The prospective ruler must come, hat in hand, to his prospective followers, asking their help. He must ask their permission before he can assume a position of commanding superiority. Sometimes the process of campaign and election seems costly, crude, and ineffective. Yet, even if we ignore the value of an expression of popular opinion and the other virtues of having elections, the single fact that they force those anxious to dominate their fellow men to obtain the permission of those dominated compensates for all costs. The act of campaigning emphasizes the fact that democracies are leadership rather than command oriented. The tradition of a fair and effective election process brings the concept of democratic leadership into the habitual thinking of the society and helps to guarantee the continuation of a free society.

THE RECRUITMENT OF POLITICAL MANPOWER

Democracy has invented its own ingenious kind of torture: the cruel path of ambition. Having opened the way to many ladders, it watches sardonically as man after man finds the rungs rising too steeply for his feet. Instead of the rigid hurdles of class consciousness, democracy substitutes another form of discrimination, that between success and failure. It would be a tragedy if, after having paid the costs of encouraging ambition, a society did not improve the quality of its political leadership. Having opened gates throughout the community, a democracy must take steps to assure itself that a substantial number of those with leadership potential find their way into central leadership positions. The liberty of diverse career choices may be self-defeating if it leads too few persons toward community leadership. If freedom results in too great a flow of talent into economic enterprise, into technology, into science, and into other talent-consuming fields that are narrowly specialized, the democratic goal of maximum participation may be damaged by the very freedom it offers. The first task of political education is to guard against this dangerous eventuality.

It is a peculiarity of democracy that, although the leaders of governance must eventually possess much greater skill and knowledge about governmental processes than the rest of us, such persons cannot be accorded any program of basic education. Potential leaders are distinguished from nonleaders by the process of political education itself; the distinction cannot precede it or be specifically recognized in the organization of a teaching curriculum. This is due to the basic character of the open recruitment process inherent in the democratic idea and also to the very nature of the task of a political leader. Such a person will learn to become an expert in the processes of governance, but in other respects he will be the very model of the "compleat amateur." His field of knowledge, outside those specifics of political maneuvering which are largely learned by in-service training, is the community as a whole. As a result, there is no profession more in need of an initially liberal education—liberal both in the sense of breadth and in its association with the idea of liberty. Future leaders cannot be identified at birth, but it is necessary somehow to ensure that all who might be raised to power in a democracy will be trained in the liberal arts.

The initial step in democratic recruitment is the attempt to instill in the right persons at the right time a love for the political life. It is desirable that such persons are motivated equally by an interest in social objectives and by an enjoyment of the political process. A stratagem must be devised to keep interest in political mechanics from degenerating into cynical opportunism and to prevent concern with goals from developing into a doctrinaire fixation on rigid objectives or an unproductive utopianism. The channel between these twin shoals is narrow and treacherous, and few can steer the way without veering from the central course. Some are captivated by the siren call of politics as a game; others by the attraction of perfect virtue, seeking rightness when compromise is properly called for. Media of mass communication, schools and universities, and textbooks and popular writings can emphasize the better side of democratic politics, but the most important feature of political education will remain political practice. If the actual path of political life is a balanced one—an intriguing game never entirely separated from social direction—the facts will speak for themselves, politics providing its own school for future leaders.

Leadership is in many ways its own creator; "great men," according to Emerson, "exist so that there may be great men." One aspect of leadership usually underemphasized is its role in creating future leadership. In any society, leadership is to a major extent co-opted. In the narrow sense, co-optation occurs when present leaders discover and train talented men and women to replace them. Although the practice is not openly encouraged either by the American tradition or by its political structure, such co-optation is a more normal part of the tightly organized parties that provide something like a career pattern within the British parliamentary system. There is, however, another respect in which leadership is co-opted in a democratic nation: this occurs when dynamic, colorful leaders—men who obviously love the game of politics and who show deep concern with the direction a society takes—encourage others through spontaneous enthusiasm and dramatic action.

Political enthusiasm is contagious. When, instead of choosing politically oriented men, democracies turn for leadership to men who do not genuinely enjoy the political process, as Americans have done on several occasions, a smothering blanket may easily be thrown over the spirited pleasures of political life that normally act as attractions for young blood. The contrast between the late 1950s and the early 1960s is a case in point. In the late Eisenhower era public discourse took on a dull, gloomy air, with a decline in political interest and much talk about a loss of national purpose. In the short years before the Kennedy era ended in tragic assassination, in the frustration of a war that could not be won, and in an unsolvable race problem, there was a new spirit, a new interest in political life. The crime of the dullard in public office is that he drives potential new talent away, much of it permanently. But the rare man who can set a society on the move by providing the spark of leadership strengthens the community for years ahead, making public life attractive as vocation and avocation for young persons with high ideals.

Democracy does not make the recruitment of political manpower an easy task. The profession of political leadership is a chancy one. A democracy purposely interferes with men's ambitions to govern their fellows. It is the privilege of no man to succeed of his own volition in becoming a ruler. Neither ambition, training, conscientious effort, nor strong social purpose is sufficient. Among all the professions, democratic politics is the most open and yet the most exclusive: anyone may make formal application, but admission is determined by a high-handed community that has so many criteria that rarely can anyone find the precise formula for continued success. The career of a democratic leader must, perhaps fortunately, begin in some area other than politics itself, in a tangential field of endeavor. This is less true in Britain and is particularly the case in the United States, where the chief channel of political careers, the political party, is so fragmented that it can give little more than minor help to the aspiring politician. In fact, it is commonplace for American political parties to be unable to protect even their elder statesmen. Senators, governors, and presidential candidates are often put out to pasture at the height of their careers, with potential for service unfulfilled.

Few men can contemplate unemployment or a life of leisure as alternatives for failure to achieve public office; only men with the resources of a Kennedy or a Rockefeller can deliberately set out to undertake a political career. Although it is fortunate that the rich are becoming public spirited and that American democracy is well enough established not to have fear of potential plutocrats, a properly functioning democracy must keep the doors open to all levels of society. It must concern itself with encouraging potential leaders to move from adjoining careers into public life. The crucial need is to encourage men and women to enter those kinds of tangential professions which demand a humanistic kind of training, in which they are trained to see society as a whole and not to concentrate on some small, technical segment for intense specialization. It would be disappointing if the liberty that democracy offers became merely the capacity to keep busy—at one moment operating the economic machine and, in the next, desperately seeking ways to consume its generous product. One of the most disturbing results of a society that gains abundance through technological specialization is the prospect of a decline in the proportion of an educated class that is broadly oriented. A large body of liberally educated men and women is essential to provide the community with a meaningful sense of direction. It is possible to offset potential overspecialization, but it will require careful attention to the whole educational machinery.

No one would argue that public leadership in a democracy should be made the exclusive province of any profession—of lawyers, butchers, bakers, or candlestick makers—but the conventional stress on the legal profession in the American scheme, although not typical of all other democracies, does possess a certain logic. Law remains among the most liberal of professions in an age of fragmented specialties. Trends in American legal education are taking a broadening direction, and legal education has always encouraged the critical mind as well as the art of democratic discourse. Although the prominence of economic institutions in an abundant society necessarily forces most lawyers to adopt a business orientation, law continues to reach as thoroughly into all corners of life as does any other profession. It is inevitably linked, furthermore, to the process of governance, both because its rules come from government and because law provides the means of controlling the governors. Although a democracy would be foolish to depend exclusively on legal training for the political education of its leaders—law is, after all, backward-looking in its reference to precedents and ancient codes—it is encouraging that at least one profession still stresses the virtues of liberal education.

Before modern democracy addresses itself to such questions as those involving particular kinds of schooling or with the way to make politically oriented professions such as law into better sources of political recruitment, it must be concerned with the fundamental nature of the aristocracy it is trying to create. The aristocrats of society, those who must show us the way, have in the past, by and large, been found among that class of persons who were well situated in terms of wealth. During the period when democracy was arising in Britain and elsewhere, leadership strength was located among a small class of comfortable, educated men and women who happened to possess a public conscience. But now we find, despite the extreme disparity of disadvantaged minorities, a situation in which abundance is remarkably widespread throughout the community. It is to be hoped that out of this larger mass of comfortable people, presently much concerned with learning how to consume increasing amounts of worldly goods, a new kind of aristocracy of civic talent will emerge, one that no longer needs to stand on the shoulders of a poverty-stricken mass.

When we speak of a new aristocracy we should not have to apologize. If abundance were properly distributed throughout the community, as it can now potentially be, each man would have a better chance to choose his own path; he need not be jealous of those who make their choice in the direction of public leadership. To paraphrase President Kennedy, a society can be safe both for personal distinction and for democracy—the two are not incompatible. Although there are sufficient historic justifications for democrats being levelers, times have changed, and our concept of aristocracy also needs to change. An open aristocracy of political talent can be quite different from a closed one built on inheritance or on extreme differences in wealth and in education. A potential equality of educational opportunity, which now seems not far ahead of us, will change the role of the leadership echelon in society. The concept of a Platonic guardian class will be totally altered when it is assumed, not only that wisdom can come from anywhere, but that the community will take upon itself the task of making such wisdom generally available by creating sophisticated institutions of low-cost schooling. If anything, future need for excellence in civic leadership will increase, so that an elite will continue to be demanded. The democratic community can, however, make that elite into a totally open category, admitting all those with ability, with energy, and with the desire to assume a public conscience.

THE MAGNETISM OF GOVERNMENTAL POWER

"Authority intoxicates, and makes mere sots of magistrates," says Samuel Butler. "The fumes of it invade the brain, and make men giddy, proud and vain." The problem is ancient. Its solution is a central challenge to the democrat. There are numerous instruments that can be brought forward to harness it, but none of these, or at least none with a significant hope of success, attempts to repudiate power itself. The phenomenon of government has, in these pages and elsewhere, been conceived in terms of power; it is distinguished by the unique superiority of that power. Having established government as a central source of power designed to bring order to the community, men are seldom satisfied until it has been put to broader use. They cannot, as has already been implied, avoid seeing enticing potentials in the ability of governmental power to utilize natural and social resources for endless new private and communal purposes.

Government can, if it wishes to be so foolish, attempt to undertake virtually all economic activity in the community. It can take from the poor and give to the rich or take from the rich and give to the poor. It can distribute resources among groups, classes, and geographic areas for the wider benefit of all or, if it wishes to be perverse, for the special benefit of a favored segment. The fact that no government is absurd enough to exercise its powers to the ultimate, that most western governments are circumscribed by law, and that many governments are strongly influenced by private groups within their boundaries or by other governments beyond their frontiers—none of this alters the basic theory behind governmental authority. It remains, in our world of nation-states, the superior power, irrespective of who dominates it and of how inhibited its citizenry have made it through legal or political limitations. Despite particular restrictions on specific governments, government in general remains unique in its ability to act with uniformity over all people, over all groups, and everywhere within its geographic limits.

Although some governments may be ineffectual, the general phenomenon of governmental power appears to be subject to a long-term inflationary tendency similar in some ways to that which has affected monetary systems. We are aware, for example, that the French government floundered for a decade or so after World War II, that the American government seemed lacking in a sense of domestic policy direction during the same period, and that other governments have had similarly impotent periods; but such specific instances of decelerated growth do not refute the trend. Sometimes periods of apparent decline in governmental activity are actually times of consolidation; this may well have been the case with the American experience in the 1950s. If this general assumption of inflation in governmental powers is true, what is its cause? In large part, of course, it is the result of dynamic social changes that have required new governmental actions. But the cause can also be found in the nature of government itself: the vigorous powers of government are a temptation, attracting all those who wish to see social action carried out on a comprehensive scale. Governmental power is not simply superior; it is also magnetic in its attraction to those in the society who want something done.

The magnetic attraction of government comes from its inherent power and from the increasing indispensability of its major activities. This is well demonstrated in its function as agent of the community in relation to other communities. Nationalism is partly caused by and partly a cause of expanding governmental power; it has spread, in a highly dynamic manner, from the European heartland to older fringe nations such as America and Russia and, more recently, to non-European communities, which appear to have adopted it with almost fanatical enthusiasm. The great temptation to utilize the monoply of military force that all governments possess demonstrates an area of governmental power in which the inflationary tendency is particularly frightening to democrats. Success in nationalistic endeavors appear to demand, simultaneously, great secrecy in administration and policy development and a vast expansion of the concentration of decision-making power. Democrats are justifiably unhappy with the bits and pieces of knowledge that sometimes escape such nationalistic enterprises as the American Central Intelligence Agency and the Green Berets.

The essential internal function of government in the preservation of order and in the mediation of social conflict displays an equally dynamic pattern of growth. This expansion of domestic ordering functions is but one element in a generally increasing sophistication of all human collectivities. Technology has made possible vastly more powerful and expansive industrial and commercial corporations, farm associations, and labor unions, while simultaneously requiring more governmental activity in their control. In capitalist nations governmental expansion remains relatively haphazard, more a reaction to technology than a generator of it. But, in both socialist and capitalist communities, government has expanded: in one case to direct more closely a developing economy and in the other to soften the harshness and temper the conflict resulting from an almost too rapid technological evolution. Even those western societies which have not been so foolhardy as to move toward anything like total control of the economy are learning that the task of manipulating a complex society is almost too great for the unsophisticated tools available.

Government has also expanded with rapidity in its nonregulatory service function. Once men and women have discovered the potential power of government, the extent of its resource base, the ability it possesses to distribute the wealth, and its value as a cooperative mechanism to enrich their lives, the pressure builds for the expansion of activities aimed at the general welfare. The long history of governmental expansion of activities in the realm of education is a good example. Beginning in a small way not much over a century ago, each expansion of the governmental role encouraged education-minded publics to ask for more and to ask it, increasingly, from a more centralized unit of government. The Johnson administration's Elementary and Secondary Education Act signaled a major increase in such expansion, but the long trend has been a steady one. More and more groups have learned of the potential largess government can provide, and no community and no possible governmental function seems immune from this inflationary trend. The expansion of governmental activity thus becomes cumulative. Its functions tend to increase in geometric progression: the more people learn about the latent riches government can harness for public purposes, the more they demand—without wishing, quite naturally, to give up any past services. In free, pluralistic societies, organized groups find ways to press for such advantages with increasing effectiveness, and their influence is difficult to resist.

The expansion of government functions is not, however, precisely equivalent to the expansion of governmental power. Any recent secretary of agriculture is likely to have experienced not so much a feeling of great power as one of nagging frustration, resulting from the fact that the government's enormously expanded agricultural functions have themselves created almost insoluble problems. The existence of prepaid medical care in Great Britain added some power to the governing officials; yet it also created severe headaches that have sometimes made cabinet ministers feel almost powerless. A fat government, overloaded with complex functions, is not necessarily stronger than a lean one, its powers concentrated on a few objectives. On the contrary, some of the expansion of government displayed by the growth of the bureaucracy, by the increase in spending, and even by the expansion of police duties has made the tasks of government more difficult and has brought a feeling of impotence to the officials who are supposedly enjoying increased power. The fact that a complex organization like government has more and more work to do and spends more and more money does not mean that an equivalent increase in influence has accompanied it. Power and function are by no means identical.

The growth of the functions of government, with a burgeoning public payroll and a variety of new services, is also an expansion of power in the sense that government has been charged with channeling a greater share of the human and material resources. It performs new functions that might, hypothetically at least, be performed by nongovernmental agencies, which could provide more potentially competitive sources of power. It does not follow, however, that every functional expansion adds exactly that much to the concentration of power within the society. Officials in governmental agencies perform increasingly numerous important social functions. Yet the particular officials are not always tightly controlled from above as in a perfectly pyramidal hierarchy. Influences on government from private, outside agencies and interest groups seem to increase in democratic societies at almost the same rate as the expansion of governmental functions. Furthermore, large and complex organizations, like modern governments, frequently permit generous grants of autonomy to subordinate officers. There are, as it were, a myriad of little hierarchies operating semi-independently of the master one, which, in popular mythology, oversees them all. There remains an all-important question, however, even in the most decentralized of such structures: to what extent are these little hierarchies controlled or controllable by the elements in society they supposedly serve and by those who are taxed for their support? The problems of freedom from arbitrary control do not disappear simply because a number of small organizations are only very loosely united in a master organization. This will be important to remember when judging the effectiveness of democratic practice. It will also be an important consideration in our later review of problems of accountability (Chapter 6).

As the final quarter of the twentieth century approaches, the traditional concern of libertarians with excessive power has encountered yet another confusion. The current epoch frequently seems to display a problem describable as a failure of power or as a crisis of nongovernability. Governments (including but not limited to those called democracies) have often appeared almost incapacitated in the face of the difficult problems confronting them. In the mid-1950s this was a major theme of Walter Lippmann's *Public Philosophy;* in the late 1960s it was a central point of Theodore Lowi's *The End of Liberalism.*[4] Modern governments seem often to be as confused as their citizenry by the increasingly severe problems confronting the community, and democratic governments have no way to hide their confusion. There was once a time when democrats were so critical of overgovernment, so frightened of the abuse of power, that they could not recognize the potential existence of a counterproblem. Some of them, later on, learned to praise the kind

4. The former was published in 1955 (Boston, Little, Brown); the latter in 1969 (New York, Norton).

of activist government that made serious efforts at meeting freedom-depriving social problems. In neither case was the capability of government the issue. The postwar period has, however, been one of almost continuous strain on governmental processes from both domestic and international tensions. One of the major postwar trends among western nations (one to which this book will return in Chapter 7), is the rising affluence that does not extend to everyone in the population but affects the nature of the whole culture. Its high costs were not immediately recognized. In the United States, when they did begin to be observed, there was ample room for concern. The new opportunities often seemed to turn sour. For example, mechanized agriculture in the rural South along with potential jobs in the cities had, at first, seemed to mean new opportunities for poverty-stricken blacks. But it was soon discovered that many of the blacks had moved into what were becoming ungovernable, urban wildernesses, instead of into areas of new opportunity. Nor did Americans realize, at first, the price of the commercialized affluence in uglification and pollution, in physical and psychic disturbance. Nor had it occurred to many to ask what would happen if the young should inquire, in their own confusing way, about the deadening spirit of a commercialized society.

The New Dealers and others had taught us to demand practical action from our governments. But, amidst this rapid but delayed awakening to the ills of the world around us, those governments now seemed incapable of action in every area but the international one (where they seemed, instead, merely to become involved in nonresolvable conflicts). The burst of policy-making early in the Johnson administration had the flavor of a New Deal revival, but new deals hardly seem adequate any more. By the time that there were hints of a policy of "benign neglect" from the Nixon White House, many were too cynical to care. Whether or not it was deserved in the circumstance, such cynicism is dangerous. It results, in part, from a failure to realize that democratic governments attack their more serious problems, first of all, through extended discourse, a slow process under the best of conditions. Reaching solutions in such a manner can be a frustrating experience. Planning will be crude, policy will have the appearance of muddling through. The community, itself often slow to recognize its problems, cannot expect dramatic resolutions the moment it comes awake. As both Lippmann and Lowi were so fully aware, a community needs direction at any time but particularly at moments like this. It needs a sense of general policy direction. But, as both would recognize, even with active leadership and coordinate direction, there can be no guarantee against fumbling.

A free press makes the crisis of nongovernability more apparent. But this does not mean that it is nonexistent elsewhere. In this fast-moving age all communities are confronted with consequences of new social changes before they have begun to adjust to the last ones. Pluralist societies will, under such conditions, appear to flounder even more than is their norm. Even if the solutions were more obvious than they happen, in fact, to be, pluralism could (by definition) provide no coordinated structure that could be commanded for quick action. And the United States has carried pluralism to an extreme. It has created a near infinity of bureaucracies in the national government. This is not so unusual, but to these must be added another near infinity of separated state and local units of governance. Even the many legislatures are fragmented into near-autonomous centers of committee power. To manage such a system would require remarkable coordination of numbers of leaders as well as political skills not often apparent. But there is yet another question, one too easily ignored at times such as these. Precisely what would we have our governments do if they were more manageable? To whom do we credit the wisdom for their coordinated direction? Instead of answers we get more problems, and they are complex ones; so are the instruments devoted to their solution. There is reasonable ground for fear. The only immediate recourse, however, is to continue the discourse: to continue demanding action and suggesting solutions. This must be done in full awareness of the inherent complexities of the democratic process, and if one continues to prize the virtues of dispersed power, he should not be totally surprised when he suffers some of its consequences. Will the next crisis be too overwhelming for pluralistic institutions to survive? It would be foolish to have blind confidence; it would also be foolish to discard the entire structure in a moment of panic. Reforms in the structure of power, in the leadership system, and in the policy-making mechanisms need to be explored continually, but it is dangerous to do so entirely in a mood of fear and anger.

CHAPTER 3

The Public Life: Democracy as Participation

SOME slight, sardonic amusement might arise from placing all the volumes a democratic society has produced concerning one of its uncommon men, a democratic hero like Abraham Lincoln, in a scale balanced by all the books, bad or good, ever written in praise of the common man. One could add, for good measure, every book written on the role of the public in a democracy without redressing the equilibrium very substantially. For every Walt Whitman, one of the rare poets of democracy, there are perhaps a hundred singers of praise for now-forgotten heroes. Such comparisons emphasize the obvious. One of the best efforts of a journalist to describe the democratic system in action is Theodore White's *Making of the President, 1960.*[1] What makes that book so useful is, in part, that it displays the close relation between personality and process in an election campaign. As a more academic example of the paradoxical fact that democracies spend more time thinking about leadership than about masses of men, one might look at an important, scholarly work, *Public Opinion and American Democracy.*[2] The author of that work, Professor V. O. Key, found himself, perhaps unconsciously, concluding almost every chapter on the role of publics in a democracy with discussion of the function of elite elements in the formation of publics and in the development of their opinions.

1. (New York: Atheneum, 1961).
2. (New York: Knopf, 1961).

There is no question that a democracy must concern itself with leadership. Chapter 2 has stressed that democracy may be seen, from one perspective, as a particular structure for the development of leadership. But it is not possible to stop there. A student of the political history of medieval Florence might tell a large part of the story of that republic in terms of the comings and goings of the great families, but, if he forgot about the role of those lesser men who made up the great and small guilds, he would never quite understand events and their causes. In a democracy such as the United States much of political history is found in the story of presidents, of presidential candidates, of a scattering of great leaders of Congress, and of stray military leaders now and then wandering onto the stage. But leadership in a democracy such as the United States arises from the community, responds to it, is elected by it, and must learn to work with it. Perhaps more importantly, the goal of democracy is different: it focuses on the mass of citizenry. It is their freedom and their fulfillment that provides the value orientation of the democratic community.

THE FUNCTION OF EVERYMAN

Although democrats are inclined to be skeptical concerning eternal truths, they must start somewhere; they generally hold certain truths to be self-evident. They believe, for example, that men are endowed by their Creator at least with the capacity to be free. They need not make the categoric assertion that "all men are created equal," but they can edit the Declaration of Independence to assert that men are basically alike in capability of conscious choice and in potential awareness of the consequences of their decisions. When any assertions of equality or liberty are made, however, there must be qualifications immediately. There can be no assumption that man possesses perfect rationality or even the capacity for it. There need be no claim of either universal wisdom or natural goodness. The presumption is less pretentious; it merely describes the human beast as a choosing animal, as a creature capable of self-development through personal decision-making. Two consequences follow: first, that men will be able to develop more fully if the community stretches its tolerance so that each individual has the liberty to find his own road to success or failure; secondly, that men, viewed in the mass, demonstrate many of the requisites for participation in collective policy-making.

On the basis of such presuppositions democracy undertakes an experiment in participation, bringing the commonality of men into the process of government at certain points in the process. Needless to say, the whole venture is a profoundly challenging one. The very concept of the common man has sometimes become a cliché. While the leaders of men stand out as distinctive personalities, the democratic everyman is nothing more than a faceless abstraction. He lacks an ego. The best way to find one for him, to convert him into a "somebody," is to picture him as a mirror of our own individual self. We cannot expect this mirrored creature to stand forth bedecked with ribbons and medals; after all, no sane man is a hero to himself. But, as men learn to respect their own selves, they can reflect that respect in their vision of the everyman. The dignity of self, despite the difficulties of its achievement, has the potential for converting this otherwise quite mythical being into a creature real enough for discussion. By personalizing its everyman, democracy can convert him into something beyond a mere speck in an anonymous agglomeration of mankind.

As stated earlier in this book, democracy attempts to give a distinctive significance to the collectivity, converting it into a humanistic community. It seeks to change each member of that community into a valued personality. Its aim is to bring forth self-knowing, self-directed human beings by creating a setting in which men and women can achieve maturity. The democratic purpose, as seen here, is both personal and collective. Both for his own sake and for that of his community, the individual must learn to become responsible through making careful choices; he must learn to exercise his freedom wisely. But he cannot do this single-handedly. To find one's individual self, to find personal meaning, requires a balance of ego and love: a sense of self-comprehension and self-appreciation accompanied by enjoyment of the company of others. If a society is to create a multitude of mature personalities, both individual, self-directed effort and communal engagement are required. Democracy must stress both man's separateness as a personality and his function as a participant in the larger society.

But this concern with broad purpose seems overly abstract when viewed in relation to the down-to-earth kinds of problems that face operating democracies. One practical problem is to find means of assuring that the democratic everyman will become what Aristotle believed that man must be—a "political animal," "an animal intended by nature to live in a polis." All communities demand that their members make numerous adjustments to accommodate their fellows, but a democracy asks something more. It insists that large numbers of men enter consciously into the processes of social action, requesting of them at least a small role in the choice process by which the whole collectivity finds its direction. Democracy asks this of men in part because it is good for them, because they will be better able to fulfill themselves as mature, responsible beings by relating closely to the community. But it demands wide participation for another reason as well: because its processes require a leadership responsive to the citizenry, something that can take place only if there is sufficient public stimulus to provoke such a response.

The existence of a politically active community, of a participatory society, does not require a uniformly applied formula for balancing the individual's public responsibility against his private life. A democracy is marked off by both freedom and participation. The freedom component prohibits, however, any precise prescription of the extent of participation. There undoubtedly exist men who are totally deprived of the capacity to cooperate with the larger community, total *idiotes,* in the original Greek meaning of the term, and there are perhaps even public-minded men who seem to have no observable sense of privacy or of family life. But these extremes are so rare that they appear to be perversions, mere pathological aberrations. The problem is not found in these extremes; it is a matter of the balance, for which the democrat suggests a typically democratic solution: he makes no attempt to legislate how much of himself any man should devote to either realm. The right of nonparticipation remains as sacred as the opportunity for any man to make himself into a largely political creature. If, however, democratic education is successful and the processes of democracy are working well, most men will wish to give a share of their mind and energy to the public life. The tradition of involvement is essential to a free community; yet it is not sheer quantity of participation that distinguishes it from other patterns of society. In fact, active social involvement may be greater in an army squadron, in a prison, or in a mass-production factory than in a democratic community. After all, even a totalitarian regime aims at maximizing participation. The question is: participation of what kind?

Democratic participation is distinctly voluntary and is not exclusively governmental. There is an infinite variety of social roles that an individual may play in a pluralistic society; hence, participation has an infinite variety of meanings. As an abstracted being, democratic man may be described as a participating animal, but this says nothing about the kind of participation he is expected to undertake. As a rule, citizens of a functioning democracy will take part in community decisions, but such communal activism cannot be the product of coercion. To require participation is to convert it into a purely formal act. If voting, as a significant act of involvement, is compulsory, as it is in some nations, it may eventually degenerate into mere ritual, as mechanical a requirement as that of registering for military service. Rituals have their place in a free society, but any act of participation must be more than a formal acknowledgment of communal responsibility. A democracy will surely decline if its citizenry fails to fulfill its role in the process, but the choice and form of participation (voting, campaigning, talking, publishing, petitioning, protesting, or lobbying) must remain a voluntary one.

THE DEMANDS OF DEMOCRACY

For the United States, this is an era of endless community problems, but one of these is not that of overoptimism. A long depression, a series of wars, threats of overpopulation, domestic violence, and unresolved racial tensions have obliterated what little was left of the image of a possible omnicompetent citizen. A cynical view tends to predominate. Yet just as much caution is required by the pessimist as by the optimist. The long view is no less valuable today. It is still possible, with a vision tempered by history to say, with Edmund Burke, that, although a depressingly large number of individuals may look like fools and the unwashed mass may frequently seem idiotic, the species remains wise—from the viewpoint of the long ages it appears to act rather sensibly.[3] Even with a long historical perspective, however, this can be nothing more than a hunch. Any such conjecture can be made more useful only if we first ask what is likely to be demanded of the multitude of men; our judgment will be colored by what we expect in the way of mass participation. Although the nature of specific electoral demands will require particular attention in Chapter 4, it is worth taking a preliminary look at this stage.

Even without the empirical evidence provided by the pollsters, it would be a violation of common sense to claim a sophisticated kind of knowledge on the part of those asked to make decisions as participants in a democracy. How, then, can we be so foolhardy as to put confidence in "a community of common men," operating (in Carl Friedrich's terms) through "common judgement upon matters of common concern"? [4] It helps to realize that it is precisely in those areas, in matters of common concern, that decisions are being asked for. Who is better qualified to express the meaning of "common concern" than the multitude of common men? This is a traditional answer; yet it is none the worse for the wear. If we are foolish enough to ask highly sophisticated questions of an unsophisticated general community, we can expect to receive unsophisticated answers. It is the simplest kind of sanity to ask questions within the competence of those being questioned.

3. See, for example, Burke on representation, in Ross J. S. Hoffman and Paul Levack, eds., *Burke's Politics* (New York: Knopf, 1949), p. 227.

4. Carl J. Friedrich, *New Belief in the Common Man* (Brattleboro, Vt.: Vermont Printing Company, 1942), p. 42.

The question of democratic competence has all too often been stated in terms of a rigid concept of rationality. If popular choice-making were to be rational, in the strict sense of the term, the participants would have to be fully informed, with a clear idea of the specific objectives being sought. Strict rationality would require an awareness of alternatives available and an ability to compare relative costs whenever one goal had to be sacrificed for another. Such a concept is apparently useful to the economists, although they admit that genuine rationality is rare even in the world of hard-minded moneygrubbers. If political rationality is a useful idea, the standard, as has been implied, will depend upon what decision is demanded of the participant. In Britain, for example, the major act of the voter is to choose between two or three candidates who are closely affiliated with a well-knit party and whose actions are partly predictable in terms of party. Understanding the parties and their relation to public policy (itself a task of major consequence) makes it less important to be able to predict the behavior of a particular personality. Quite a different capacity is demanded of the American voter, who is forced to fill dozens of different offices from among candidates only remotely party affiliated, not to mention the frequent additional decisions he must make on referendum issues.

Without being tied to some specific political function, the nature of the rationality requirement can bring only a circular answer: the participant must act as rationally as required by the functions he performs—a statement that goes nowhere. To say that there must be sufficient intellectual equipment to uncover the needed information concerning alternative goals, alternative costs, and alternative means of achievement means very little when the diversity of situational needs is considered. Even among legislators, the role of the back-bench member of the British House of Commons, with a strong party to lead him, is entirely different from that of his more independent counterpart in the United States Senate. And surely the voter who can understand the antics of coalition formation in a multiparty assembly has a task quite unlike that of the voter in a United States presidential election.

It may well be that the idea of rationality is too deeply associated with abstract technological and economic thinking, too closely related to quantifiable factors, to have much usefulness in a discussion of political life. What needs to be asked of the participant in democratic politics is perhaps a kind of reasoned consideration or, in a more optimistic mood, some vague sort of social wisdom. It may well be, in fact, that the antique metaphor of the shoe that pinches is still not without usefulness. The purchaser needs to know only which shoe cramps his foot and which one grasps it snugly but comfortably; it is not necessary to know all about their manufacture or even that they come in numbered sizes. He needs to know when to change cobblers, but the ability to know this does not require the same specialized training that would be necessary for him to be able to construct the shoe himself. Like all metaphors, however, this one fails if taken too literally. It may often take a very long time for members of a community to judge whether a particular set of policies "pinches." Whereas an experienced shoe buyer can predict the comfort of the shoe after a half hour of walking, voting requires quite different, more challenging predictive arts. The voter must test the product with the mind and not with the foot, with some kind of crude reasoning rather than with simple sense perception.

It is quite clear that the citizen-participant in a democracy does not need to know how to perform the acts of government. But he needs several other things not demanded of the wearer of shoes. It will be necessary to comment more fully upon some of them in Chapter 4. It will then be appropriate to examine the citizen's role in connection with the all-important process of voting. But it is worthwhile remembering at this point that the act of voting is by no means all that is demanded of the citizen of a democracy. All of his social actions will affect the nature of his community and its success in achieving democratic goals. Social attitude may be just as important for continuing progress toward freedom as an ability to act with wisdom in the polling booth.

Perhaps social maturity is the term that best describes the personal quality required by a democracy. Such maturity has already been discussed (in Chapter 1) in terms of the purpose of democracy—as a resulting product of liberty and responsibility—but this may turn out to be something less than a paradox. It could well be that the end result of democracy and its prime prerequisite are identical. In actual social situations, we do not move from causes located at one point in time to effects located at another. We deal, instead, with a mixture of causal relations in which the same factor can be both cause and effect: this might be called mutual causation. A society can learn to be free because its citizens tend to be mature and, in the very act of freedom, it may teach itself maturity. This is as true of a community as it is of an individual. We do not know precisely what makes one man mature and another immature. The individual who demonstrates self-awareness at a late stage in life is one who has had sufficient self-awareness earlier to permit him to grow up in a healthy manner. A society, like an individual, must learn to understand itself, to meet its problems with self-awareness. This will require maturity on the part of its citizens. At the same time, such maturity, once gained, will help to make conditions right for the proper functioning of democratic processes.

It is not feasible to elaborate further on what is meant by social maturity. It may, however, be worthwhile to warn against one misunderstanding that may arise out of the concept of mature self-understanding: the confusion of self-awareness with introverted self-pity. Self-knowledge of the kind that is both the end and the means of a democratic society can rarely be achieved without a sense of humor. Freedom creates a plentiful supply of strange people who make apparent fools of themselves. The democrat who fails to see his fellow man and himself with a touch of whimsy will very likely have a distorted view of the world. He who possesses a sense of humor can, however, without deprecating himself, look with some amusement on the fact that he is frequently responsible for his own predicaments. He is unlikely to search for others to blame or to sit back wringing his hands on seeing what God hath wrought. If a man can contemplate the absurdities in his own life with a genuine smile, he will be more capable of seeing his fellow men in some balanced perspective, and he will be a safer social creature. There is more than a linguistic tie among humor, humility, and humaneness. The ability to contemplate the incongruities of life (the essence of humor, according to Stephen Leacock) is most surely the beginning of human understanding and sympathy. The requirement is not one of laughter; as Leacock warns, all primates are capable of laughter, "not only archbishops and bishops, but orangutans, gorillas, and chimpanzees." Humor is peculiarly human. Possessing a genuine sense of humor is much more than possessing the mere ability to laugh; it is something quite different, something more useful for a continuation of sanity in an often disturbing world. Humor is important because it is death to fanaticism; it deflates the true believer who so often threatens freedom in a community. It offsets, incidentally, some of democracy's tendency to elevate the "bitch goddess" of success on too high a throne and helps to keep the sin of failure from becoming too overburdening.

Perhaps democracy expects too much of its everyman, asking him to have sufficient maturity to see himself clearly, to perceive himself in a social setting, and then to examine himself at least occasionally through wit-colored glasses. Americans not only ask for qualities such as this in the common man but compound the difficulty by placing him in the midst of an overstuffed society. He is provided with an overabundant environment: there is too much to consume, too much to comprehend, too much art, too much science, and too much insistence that he take advantage of it all. (Even those deprived persons living at or near the poverty level are affected by this overstuffing despite their inability to enjoy all of its rewards.) Modern society seems determined to make personal life more difficult to manage at the same time that participation in increasingly complex political situations adds to the burdens of choice-making. Adding to a man's opportunities, increasing his options, inevitably makes both choices and responsibilities more difficult to manage. It is perhaps less surprising that democratic man in a technologically rich community has difficulties in adjusting than that he performs as well as he does. The modern democratic community brings newfangled forms of anxiety, but the insecurities of freedom in a bewildering environment are not quite like the older chains of slavery. The confusing world provides novel kinds of insecurities and fears as well as new modes and potentials for self-development.

THE COLLECTIVE DECISION

Up to this point, there has been more consideration of soul than of body, more stress on democratic purposes than on participatory processes. It has been important, at an early stage, to become aware of the nature of the democratic spirit. Now it is time to take a closer look at some of the flesh and blood of democratic government. Democrats need to be somewhat concerned with the pure ideals of a Platonic Republic, but they also need to be a bit Machiavellian, giving attention to princes, to politics, and to instruments of collective policy development. Since democracy is productive of both freedom and popular participation, it becomes important to be concerned with practicalities, particularly with how a democratic citizen can effectively be brought into the governing process. This will lead, in Chapters 4–6, to consideration of the act of voting, of the nature of political discourse, and of the dynamics of influencing public officials. Before discussing those peculiarly democratic processes, however, it may be fruitful to examine a preliminary question: how can any community take collective action, and what are the primary modes by which a large body of men can act as a unit?

There appear to be three basic ways in which a collectivity may be said to act as a unity, three modes of setting communal direction. First of all and most simply, it may act through an agent who supposedly expresses the social will and acts for the whole group. This agency process is surely the most common form of socialized action, even though it entails the least involvement by members of the community. The society can act also in almost an opposite fashion, through the largely uncoordinated activities of numbers of individuals and subgroups. This pluralistic mode of social activity is not very *communal* in that there is a minimum of organized agreement on collective direction. In either of these two modes there is a communal direction; yet the community, as a community, has not taken an active part in it. Only with the third mode of action do we find something that is truly communal, both in participation and in effect. Only in the third category is there a structured effort to bring a collectivity of men into something akin to agreement on means and ends of common interest. Clearly, it is the processes of politics involved in this third kind of collective action that are of particular significance to democrats; it is well, therefore, to let discussion of it wait until there has been consideration of the other alternatives that may, formally at least, seem less democratic.

History does not provide a date to indicate when those who acted as chiefs, emperors, kings, princes, dictators, or mere committee chairmen began to assume something beyond a personal privilege to rule; it does not tell us when rulership ceased being a matter of right and began to be a matter of social obligation; it does not reveal when governors began to conceive of themselves as representatives. The reason for this lack of knowledge is, quite probably, that the idea of ruler as agent predates history. The idea is too universal to have a date of origin. Agents have come to their positions in a wide variety of ways and have maintained power under widely divergent terms. The agency may be hereditary or self-assumed by conquest, and the agent may be chosen because he is the "elder man" or by some form of election. He may be removable by election, by failure to win a majority vote in an assembly, or by the always available device of a revolutionary firing squad. He may hold office as executive, legislator, judge, dictator, military commander, or bureaucrat. Representation by agents is universal; democratic representation is something more rare. Although there are no hard-and-fast rules prescribing methods of choice or control of democratic social agents, such methods are clearly a critical question. There is great variation, even among western democracies, in selection and accountability techniques as well as in constitutional restrictions on the power of officeholding agents. The chief principle seems to be that, having accepted the necessity of agents who act for the community, a democracy tries to make them also act in accord with community wishes, a task the difficulties of which, if not already obvious, will become clearer in Chapter 6.

A second mode of possible collective action was mentioned in Chapter 2 in connection with the idea that a society could move ahead in a vague *trend direction* as well as through specific policy decisions. The example used there, of the development of a Jim Crow system for dealing with the American Negro after Civil War and Reconstruction, is also useful here. The whole pattern of strange taboos and rules were not merely the result of agents acting for the community or of votes taken by the society or its representatives but arose, more importantly, out of a series of apparently fragmented, semiautonomous individual and small-group acts. This is only one kind of fragmented social action, however. Another type might be called *negotiational,* the kind of policy set through something vaguely like bargaining or diplomacy. That the diplomatic manipulations and haggling that take place in a labor dispute can become a major social decision is evidenced in a small way by any auto workers' strike in the United States and, in particularly dramatic fashion, by the general strike that brought France to a state of near collapse in May 1968. In a more fragmented and autonomous way, the thousands of single negotiations that occur every time someone sends his son to college, or buys a house, a car, or a television set are social decisions. Purchasing a color television set in preference to the *Encyclopaedia Britannica,* buying cars too fast and too large for existing roadways, moving into a house in a suburb in preference to the central city, enrolling in a particular university—all of these actions change the pattern of society when combined with millions of other such fragmented decisions going on more or less simultaneously. The historic social decision of Americans to produce the number and kinds of cars they now drive has reshaped the landscape, redesigned the economy, altered recreational activity, and even remade the nature of family life. This was a community policy of monumental consequences despite the fact that presidents and admirals, governors and senators had only an infinitesimal part in the decision.

Americans have become accustomed to drawing such arbitrary lines between private and governmental spheres that it seldom occurs to them to consider as anything but "private" an act such as the purchase of a large, powerful car or the refusal to rent a house to a member of a minority group. In this failure to see the social consequences of personal actions the community is allowed to drift in certain directions to which many might have vigorous objection if they were proposed as conscious matters of public policy. It now seems futile for a society to attempt to erect precise and rigid barriers, with a bold sign saying: Government, keep out! The totalitarian experience gives warning that man is hardly human unless he retains a wide sphere of activity immune from direct governmental direction. But democrats also know that all community action need not be governmental action. They must realize that the line between private and public spheres is hazy at best and that little is gained by blind opposition to increased governmental activity or by the hope that precise line drawing will preserve the private area intact. It is vital to keep in mind that so-called private decisions may have overwhelming social consequences that only collective action can remedy. The problem is a perplexing one for a democracy. On the one hand, personal autonomy is a high goal of democracy. On the other hand, such liberty brings a responsibility that is implicitly expressed through the other high goal of participation. Citizens of a democracy must learn to recognize the social significance of their private acts if they wish to retain a zone of private choice. They may try to avoid expanding the governmental zone; yet this can be accomplished only by a heightened sense of communal responsibility and a developed social knowledge in regard to seemingly personal actions.

THE ACT OF POLITICAL COMMUNION

The citizen of Athens was, in the words of Aristotle, "a man who shares in the administration of justice and in the holding of office." The man "who is without a *polis*" is, for him, either a poor, deprived, almost subhuman creature or else a "being higher than man."[5] The Athenians lumped together the goals of liberty and participation, stressing the latter. The important rights were not private but public, not freedom from government but freedom to act as a part of government. The *polis* was "so omnipotent that a man could be nothing," according to the classic scholar, Fustel de Coulanges, unless he was part of "the collective sovereign."[6] The act of suffrage, which for us is merely an occasional act of political communion, then had "a value incomparably greater than it can have in modern states." Voting was but a part of it. Civic participation made an individual into a man, someone to respect, with dignity and fullness of personality. The large nation-state of our era has moved a long way from the Greek participatory concept of democracy. If there has been any corresponding gain in personal freedom, as seems surely to be the case, there has also been a loss, a loss of understanding of the meaning of the kind of liberty that may be called freedom-in-community.

It is too late to conduct a wake for ancient Athens or for the New England town meeting. Most modern governments have become too complex and their territories too wide to allow the same kind of day-by-day political communion to be achieved. It has been necessary to find substitutes. The major substitute is undoubtedly a cheap imitation when seen as a mere mechanical act of participation, but, when viewed as a larger act, one tied with symbolic meanings, it may be more significant. The substitute is, of course, the act of voting—an implement of communal action that antedates the Greeks. The act of voting, in the broad sense, includes a development and presentation of alternatives, a process of free and open discourse of the alternatives, and then a more individualized act of choice-making. It focuses with particular sharpness on personal responsibility at the final stage. If properly performed, however, it can be a highly communal process in its earlier stages, as

5. Aristotle, *The Politics*, trans. Ernest Barker (Oxford: Oxford University Press, 1946), pp. 93 and 5.

6. Numa Denis Fustel de Coulanges, *The Ancient City*, trans. Willard Small (Garden City, N.Y.: Doubleday, Anchor Book, n.d.), p. 328.

alternatives are developed and discussed. This act of decision-by-citizen can become democracy's great ritual. It can express the communion of individual and society at the same time that it expresses the idea that the community constitutes a cooperative unity.

The formal act of voting (a topic of Chapter 4) is not fully understood when viewed alone. It is important to see it in the broader light of other kinds of communal decision-making and particularly in relation to something that may be called *unanimous accord*. Voting could be described as an act of collective settlement —the result of an agreement to make a decision despite continued disagreement. It normally occurs under conditions that demand some kind of decisive action. Minimum damage is done to our sense of social justice and to the solidarity of the community when its leaders act on the basis of tabulated individual decisions. It is, as an ideal, still preferable, however, for the group to reach actual agreement, unanimous and unbegrudging. Sometimes by discussing the shape of an issue and exploring new alternatives, members of a group can come to complete agreement after an initial state of discord. If some members of a club want to plan a picnic, others a dance, and still others a bingo game, it may be possible for them to find a combination of the three or for those who prefer a dance to convince the picnic lovers of the inevitability of rain and the bingo lovers of the risk of violating a gambling law. The social event that follows will be a much happier one if everyone agrees that the final choice is the best one and does not remain in a state of anger, pouting at having lost to the majority will.

The conversion of voting into a ritual act—one that is repeated on endless occasions in a myriad of groups in a pluralistic society—tends to hide the practical significance of unanimous accord. But the reflection of anyone who has been a regular participant in committee work will bring to mind numerous occasions when disagreements, strongly voiced at first, have evaporated as discussion has proceeded. Despite one's painful memories of long-winded committee sessions, it is clear that patient talk can frequently result in total agreement. Sometimes cooperation is so essential for the success of an undertaking that nothing short of wholehearted agreement is practical. It is often better not to act than to act after a split vote. But even when this is not the case, in thousands of democratic situations unanimous accord may be attainable at a minimal cost in delay. This kind of agreement is significant, however, regardless of the extent of its use. It is symbolic of the ultimate in democratic achievement. The Quaker sense-of-the-meeting concept, while utopian in many situations, provides an ideal that makes actual voting more comprehendible. Among other things, it makes it easier for the minority to understand why it must accept the majority wish. The feasibility of reaching unanimous accord without any curbs on free expression or voluntariness of choice gives strength to democracy's goal of liberty through participation.

When a president faces a new crisis in foreign affairs, he is quick to consult leaders of the opposition party as well as divergent factions within his own party. What he desires is not the assurance of winning a test vote but the near-unanimous support of the community in crucial trouble. A single dissenter can, under some circumstances, be a sign of a failure in leadership. Not majority support but the backing of as much of the total community or set of communities as is humanly possible is called for when a labor leader embarks on a long, bitter strike or when a leader of government is working in alliance with other nations in a world at war. Voting has sometimes been described as the alternative to fighting, but this does not state its entire purpose. Its more basic function is to unite the community behind an agreed-upon action. Democracy has, through voting, found a way to bring the community into action even when there is continued disagreement. This does not mean, however, that unanimous accord is not preferable. Knowledge of this fact helps leaders to ascertain when to call a vote and when to postpone the decision; it tells them whether, in a given situation, a 51 percent majority means to go ahead or whether it suggests, instead, to hold back.

It should not be forgotten that unanimous accord means a complete agreement freely and wholeheartedly joined. It does not mean that some members of the group are grudgingly willing to go along because they do not feel excited about the issues or because they observe a well-set drift in the direction of group opinion. Agreement of this kind is something quite different. Let it be called *implicit voting*—something halfway between formal voting and unanimous accord. Unlike unanimous accord, there continues to be disagreement after a choice has been made; unlike normal voting, there is no formal count of ayes and nays. One of two kinds of assent are involved in implicit voting. Discussion may make it clear, without any vote, that certain members of the group are definitely in a minority, and they may feel that, having made a reasonable effort to convince others of their viewpoint and having failed, their only sensible action is to go along with the viewpoint of the larger number of members without making a formal issue of it. Or certain members of the group, possibly even a majority, may discover through discussion that others feel more keenly about the issue or have demonstrated a larger stake in the outcome; under such circumstances those with less deeply felt interest may allow those with intense feeling to have their way without calling for a vote. In the one circumstance, implicit voting is very close to the normal voting process, except that it avoids going through the formality. In the other, the voting is concerned not with numbers but with another, very significant, factor in the political process—the intensity of interest of various parties to a dispute.

It is obvious that implicit voting, based on either numerical reasoning or on intensity reasoning, works best when there is a regular custom of taking formal votes. In a democracy the right to reach a full vote must always be retained at some proper point in the process, but there may be advantages in avoiding its actual use. Even when unanimous accord is not feasible, as will often be the case, there may still be advantages, for the communal spirit of the group, in not formalizing the vote. The informality of the implicit vote has a very substantial argument in its favor: it permits flexibility in decision-making. In particular, it allows the consideration of numerous factors other than numbers of supporters behind a particular alternative. As in formal voting, there is compromise for the sake of action, but the disagreement that continues to exist is not intensified by using the last resort, which in the case of democracy is the ballot, not the sword. In implicit voting, with less tendency to force anyone to take a firm, formalized stand from which he cannot back down, fewer feelings are apt to be hurt than in formal voting; it will be simpler to achieve agreement next time, easier to work toward unanimity in future situations when harmony is of particular value.

It is very likely that implicit voting and unanimous accord are more frequently used in decision-making situations than the formalities would indicate. City councils, legislative committees, executive cabinets, not to mention the endless numbers of special commissions and committees that dot the political landscape, frequently make decisions this way. But we must be cautious. When the rules require that a formal vote be taken, as with the passage of a legislative enactment, the form is often followed when, in reality, there is implicit voting. The frequent existence of a formal vote resulting in unanimity is no indication of the frequency of complete agreement. In many instances, it may be, instead, a sign that implicit voting has taken place beforehand, eliminating the necessity of anyone's voting openly against the measure. For the nonsophisticated assembly watcher, the use of this sleight-of-hand trick is confusing. He will be much the wiser if he learns, early in the game, what is being stated here: formal unanimity is not identical with actual unanimous accord. There is, in fact, no easy way to determine whether a dissenting group has, after a formally unanimous agreement, decided to continue disagreement but to go along for the sake of goodwill. This undoubtedly happens, however, more often than most of us realize. The fact that voting is central to the democratic process does not mean that every vote is a true index of the status of opinion within a group. In any aspect of the political process it is dangerous to allow oneself to be taken in by outward forms, even forms as important as those involved in casting some type of vote.

CHAPTER 4

Voting: The Fundamental Ritual

HISTORY has need of dates as pegs on which to hang social changes, devices to jog the memory of the schoolboy. In American history those dates are not coronations or inaugurations, despite the elaborate ceremony that now surrounds the latter. Americans think of 1800 as the initiation of Jeffersonian liberalism; they think of 1860 in connection with Lincoln and the Civil War; they think of 1932 as the beginning of the New Deal era. Yet Jefferson did not become president until March 1801; Fort Sumter was not fired upon until April 1861, Lincoln having been inaugurated the month before; the New Deal did not begin until the spring of 1933. Americans tend to mark off eras with dates of elections and look upon them as others have looked upon great battles. These are great events in American history; they are the democratic equivalent of such battles—they bring change to the society.

In America election days are working days; it is not the custom to turn them into special holidays, even though other nations often go to the polls on Sunday. Although there is considerable logic in closing down factories, shops, and offices, the day is not a festival; its purposes are serious. It is not intended for picnics and games but for the serious task of registering an important decision. It is appropriate that the great rite of democracy not be a day of parades and music nor of speeches by great leaders. It is the silent day, the day in which people trudge to the polls, cast their ballots, and return home for an evening of intensive watching and listening.

The morning and afternoon has a subdued tone: each man and woman is made aware of his individual inadequacy as a citizen. The daylight hours will, ideally, express a quiet intensity, a surge of public responsibility. The evening hours, after the polls are closed, are different; the individual act of the day is over, and it is now time to see how the community has acted. Having judged himself as a civic being during the day and felt all the doubts of decision-making, the voter can sit back and watch the strange behavior of the whole society. The family gathers before the television set; the work is now done; it is time for the show to begin. The moment of individual doubt is past and, hopefully, the time has come for renewed confidence in the decisions made by the community as generality.

THE MEANING OF THE VOTE

The child of democracy learns to vote during the first days of his social life. Most Americans have been voting for one thing or another as far back as memory will take them—sometimes for Queen of the May, sometimes for railroad and warehouse commissioner, and sometimes for president of the United States—in any case, the act becomes habitual. Much of this voting is trivial. Some of it is mere form, the decision having already been made by a nominating committee proposing a single slate of candidates, as in many professional organizations and labor unions. Although there may yet be a problem of insufficient familiarity with this democratic ritual among the deprived classes, among the large middle and upper levels of society any active citizen will very likely have voted hundreds of times and, very likely, have been elected to at least a committee chairmanship.

Voting is both an act of social usefulness and of ideological symbolism. If its inventor were known, he would rank not with the creator of television or the phonograph but with the man who discovered the wheel or the use of steam power. In the absence of voting, the only practical last resort, short of bloodshed, for settling political disagreements, is the arbitrary decision of a stronger man —a great king, priest, or judge. Now, however, voting has become so universal that even totalitarian regimes have adapted it as a device to consolidate public support. Voting symbolizes participation, something upon which all modern regimes, whether or not they are democratic, place great reliance. But for a democracy, the vote, being competitive and free, is the greatest of teachers. It instills the idea of fair play for winners and losers; it stresses the acceptance of socially determined decisions; it emphasizes the importance of free expression and the right to organize political groups. In fact, it becomes the central symbolic act for the whole pattern of democratic practices and ideals.

The mechanics of voting are known to everyone; a determination of the number of individuals supporting each of several alternatives permits the collectivity to adopt one choice as that of the whole community. Variations in the types of voting are numerous. A vote may be anonymous; there may be a public show of hands or a roll call of names; there may be an attempt at precise accuracy or merely an impressionistic count as in the case of the voice vote. Each method has different practical consequences. Yet they are alike in that the democratic vote (as contrasted with a mere plebiscite pledging support for the regime) requires three elements of action: there must be a free act of proposing competitive alternatives; there must be uninhibited discussion of alternatives; and, at the end, there must be an act of deciding and counting decisions. This means that the formal participatory act of democracy requires three kinds of freedom: freedom to place one's proposal before voters for their consideration, freedom to discuss alternatives in all stages of the process, and freedom to choose between proposals. For some persons participation through voting will take the form of running for office. For others it will mean joining in a nominating caucus, making a parliamentary motion, obtaining signatures on an initiative petition, or perhaps moving an amendment from the floor during a meeting. For still others the most significant act will be that of talk: discussing and arguing about alternative proposals or about the merits of rival candidates. For the majority, however, the primary act will remain that of decision-making when the official moment arrives. Although the functions of shaping alternatives and the vital activity of public discourse precede the decisional stage of voting, the discussion here will deal with the decision process first so that this may be well in mind during an examination of the essential preliminaries.

The election of madam chairman for a church circle may be the most insignificant of actions if, as sometimes happens, no one wants the job and no one really cares who is elected. The election of President Nixon in 1968 was, by contrast, vitally significant to the nation because of the critical nature of the times; each vote was crucial because the outcome was breathtakingly close. Between these extremes a variety of degrees of significance may be attached to the single moment at which some group of individuals undertakes this central civic act. The time involved in actual voting is minuscule; yet it is remarkable how much civic satisfaction is crammed into this singularly socializing experience. Men and women do not vote in the abstract. They vote under certain given conditions, which can make the act a mere gesture of good citizenship or an act of major political and social consequence. This raises an important question: just when should a vote take place? Not all civic decisions can be the result of voting; as has already been stated, most community actions must be performed by agents of the community rather than by the members of the community acting in unison.

Ideally, there should be a vote whenever members of the group feel that a decision is a significant one and disagree about what the action should be. The key criteria are *importance* and *disagreement.* Citizens should vote for the more important officers of the government, those who make the kind of decisions that are commonly the source of major disagreement and that shape the future of the community. The best word to describe this criterion is "controversy." Votes are designed to settle controversies and should, ideally, occur whenever there is controversy. To say this is to make it immediately apparent that no precise criteria can be developed. It was once fashionable to delineate the distinction by drawing a line between matters of policy and matters of administrative detail. This did not work. A minor matter at one moment or to one individual may be a major one in another moment or to another individual. The installation of a sewer line and the assessment of its cost to the property owners is a matter of routine administration to the city manager; yet it can be a vital and controversial issue to the citizens. The possibility of a political explosion over a small act of government is always present. There have been, by way of contrast, long periods when major decisions of foreign policy have been made without significant dissent.

Part of the process of constitution-making involves drawing arbitrary lines to separate the area of vote-taking from that of bureaucratic decision-making. It is difficult, however, to see how any simple rule can be formulated that will be of much help to the founding fathers of a new nation. The best that can be suggested is an examination of the pragmatic answers developed in the long history of decision-making in such well-established democracies as the United States or Great Britain. Votes cannot always be taken when it is ideal from the standpoint of participation. On the other hand, some voting will inevitably seem nearly pointless to those who must go through the motions. There is, furthermore, a necessity to insulate certain kinds of decisions, such as those made by judges, generals, and perhaps even bureaucrats, from the kind of public pressure the act of voting implies. Needless to say, it is sensible to delegate much decision-by-vote to a representative assembly; greater expertise may then be brought to bear on policies and politics, and the members of a voting community will not be overly burdened.

THE ASSEMBLY AND THE ELECTORATE

The reader of history, studying Thucydides, might well receive the impression that each moment in an ancient Greek assembly was one of eloquence. The impassioned speeches at the Congress at Lacedaemon at the beginning of the Peloponnesian War and the great funeral oration of Pericles may mislead the reader into assuming that every statement uttered at a meeting of ancient Greeks was a heroic one. It is quite possible that there were as many moments of trivia, as many stupid speeches, as many evidences of personal jealousy, and as many displays of egotism as there are in an electoral campaign of our own day and age. Yet the Greek assemblies must have been tremendously effective implements of mass education. Even the New England town meeting was described by as astute an observer as Tocqueville as being "to liberty what primary schools are to science; they bring it within the people's reach, they teach men how to use and how to enjoy it." [1] There can be no question but that much was lost to democracy and the community spirit when the political society became so large and its functions so complex that men could no longer gather together in the marketplace or town hall to conduct its business. It is nonetheless foolish to assume that, in either Athens or New England, a large group of men governed themselves directly. Matters have seldom been that simple. There is, however, a major contrast between assembly situations and electorate voting. The differences are important despite the fact that they both require leadership and that all business of government has seldom been conducted in a general meeting of citizens since the day society passed beyond the tribal stage.

Much can be learned about how democracy works by using comparisons. For example, any course of study in American government that did not make frequent references to other major democracies, such as Britain and France, would surely be superficial. Likewise, it is valuable to compare kinds of voting situations when examining the meaning of voting in a democracy. Now that the town meeting is largely an anachronism, we have not one but two common settings for decision-by-vote. One is that in an unassembled collectivity (the electorate); the other takes place among

1. Alexis de Tocqueville, *Democracy in America,* trans. Henry Reeve (New York: Oxford University Press, 1946), p. 53.

men and women gathered in one location (the assembly). In the former, each member of the electorate makes his decision—performing the ritual act of communal participation—alone and separately. The elector's vote is a solo performance. Whatever part he may have played in the discourse or selection of alternatives which precedes the vote, it is unlikely that his voice will have been heard by the entire voting community. By contrast, although an assembly may not work together in daily participation as does a college fraternity, often meeting no more frequently than an American party convention, a vast difference remains—one created by the possibility of face-to-face discourse. Some assemblies meet only once and then dissolve. Others assign much of their work to subassembly committees. These and other differences between types of assemblies are generally minor when compared with the differences between the processes in any assembly and that of any electorate.

The best opportunity to see the dissimilarity between these two kinds of democratic process comes when the entire voting community does what assemblies normally do—when an electorate votes on policies rather than on candidates for office. There must be some preformulation of alternatives when either assembly or electorate votes on policies. Choices for action must be developed into concrete proposals. Proposed statutes must be drafted in proper legal form. In an assembly this preliminary development is usually a regularized process: a British cabinet minister brings a proposal to the floor of Parliament; a city manager makes recommendations to his council; a standing committee reports to the United States Senate. In less formal circumstances, any member may rise to make a motion, but, if he desires to do something more than muddle through and wants to make certain that his motion will achieve what is intended, he will have worked carefully on it in advance, preferably in caucus with several allies and with the help of experts. In the case of electoral plebiscites, either an agency of government (the legislative assembly in an American referendum) or a private interest group (under initiative procedures) will have undertaken the advance work that must precede a vote. In either case, there must be some act of leadership before a proposal can receive a vote. A process of refining and defining must occur before any large body of men and women can indicate assent or dissent, but the procedure will differ in important respects when the vote is in an unassembled electorate rather than in an assembly hall.

One of the first striking comparisons is the fact that proposals made to an electorate must be handled in a more formal manner than those offered for consideration to an assembly, where leadership can arise spontaneously after discourse has begun, and new alternatives and refinements can be brought forth at any time. Permanently established assemblies tend to institutionalize (and hence formalize) their modes of action. Paradoxically, however, the existence of established routines makes it easier for numerous less ritualized processes to exist. Because formal patterns are so thoroughly established, various types of nonformalized activities can accompany official processes. Most informalities common to an assembly, however, are not feasible with an electorate made up of distant strangers. Since electorates are composed of individuals scattered over a wide area, for them to be able to act in unison, their choices must be sufficiently predigested. Hence, no member of the electorate can stand up on the spur of the moment and say: "The proposals we have before us do not meet the problem, but, with the changes I am about to suggest, they will work very well." Discourse in an electorate takes place about a fixed proposal, which cannot normally be altered. In an assembly, discussion will frequently inspire changes and entirely new approaches to the problem at hand. It is possible to alter assembly options in midstream. Such is not the case with an electorate.

A substantial number of pages in any legislative manual will be devoted to amending processes—a fact that well illustrates the difference between decisions in an electorate and in an assembly. To understand the importance of amending, it is useful, first, to be aware of the yes and no aspect of voting. When more than two alternatives are available—for example, when there are five candidates for an office in an American primary election—the voter says no to four of them and yes to the fifth. Although there are complications provided by systems such as preferential balloting, the affirmative-negative alternative is the general rule. It is certainly the rule when the voting is on issues or laws as opposed to candidates. A voter in the electorate or a member of an assembly must vote for or against a motion, resolution, statute, or ordinance. But this for and against kind of voting can be made infinitely more subtle by the possibility, in assemblies, of an amendment process permitting small, refined changes as well as a major redrafting of the proposal. Improvements and alterations may eliminate weaknesses and add strengths that make it unnecessary to reject a proposal *in toto* when objection is aimed at specific parts. Most members of a democratic assembly would not dream of functioning without amendment procedures (even though amendments may, at certain times, be restricted). Yet this absence of amending possibilities is the normal rule for plebiscites, referenda, or initiatives voted directly by the electorate.

Assemblies also have advantages over electorates in the discourse stage of the voting process, although the comparison seems less black and white. Direct confrontation, arguments providing both attacks and rebuttals, queries and responses, efforts to achieve mutual understanding—all of these are vastly more difficult when the participants are remote from each other. Despite the frequent superficiality of the debate, it does permit a more sophisticated process of collective reasoning to take place than that which occurs in an electoral campaign. The face-to-face confrontation has obvious advantages. When every voter is present in person, he is able to speak with proposers or nominators, who themselves may wish to clarify points that are notably bothersome. To be able to converse with those directly involved—with amenders, critical opponents, special-interest spokesmen, or experts—is an advantage any intelligent voter should desire. The campaign process may sometimes be quite excellent for explaining issues to the electorate, and some voters may be skilled in keeping themselves informed, but the lack of face-to-face confrontation with major participants can be a distinct handicap.

In one kind of assembly, that typified by legislative bodies, where a leading segment of the membership remains stable over a period of years, legislators can accumulate knowledge and experience in substantive policies and problems and, equally importantly, in methods of debate, amendment, and parliamentary procedure. Skills of judgment can be acquired concerning the intricacies of the political personality, making it easier for lawmakers to evaluate the kinds of men and women who take part in civic life and to understand the way they think. Members of regularly meeting assemblies can become knowledgeable in the nature of political pressures and the techniques of propaganda, enabling them either to resist such techniques or take advantage of them. Some of these skills may be gained by the sophisticated voter-in-electorate. Surely this is a function of political education, even though such skills are more common in those who make a vocation of politics than in those for whom it is an avocation.

The amateur, it may be noted, has a very definite place in democratic governance. Although the committee system does make American legislators more efficient because it permits specialization of function, a good legislator must resist the temptation to become overly expert and narrowly specialized; there is always a need for generalists. It is a virtue of democracy that it increases greatly the amateur's role in government. However, it is important not to forget the sharp distinction between the role of legislator and that of the occasional voter.

This discussion is not intended as an attack on direct legislation as it developed out of the Progressive era in the states of the American West. Although there is reason to have doubt about some of the virtues once claimed for direct democracy, the comments here are not meant to be a polemic against any political reform. Nonetheless, it is important, when deciding how to use direct legislation, to know its limitations, to know how it differs from legislation by assembly. Referenda for establishing new constitutions and amending older ones are now very popular and are so well known that they do not require elaboration here. Furthermore, whenever a representative assembly ceases to be truly representative or is in need of other kinds of self-reform (as exemplified by the failure of American legislatures to reapportion themselves in accord with shifting population), it is clear that initiatives originating from outside interest groups can be of inestimable value. Sometimes direct legislation is the only means of solving a problem, and, since democracies must be pragmatic to survive, it may be wise to provide mechanisms for almost every contingency. At its best, direct legislation makes it possible to solve problems that the other mechanisms neglect; at its worst, it is a tool of competing pressure groups seeking policies a legislature is too wise to adopt. But the results have not been horrendous. The fact that such implements work, despite their inherent clumsiness, is an indication of the flexibility and adaptiveness of the general democratic idea to an infinite variety of political circumstances.

THE POPULAR MANDATE

Prophets are seldom underemployed in modern democracies. They work especially hard during election years. As the campaign nears its climax they find themselves facing an audience large enough to evoke the envy of a Hollywood star. Then, for a few short hours on election day, no one wants to hear their voices. It is time for action, not talk. But business revives after suppertime. Forecasting from early returns provides a few final hours of prediction. There is new work for prognosticators. The subject shifts. The diviners of coming events now tell us what to expect from those elected. In a presidential election year, particularly when a new president is elected, this endeavor absorbs a major portion of the time of the pundits. But they also find time for another kind of analysis. They begin searching through the haystack pile of election returns to uncover, somewhere amidst the infinite number of factors that might have influenced millions of different kinds of voters, some small clue indicating how the community wants its government to act during the next few years. This hidden key is called the people's mandate. The search must go on, despite the obvious difficulties, because it is democratic dogma that there exists a public will and that elections express it through a mandate.

Analysts are, quite reasonably, not expected merely to prophesy what the voter will do and explain what he has done; they must also criticize the system itself. Some of these attacks on the American system are founded upon a conception of the electoral process not unlike the original Latin meaning of a mandate. The critics expect the election, like the orders of a Roman emperor to his provincial governors, "to give something into the hands" of those charged with responsibility, a kind of authoritative command for action. Much modern discussion of democracy, of democratic parties, and of electoral processes, is based upon one form or another of this mandate theory, a theory that pictures voters as giving authoritative commands to their governors. No one really expects the voters, in their collective wisdom, to inscribe a parchment with a series of specific orders, but a similar result is somehow expected to take place through the process of voting for governmental officials. Although no reform-minded analyst has taken the argument to such an extreme, the logical, idealized mandate would be most feasible with some kind of elective monarch, a single officer elected on the basis of one sharply defined issue with specific policy alternatives on which each candidate could take a definite stand. A fresh election would need to occur each time a new issue arose, and, each time, one candidate would present himself for each conceivable alternative policy. The elected officer, in such an idealized situation, would then dutifully do what he was told to do—supposedly an action identical with what he has promised to do—a simple matter of following prior orders.

To describe the nature of a true democratic mandate in its simplest and most idealized form, rather than in the more moderate language of responsible-party reformers, helps to make it clear why it is so difficult to achieve a perfected mandate system. Who would be satisfied with one elected governing official? How effective would officers be if they sought election every few months? How tiring would be the efforts of citizens asked to vote on every conceivable new issue? How many communities face only one policy issue at a time? Actual democracies have, universally, evolved methods of plural representation through legislative assemblies. They have segregated voters in constituency districts and thus divided up the prospective mandate. They have provided for elections several years apart, not attempting to obtain an expression of voter will as often as political conditions might change. Yet the mandate idea remains. It is never suggested in such a perfect form, however. A frequent version of the theory asks merely that political parties be somehow strengthened sufficiently to offset the divided power structure within the legislative assembly. This would be done so as to achieve a more strict discipline over party members who are legislators, a reform that would supposedly allow the voter to ignore individual candidates and vote for the party as a unit. Totally disciplined assemblymen, operating under hierarchical party leadership, would permit the elector to vote for the equivalent of the elected monarch mentioned above. The party in such a scheme acts like an elected king: rival monarchical candidates are replaced by tightly disciplined rival parties between which the voters may choose. If, continuing the logic of the perfected mandate, there might also be a guarantee of a simplicity of issues, if elections could be held whenever major issues change, if political personalities were never as significant as policies, if the moon were made of blue cheese—the political world would, quite naturally, be an entirely different kind of place and, for some critics at least, more nearly ideal.

Now that men have left footprints on its surface, no one believes that the moon is made of blue cheese, nor do many people believe that the model of an electoral mandate system is possible. The great success of the highly pragmatic British system has, however, encouraged political analysts to search for the abstract principles behind it so that it can be copied elsewhere. The British legislature has become virtually unicameral, and members of the House of Commons are the only nationally elected officers. In recent years, each voter has only one vote for one national office, for his member of Parliament. Candidates are so thoroughly party oriented that the voter can vote for the party (or the prime minister likely to run the party) and not for the man, the candidate in their district. It is possible (though no longer likely) for an election to be called because governmental problems have changed so much that Parliament rejects present leadership and votes itself out of office, calling for a new election. Elections focusing on a single issue have taken place; the best example, however, occurred over a half century ago, when the House of Commons desired a mandate allowing it to limit the powers of the House of Lords and held an election on that issue in December 1910. Finally, since the parties do vote as blocs in the Parliament, a party could (if it were so foolhardy as to desire to be held strictly accountable) take a precise stand on particular policy issue of the day; it would then be expected to put that policy into effect as representing the people's will.

Scattered throughout several centuries of British political history are events and political practices that, if gathered together by a political scientist, could present an approximate picture of mandate government. But such a collection of historical processes would also distort the facts. The difficulty is that British government is a dynamic, living creature. Our Founding Fathers looked at the British government of their day and thought they saw a principle of separation of powers. American political analysts of the first half of the twentieth century saw something called party government or a responsible party system. There are undoubtedly many advantages in the British system of government—the chief of which is that it is the handiwork of no generation of founding fathers. However, it is the fate of those who abstract great principles from that system to have their studies deflated by the next generation of analysts.

This is what happened to those students of politics who thought they saw a way to achieve a true mandate system through disciplined parties. Near mandates are rare creatures even under the relatively efficient British system. The Labour government was, after 1945, able to act on the assumption of a mandate, but most of the time issues are too complex, too numerous, too interwoven, and too ambiguous for any candidate or party to be able to spell out the precise path he or it will follow. No wise candidate or party wishes to increase its vulnerability to critical attack by being more specific on programs for governmental action than is essential. The usual obfuscation of issues in an American campaign is not the result of some Machiavellian deviousness on the part of politicians; it is an almost natural result of a competitive electoral process. Issues can play an important part in elections, and voters do remember such issues, as President Johnson learned, to his loss, when he violated his 1964 pledge to avoid full-scale involvement in the Vietnam conflict. It is quite permissible to look for something like a mandate in election returns. It is fitting and proper to attempt to seek trends in voter opinions in elections. But we should be cautious about building any model democracy around dreamlike concepts of what an election *could* do, under certain unique or hypothetical circumstances, to express the popular will.

THE VOTER'S CHOICE

Three men faced television cameras at 8:30 P.M., on Monday, September 26, 1960. Two of them were about to place their political futures on the firing line. Richard M. Nixon and John F. Kennedy were ready to start the first of four "great debates"; the third man, commentator Howard K. Smith, was acting as steersman for the confrontation. The words and pictures that followed have been among the most analyzed of American political events. The audience was the largest for any single campaign event in previous history, and the event contributed generously to Kennedy's later success. But some critics were unsatisfied. The confrontation on issues was less than dramatic: public problems were discussed calmly and with high intelligence; yet it would be incorrect to say that voters were given sharp alternative courses of action. The basic confrontation, the one that most likely affected the voter's viewpoint, was one of political personality. Two quite contrasting kinds of public character were displayed by men competing to solve problems, the nature of which were as yet unpredictable. The voters responded by shifting toward the man who, up to that time, had seemed the weaker candidate. The voter learned and he responded. It was not, however, the response certain students of democracy, with the mandate concept in mind, were anxious to see.

If the mandate theory in its idealized form is not very helpful in understanding the democratic electoral process, what does the voter do when he trudges his faithful way to the polls to perform his citizenly duty? What did he do in 1960 and in the elections that have followed? On what basis does he act? It has already been said (in Chapter 3) that we should not picture the voter as performing a strictly rational act in a precise sense. Yet it has also been implied that there is a prevailing common sense in the behavior of the voters as a total group. The choice appears to be rooted in a shifting amalgam of three considerations: the man, the issue, and the party. The relative balance between these three elements will differ for each voter from office to office and from election to election. It will vary between voters. Furthermore, the voter will not often be able to explain exactly how he makes use of these factors, since they are not compartmentalized in his mind. Political personality and party association are guides to policy prediction. Each factor helps to clarify the others; they are not usually three separate considerations. The choice is further complicated because it is sometimes based on an ex post facto review of past performance of an incumbent and, at other times, on a predictive speculation, with no record of issue stands on which the voter can make a forecast. The chief concern of the voter is: "What will government do for me and to me during the next term of office?"

With this question in mind, he might wish to vote on the issues and to help present a collective mandate, giving orders to those elected. To some extent this is possible, even when a candidate is not an incumbent and has not served in some other position that would indicate his position on policies. Candidates must talk about something during their campaigns, and this something will likely be somewhat issue oriented, even when problems and policies are dealt with in sweeping generalities. The astute voter can often see through campaign oratory to detect a pattern of thinking indicating a candidate's approach to policy problems. A campaign as lively and overloaded with talk as that for president offers the voter an impression of each candidate's feeling for the issues, even when the issues do not come forth directly as clear-cut promises regarding specific action. The wise voter knows that the officeholder will face numerous unpredictable problems, that it may be more important to take the measure of the man than to listen to his promises on issues that seem, momentarily, important. Particularly in times of crisis, a presidential candidate must be judged on how he will respond to a future unforeseeable situation.

The 1960 debates were a fascinating study of two tense personalities faced with a crucial confrontation before a remote audience of men and women waiting to seal their fate. The debates were, most of all, a study in political personality: those features of a man's character necessary for predicting his political behavior. Good looks are pertinent under such circumstances, if good looks is taken to mean not the physical structure of the face but the look in the man's eyes, the smile and the timing of the smile, the appearance of self-assurance or the lack of it. Even the way a man parts his hair, the classic example of an incorrect basis for voting, may be relevant. So may be the way a candidate dresses. A man's face, his dress, his demeanor—these and other characteristics are keys to personality that people learn in everyday life. The typical citizen is doing what he knows best when he sizes up a candidate. Granting that it would be foolish to turn an election into a beauty contest, should not the voter utilize all of his skills in choosing a candidate for public office, skills he has learned while finding friends and selecting business partners? Is this candidate capable of decision-making? Does he have enough self-confidence to act? How will he get along with other statesmen with whom he must cooperate? Will he rush into action when wisdom lies in cautious waiting? Will he be too unsure of himself to act? Is he aggressive or cautious, radical or conservative, in demeanor? Is he tolerant of the opinions of others and hence liberal in leaning? Is he genuinely sympathetic and thus likely to look for solutions to social problems? Is he doctrinaire or pragmatic, more anxious about being right or more concerned with solving problems? These are all matters of political personality. It is quite obvious that the personal element in political character is relevant to governmental policy, even though it is too unspecific to be used to predict that a candidate will vote for the repeal of Section 2, Paragraph 6, Clause 16, of the Taft-Hartley Act or to foretell exactly how he might find a way out of a nightmare like the Vietnam war.

The voter is interested in political behavior. Among his tools are a capacity to judge character. Democratic participation does not require that he put aside this natural interest in personality and substitute a concern solely for the issues. The voter needs, however, to learn to judge personality in a political context. The businessman develops a quick sense for judging character in financial dealings, looking for a trustworthy economic personality; the task of the voter is to develop a similar skill—an ability to examine men in terms of political behavior, to think in terms of political character. The voter's task is made considerably more difficult by modern expertise in the "packaging" of candidates. The significance of a report like McGinnis' *The Selling of a President—1968* for democracy is that it requires that the voter become aware of an additional factor when he judges political character: he must learn to be alert to the media and its capacity for manipulation.[2] The proponents of modern advertising techniques usually overstate

2. Joe McGinnis, *The Selling of a President—1968* (New York: Trident, 1969).

their ability to influence an election (after all, Nixon's strength with the voters declined during the campaign despite the enormous sums spent on television and the shrewdness of its managers), but they do make matters a trifle more complicated for the already burdened voter. The main point is that the man on the speaker's platform or standing before blazing television lights is, quite properly, judged not only by the policy content of words coming out of his mouth but also by his mode of speaking, the sincerity of his gestures, how he laughs, how he responds to questions, and the like. If the voter adds to this a study of what is known about the life of the candidate in and out of politics, he will have a useful set of tools.

Although the voter has means of deciding that are not specifically policy oriented, it is important not to fall into the error of cynicism, assuming that policy means nothing and that the voter knows nothing. Policy does enter into the voter's thinking. The election of 1968 is example enough. It seems clear that President Johnson's last-minute bombing halt in Vietnam did help Vice-President Hubert Humphrey, although not quite enough.[3] The typical voter had no specific plan for Southeast Aisa—for that matter, neither did most of the critics of existing policy, in or out of Congress—but he wanted a change of direction. Knowledge at the citizen level is often vague, but it is not nonexistent. Policy at the voter's level is closer to *direction* than to *program*, but it is no less a policy concept. The polls indicate that the citizen often does have knowledge of governmental policy in that he has a sense of the direction leadership is taking. A member of Congress does not pretend to have specific knowledge of every issue that comes before him. He learns to judge the policies put forward by colleagues with other committee assignments in a different, more general, manner than he uses toward his own area of specialty. The citizen, even more removed from specific decision-making, does not need one-tenth the knowledge of such a congressman. He does, quite often, acquire knowledge that will

3. See the analysis in Theodore H. White, *The Making of the President—1968* (New York: Atheneum, 1969), pp. 376–83.

help him to judge a candidate in terms of his *policy direction* without being concerned with the detailed facts implicit in that direction.

The voter has, in most voting situations, yet another tool, one more element in the triad. He does not need to rely entirely on the vagaries of ideological and issue orientation or upon the ambiguities of political character. A candidate can also be known by his associates. Nothing helps the voter more, in this respect, than the existence of permanent organizations of political men joined in parties. Long-established parties have their traditional heroes. They have also accumulated records based upon the positions their leaders have taken on past policy controversies. The office seeker's party alliance tells something about the kind of man he is, something about his way of thinking. This is true even when parties are as loosely united and as nondoctrinaire as they are in the United States. A Democrat is, typically, a different kind of political personality than a Republican. He may, on the average, be expected to hold a different perspective on issues of the day. The candidate has made a choice between parties somewhere along the line; in so choosing he took upon himself a political ancestry that marks him for all to see. Party affiliation gives a candidate a history, one going back, sometimes, as much as a century or more. It is a history that should probably be read backward, since the more recent past is more likely to affect present actions. Lyndon Johnson, John F. Kennedy, and Hubert Humphrey are similar in political thinking to Franklin Roosevelt, Woodrow Wilson, and Andrew Jackson. Even Dwight Eisenhower, who showed little evidence of interest in the differences between parties until he began campaigning in 1952, seems in retrospect to have fallen into the right camp. His political attitudes were generally in line with those of his Republican predecessors. The original reasons for a particular man's party affiliation may have been accidental or inherited, but, even in such a case, a political man must defend his party, and in so doing he normally comes to think like his party colleagues. He must work with party associates and, despite famous exceptions, this is likely sooner or later to convert him into a party man. Although American parties may be less useful than others in this regard, it is helpful to attach a brand name to the product presented in a political campaign. The fact that the quality of each specific product may vary without a change in the label does not make the label useless.

The voter does not sit down with a check list to judge the candidates before him. He has one act to perform, that of casting a ballot. He looks upon the decision as a singular one, not as one made up of several parts. For some offices, particularly minor ones, he would be wise to follow party lines, unless he happens to be one of those eccentric individuals who knows all of the names on the phenomenally long American ballot. For a local election in a small town, personality may mean everything, because the voter knows each candidate personally. Occasionally the voter will be intensely concerned with one or two public issues and will, to the extent that he can discover the position of candidates, wish to vote on that basis. But most of the time he will make an amalgamated judgment, a total appraisal into which all he knows about the man, the office, and the conditions of the times will enter. The choice can be stupid. It is not necessarily our own biases that make us suspect that unqualified candidates are the winners in particular elections. It should be no revelation, therefore, to discover that someone, somewhere, is not voting wisely. Error is well known as a human quality; but this does not give proof that the electoral process is thereby faulty. Nor does it indicate that, from the perspective of historical time, collective decisions do not appear to have a certain wisdom. Even without the existence anywhere of an ideal mandate, the system in many western nations seems workable. If men continue to seek improvements in the voting process, they have reason to hope that it will meet future needs.

SUFFRAGE, EQUALITY, AND MAJORITY

The United States, having once been a new nation, still suffers from some disadvantages of that newness. The short span of our history, our tendency toward idealizing the practical, and the strength of Protestantism give us a society notably devoid of national pageantry. Older communities have retained antique ceremonials that add color to the civic life of the community. Catholic countries preserve holy days for colorful pageants and high masses; Britain offers coronation ceremonies and the royal changing of the guard; India has its pujas. If the Fourth of July was ever a democratic feast day in our more rural past, the demise of the squeaky band in the park and the patriotic orator have turned it into an unceremonial day of recreation. Modern democracy has no appropriate festival for celebrating its virtues. The practical act of voting, unlike the etymologically related act of lighting a votive candle, has never been viewed as an act of prayer. As suggested at the start of this chapter, it would probably be unwise to convert election day into a noisy holiday celebration. Yet certain ritual aspects are part of that day, and there is no need to remove their dramatic quality. There are, as indicated before, two high points in the rites of election day. The first is a moment of truth for the citizen: he makes a symbolic decision, and he joins in civic union with fellow decision-makers in the notable liturgy of communal action. The second act of drama is the counting of ballots and an official declaration of the mystic popular will, the moment of truth for all candidates.

Three major principles arise out of the logic of the democratic voting process: all those members of the community legally defined as mature should be given a vote; each person should have one equally weighted vote; and victory should go to the alternative showing the largest proportion of voter support. The first of these, the principle of general suffrage, arises out of the basic concept of democracy as participation. It is inherent in the democratic idea. Democracy did not begin to achieve fullness in England or the United States until after the 1830s, when rapid strides were made toward universal male suffrage. Yet suffrage will never be completely universal. No one, for example, argues that the maturity requirement for voting is not a logical one, although there is continued debate over its definition—most recently as to whether the arbitrary lower limit should be eighteen or twenty-one years. Another kind of suffrage problem arises when communities define themselves so as to exclude certain residents—all females or all members of a certain racial category. Although such issues are by no means dead everywhere (witness the Union of South Africa), citizenship is now usually defined quite broadly, and the electorate is defined in terms of such citizenship. Despite a few unsettled problems at the boundaries, most modern democracies give formal obeisance to the idea of what is idiomatically called universal suffrage, an issue that was not long ago a major battle ground of democratic reform.

General suffrage gives most of the adult population the right to vote. It does not, quite obviously, provide them with an inbred habit of voting. Americans are quite properly embarrassed by the relatively low proportion of voters at most elections. The nonvoter may be a civic embarrassment, but he remains a member of the community. He can thus not be ignored. A large proportion of nonvoters are underage citizens who have a deep stake in the policies and leadership of their community. Others are those who have changed residence and are thus disqualified. Still others either do not know enough or do not care enough to go to the polls. Voting, for those legally eligible, is chiefly an index of involvement, and involvement is closely related to knowledge. But nonvoters cannot be ignored by elected leaders. The underage nonvoter is observing politics at a formative age, and what he observes will determine his political inclinations for a long time to come. The politician or party that intends to be around for some time will ignore him at its own peril. The line between the apathetic nonvoter, the occasional voter, and the more active citizen is a vague, undefined one. Any new issue may expand the voting population to include former nonvoters. The apathetic citizen is a potential voter, and no leader can totally ignore his presence on the scene.

If the apathetic citizen does choose to vote, his vote is as good as any man's. The principle of electoral equality follows from the idea of general suffrage. Every individual who, when he joins the political community, gains the right of formal participation through the act of voting, gains that right on the basis of equality: suffrage is not only a democratic right; it is also a right held equally. This is not, one should hasten to add, the equivalent of political equality. The need for leadership—both informally and in the formal processes of government—negates the possibility of political equality. But the general pervasiveness of political inequality makes it all the more compelling that the formal act of participation be based on strict equality. Equality is still being celebrated in this significant democratic ritual, even though no one claims that all opinions are equally wise or that all persons are equally able to exert political power.

"The conception of political equality from the Declaration of Independence, to Lincoln's Gettysburg Address, to the Fifteenth, Seventeenth, and Nineteenth Amendments can mean only one thing —one person, one vote."[4] So said Justice Douglas in 1963. Taken out of the context of the reapportionment cases in which it appeared, this statement would seem to be another way of pronouncing the accepted principle of electoral equality. But those Supreme Court cases extended the argument. They argued, partly on constitutional grounds and partly on the basis of democratic logic, that the electoral principle requires each vote also to have equal *significance* in the formal representative process. The court was attacking the well-known and ancient abuses of the rotten borough, seeking to eliminate grossly unequal population differences among electoral districts. But even if it was constitutionally sound, the action of the court was bound to be controversial. Despite the possible cogency of its reasoning, the court was taking a step forward, a step beyond giving each man only one chance to vote and weighing his vote equally. It was making the theory of electoral equality more significant by extending it to include representational equality—a step

4. In *Gray* v. *Sanders,* 372 U.S. 368 (1963) at p. 381. The landmark reapportionment cases were *Baker* v. *Carr,* 369 U.S. 186 (1962) and *Reynolds* v. *Sims,* 377 U.S. 533 (1964).

in the direction of more effective participation and thus in the direction of more effective democracy. The court formalized a viewpoint about the meaning of democracy that had been brewing ever since the debate over the first British Reform Bill in the 1830s. The new ruling is unlikely, however, to produce the kind of political equality its opponents fear and some of its advocates might wish. Members of the House of Representatives still vary considerably in their political power, and the voter in a district that has elected the Speaker of the House has surely been more effective than one in a district that has just elected a freshman congressman from the minority party. There will never be political equality; but greater official equality, expressed in the formal electoral and representational processes, moves a small step in that direction.

The third of the major principles of voting has caused more confusion than the other two combined. In simple terms, the plurality principle states that the choice indicated by the largest number of voters will become the decision of the collectivity. The beginning of confusion arises from the fact that this principle has disadvantages, which under certain circumstances, cause people to prefer a majority to a plurality. To illustrate this, a situation in which plurality and majority are identical may be used; for example, in a legislature voting on a statute. In each of the votes (on each amendment and at each reading of the bill) there are but two ways of voting: aye or nay. Unless there is a tied vote, each winning choice will be supported by more than half of the members; it will have the endorsement of both a plurality (the largest segment) and a majority (that segment larger than all other segments combined). The vote will be a reasonable substitute for communal accord. But what if the assembly is voting for a new Speaker and there are five candidates? What if there is a primary election within the Republican party with five men asking to be nominated for governor? Then the largest (plurality) supported candidate might win with as little as 25 percent of the electorate behind him, which would mean that 75 percent of the voters preferred someone other than the man chosen—a very remote approximation of communal accord. Plurality voting is not always a satisfactory solution; hence there is a tendency to substitute a majority principle. With only two political parties, or through the use of two elections in a row, the outward appearance of a majority can be attained. Voters are arbitrarily told that they can only select between two candidates in the final election, and thus the ultimate winner will have received the assent (despite the arbitrariness of the process) of over half the citizens. Freedom of choice is sacrificed in order to achieve something approximating general community accord.

Since the ideal is unanimous accord and the practical objective is to achieve as much acceptance of the final decision as is possible, a variety of devices may be used to ensure the largest possible support for winning candidates. Where two parties are the norm, when third parties only occasionally upset the system, the plurality principle appears adequate because it will normally also produce a majority. In such areas as the southern United States, however, where there has in actuality been a nonparty system; in municipal nonpartisan elections; and in some multiparty nations elimination preelections and other more complicated devices have been invented to approximate a majority decision. A system that readily produces majorities is preferred because it gives the appearance of substantial consent, supporting those who must govern. The plurality system, on the other hand, gives the impression of a more refined expression of voter choice. It is not essential to discuss how these two goals of achieving a majority and allowing all viewpoints to be expressed in the vote can be combined. The methods, needless to say, are intricate. There is, however, a peripheral problem that deserves attention: the tendency to convert the majority principle into a theory by which the majority rules. The word "rule" causes trouble. It is used sometimes to indicate a principle, law, or procedure to be followed, such as that used in counting votes. But it is also applied to the act of governing, the function of commanding others to act, the activity of control. This ambiguity in the word "rule," plus the tendency to look upon a majority as an operational group, an organized being, has led to confusion in the use of the concept of majority rule.

Enthusiastic proponents of democracy have sometimes built their propaganda around the ideal of political equality when, in reality, all that is reasonably within human probabilities is electoral equality. A similar case of overselling occurred in the conversion of the majority principle used in vote-counting into a belief that a particular group called the majority might rule the community. Almost mystically, the larger category of voters, existing for that one brief moment of truth on election day, became transformed into the kind of creature that can govern a society. The concept of majority was originally a concept of measure—the largest portion of some category. With the doctrinaire democrats, the majority mysteriously appeared as an actor on the political scene—not merely actor, in fact, but ruler. Allegedly the only disturbing element was the second, rather devious, actor called the minority who continually tried to defeat the virtuous majority. These are confusions deeply rooted in democratic mythology. They are related to another confusion: the belief that an entity called the people could and would replace a person named the king. The sovereignty of the people was to be a substitute for the supremacy of the monarchical sovereign. This was a particularly attractive notion in a country such as the United States, because it had rejected its original, royal sovereign. At the time of this nation's founding, citizens in the Western world commonly assumed that the vast body of citizenry could, in some unclear fashion, replace the hated King George III or, in France, perform the functions of the Sun King, Louis XIV.

No switch in sovereignty took place, at least not in that manner. Neither the majority nor the people have replaced the autocratic monarch. As a justice of the Supreme Court said in 1793, "To the Constitution of the United States the term sovereign is totally unknown." That term, Justice Wilson went on to say, "has for its correlative, subject." [5] In the American system "there are citizens,

5. In *Chisolm* v. *Georgia,* 2 Dallas 419 (1793) at p. 454.

but no subjects." There is in a functioning democracy—in the United Kingdom as well as in the United States—no single center of supreme power. If a king remains, his sovereignty is one of the quaint anachronisms a democratic nation may prize but not observe in practice. A complex set of institutions gradually displaced the monarch in Britain. It replaced him more abruptly in the United States and France. In no modern democracy is there any longer a supreme ruler in the sense the word "sovereignty" originally implied. People as individuals, or a few of them, act as rulers; the people, as an amorphous collectivity, does not rule because it exists as an organized entity only through mechanisms of government, through specific men in specific offices with varying roles in the processes of political power. The majority does not rule because it has no group existence—except in the fantasy sense of imagining all voters casting ballots at the same split second and then dreaming that, for that infinitesimal moment, they constitute an organized association. The act of voting, as important as it is in expressing majority opinion, is not the entire act of governing. A vote in electorate or in assembly may greatly influence how a community will be governed; it can even reshape the nature of the governing process itself; yet it cannot replace the process. Democracies, consistent with their basic purpose, make ruling into an act of many parts with endless numbers of participants. Each election, each vote in a parliamentary assembly, is a part of the act of governing, yet elections and votes are by no means all there is to governmental power. The category of citizens who make up a majority in a voting situation will, at that moment, be more influential than the minority category. But nothing makes the act of voting into the act of governing or makes the majority into a ruler, autocratic or otherwise.

The slogan of majority rule is popular. It has entered into the slang of democracy and has gained a kind of emotional attachment. Part of its misuse stems from the tendency to move from the operational notion of the majority party to the shorthand idea of the majority. Particularly in a two-party system, we are confronted with an actual association called the majority, possessing organization and leadership and constituting an active and important part of the political process. There is also an operational being called the minority, the other party, which provides the official opposition. Unfortunately, it is easy to extend these operational concepts beyond their usefulness, to imagine similar creatures dividing the whole community. It is easy to arrive at an Hegelian kind of dialectic, with two contending communal forces, the majority and the minority. There may then appear an image of the tyranny of the majority, suppressing minority rights. Or the opposite picture may appear, that of the selfish minority deviously manipulating the society for its own personal gain. There are genuine problems hidden behind these confusing metaphors, problems of mass conformity and of the power of special interests. Oppression is an evil no matter how many exert it or to how many it is applied. Like the American Negro, the suppressed element may be in the minority, or, like the colored people of South Africa, it may be in the majority: one nation's minority problem can be another's majority problem. In every society there are categories, large or small, who are trampled upon and other elements that do the trampling. The size of the categories does not make the pain any less or the oppression more justifiable. Numbers may be significant, but they are seldom a sufficient description. It is rarely useful to designate groups or categories by size alone.

We have been speaking, in this chapter, about voting. Voting is a matter of nose-counting, a question of numbers. It is the central act of democracy, in ritual and in operational process. It alters the whole political system by making widespread participation possible, by permitting effective representation within the government. Voting, in sum, makes democracy work. It makes a free society possible. Popular government must take numbers into account; it must think in terms of the statistics of popular consent. It does this, however, not out of love of numbers for their own sake, but because every individual in a democracy counts, because each is entitled to the dignity of being listened to. Democracy wants him to participate; it cares about what he thinks. To make this participation practical, repeated polls are taken in order to reveal the individual's wishes. It would rather follow the desires of the many than of the few. This is fundamental democratic justice. But democracy is still government by individual men (acting in group situations) listening to large numbers of other men and being chosen by them. It is not government by one number category (the majority) in opposition to another number category (the minority).

CHAPTER 5

Political Parties and the Public Discourse

IT may be significant that the first historical model of a democracy was developed in the same Athenian community that gave us the beginnings of Western philosophy. Both arose in a city that enjoyed the arts of discussion. Even the literary container for Athenian philosophy took a partly conversational form, through the dialogues of Socrates-Plato and the plays of Aeschylus, Sophocles, and Euripides. The Greeks apparently did not consider it a waste of time to spend hours in the marketplace engaged in nothing but discourse. But many must have occasionally become impatient with words, particularly those who saw clearly the many domestic and foreign problems that were never satisfactorily met. Some of this frustration brought tyrants and demagogues to power. In ancient Greece, in pre-Gaullist France, and in dozens of other places operating under something like assembly government, it eventually becomes obvious that talk must be converted into effective action, which requires organization and leadership. Perhaps this is why the democratic model these days is more likely to be found in London than in either Athens or Paris. The British managed to build a parliamentary system that was constructed around a talking assembly but that was still focused on the executive power. They moved to government by discourse without losing a leadership focal point. Through the development of political parties, they were able to substitute prime minister for king.

Discourse is the heart of the democratic idea. Political talk provides what Walter Bagehot called the "teaching apparatus" for democracy. Popular participation becomes more effective when collective action is founded upon thorough discussion. When ideas arising out of discourse are accompanied by effective organization and leadership, the social end product will be far superior to anything produced by a Greek tyrant, a Roman-style dictator, a Bonaparte, or by any autocrat who tries to rescue democracy from mere talk. Functioning democracy is more than talk; it is organized talk; it is talk that has a way of getting somewhere. The essence of democracy is discourse; its success depends on both the quality and the organization of that discourse. Part of this organization can be built into the formal structure of assemblies and elections. Much of it must rely, however, upon the more flexible structure provided by institutions such as political parties. In practical democratic discourse, either political parties or a less institutionalized substitute must exist to help the assembly function and to give citizen discussion a more productive significance.

THE PUBLIC FUNCTION

We have stated the obvious—that political parties provide a vital element in the democratic discourse—but the more complex question remains: what is the exact nature of these valuable creatures? Above all, it can be said that they are public organs. This is true regardless of which definition of public one has in mind. Parties are not, particularly in America, properly called associations. If they have any genuine membership at all, it is likely to be a mere core around which is built a more amorphous congregation. If one looks beyond city machines and legislative caucuses operating with party labels, he will discover *public parties*, which are vaguely defined collections of people. They turn out to be strange kinds of creatures, gathering together, for each electoral contest, as large a sector of the voting population as they can and losing much of this same bloc the next time around. They are *public* agencies because they operate in the area of civic affairs but, more importantly perhaps, because they perform a public-making function. Parties create, or help in the process of creating, a public, that is, a collection of individuals, lacking formal organization, joined together by the act of focusing attention on some central activity. Government provides one theater for such an audience; the parties provide the barkers, who call attention to the show, and also the managers, who put actors on the busy stage.

Political parties had their origins in speaking assemblies, in parliaments, and rose in significance as those bodies gained power. The history of parties is intricately interwoven with the development of parliamentary government. However, as democracy became increasingly broad in the degree of community participation, party functions and organizations extended themselves out into the community to perform their now familiar public-electoral roles. Political parties provided democratic legislative assemblies with leadership and organization. Bringing a focus to discourse, they made it more certain that action would develop out of talk. In an assembly, as already noted, leaders and followers are not far apart in either status or distance from one another. When the audience is a public, however, the situation becomes quite different. Discourse, as indicated, cannot possess the same intimacy when the audience is unassembled, when it must act through dropping a ballot in a box far removed from most of the other participants. Discourse in an electorate is not discussion in the strictest sense of the latter word because so much of it takes the one-sided form of an electronic broadcast or of words on a printed page. It bears repeating that there is a great difference between men arguing in a conference room and the unilateral kind of talk coming out of a newspaper, a radio, or a television set. Any element of give-and-take must take place at a distance, with hours or days between argument and rebuttal. A major part of the response in such circumstances occurs in the silent secrecy of the voting booth. The public, furthermore, hears only part of what is said. A speaker on radio or television is tuned out easier than one who meets his audience face to face.

Public discourse is, then, slightly blind and quite ambiguous. One can be sure neither about the size of the audience nor about the true nature of its response. A perfectionist like Rousseau had good cause to be frustrated with democracy in large communities. An assembly audience, despite the frailties of all human communication, is preferred, for sound reasons, to a community audience. But there has been a recent change of perspective. Traditional political philosophy made no sharp distinction between community and public, but, as viewed now, at least in these pages, some members of the community do not, in any operational sense, constitute part of a public-as-audience. They give no heed to what is happening at the center. If a public is an aggregate of unassembled people who center their attention on a particular activity, there will be a different public for each focal point, and, more importantly at this moment, each public will exclude those who do not pay that specific action the honor of their attention. It will also exclude all of those who perform the major acting roles, the insiders. A community, by contrast, includes those who are completely apathetic, even though they are operationally insignificant; it also includes the totally engaged persons who act as governors. A public is made up of interested outsiders. But it is necessary to add qualifying provisos. Sometimes, if one is using a different definition of community or is following a conception of public such as is indicated by the phrases "public interest," "public welfare," or "public ownership," the terms "community" and "public" become identical. Under this other, quite different meaning of the term, the public is the whole community. It is the subject of governmental action, the possessor of social resources; it is not merely an interested set of observers. The community (or the public in this other sense) includes three-day-old babies, catatonic patients in a mental hospital, members of Congress, chronic nonvoters, and the president himself. But when concern is with the part of the community that affects governmental action rather than the part that is affected by it, as concerns us here, the concept of public is more usefully limited to those outsiders who join the discourse, to those who watch closely the antics of leaders acting in the heat of the governmental spotlight while they themselves remain, more comfortably, off the central stage.

Liberty brings variety. Freedom in democratic discourse means that talk will occur in a variety of forms; it will be found in rather strange places, voiced in unfamiliar dialects. The newspaper and the barber shop, the theater and the dining room, the television studio and the neighborhood bar—in all of these places democratic talk flows freely and often disjointedly. Free speech is both a basic tool of democracy and its most glorious product. But democracy is deeply concerned with governing, and, in that perspective, the major talk activities will be the assembly debate, the committee argument, and the electoral campaign. In all of this governmental discourse there will be a defined finishing point. Unlike much of the talk in the world at large, it will usually get somewhere, coming to an ultimate conclusion in decision-by-vote; or it will arrive at some equivalent such as unanimous accord or an implicit vote. Granting that the quality of governmental discourse is not necessarily at a higher level, not more gentlemanly or more erudite than social discourse generally, it is often forced, somewhat arbitrarily, to be productive—at least in the limited sense of reaching a formal conclusion. The argument may go on after the ballot, but the existence of a punctuation mark—the act of voting—will materially affect the nature of the discourse process.

When the vote provides a punctuation point for discourse, it not only gives formal assurance of getting somewhere but also provides a note of drama for the talk, building audience interest toward a crescendo. An intense presidential campaign like the tight race of 1968 or a closely fought contest in Congress makes discourse more effective by magnifying the size and the activism of that particular public. The precise magnitude and intensity of any public response will depend upon what takes place on center stage, with political parties, even in their somewhat weakened American form, helping to build up popular concern. When the temper and quantity of interest builds to a high point, actors in the governmental arena become acutely aware that they are being watched. Public-building is, therefore, a vital part of the democratic process. Mutual awareness on the part of actors and audience is a spontaneous process. It cannot be created by adherence to one set of rules. It is normally an informal kind of happening, the kind well performed by amorphous, unofficial congregations like political parties. Political parties are effective in bringing a note of dramatic competition to the creation of publics and to the public discourse because they are, in the definition used here, competitive creatures, beings that thrive in the glare of footlights, building up public attention in order to remain alive.

Before leaving this general and brief discussion of the nature and creation of publics, some comment needs to be made about a special kind of public created in the process of public-opinion polling. From the inner sanctums of their offices, the pollsters issue questions of alleged community concern, and their interviewers carry them to the outer world in order to sample the population. The persons polled, the pollees, may quite conceivably have no interest in the issue until they are asked about it. Being aware, however, of the high ethical value placed on civic-mindedness in a democracy, they respond with alacrity if they possess the minimal knowledge that makes any response possible. Such persons are now part of a public, even though they may not have been, in any more natural sense, a moment before. The pollees respond because it is polite and because it is their civic duty. The function of the pollsters—their very reason for existence—requires them to look upon public opinion as having a somewhat autonomous existence. They are forced to see it as something to be discovered, separate from any spontaneous response to the action on the governmental stage. The focus of this poll-created public is not the doings of the governors of the society or of any other activists. The focus is on the poll and the polling question itself. In this sense, such a public might be called artificial.

The public thus uncovered by the polls is not entirely a creature arising from stimuli in government, in political activity, or in some other arena of activity. It is the product of those who ask the questions. Benefits are undoubtedly produced by such poll-created publics. This new kind of public—one made up of the handful of people polled plus the larger group that avidly reads the polls as a weather vane of civic concern—is not necessarily a bad kind of public. Because the polls emphasize the role of publics and of public opinion, they make a contribution to the political society. But it is important to know what is happening, to be clear about what the polls are measuring. The responses produced are not identical with those which leadership, by its own prodigious labors, creates in a potential audience. Not all of the responders, the pollees, have put themselves into the public-as-audience by their self-developed interest or as a result of reading and listening; some become members of the public only because they have been arbitrarily selected by a third force, the pollsters. Just as there is said to be merit in a voting population that selects itself by showing sufficient strength of interest to get to the polls, there may be, in the more ambiguous area of public opinion, a higher virtue in that type of public that has created itself through inherent concern with public affairs. Democracy, as has been said repeatedly in these pages, is defined as a participatory process, but it is a free, spontaneous type of participation. It is participation, created neither by autocratic demands for civic activity nor for the benefit of someone who wishes, as an objective observer, to dissect the public to see what makes it tick. The polls are useful to the extent that there is awareness, both in their creation and in their use, that a *public-as-pollees* is not identical with a *public-as-audience*. The latter is created by the activity on stage; the former by the activity of an objective observer, arbitrarily injecting himself into the scene of action.

The pollsters, the press, the parties, the interest groups, and all of the various leaders on stage can help to create an active public. A lively public is a talking public. It responds to activity at the focal point with free discourse, by talking among itself. In an unorganized fashion, it also succeeds in making itself felt by those at the center of action. Because it is an audience and not an organized association, the talk will not come in the form of instructions. There will not be, in the strict sense of the term, a mandate. There will be no defined voice, no specific words, no particular language or accent. There can be a dialogue only in a rather remote sense. But those at work facing the hot lights become sharply aware of the audience out front, especially in a democracy, where governmental careers are so directly dependent upon public response. They hear a babble of muffled voices. They must learn to judge and react to this obscured speech. The astute politician becomes skilled at hearing strange sounds, at interpreting their practical meaning. The impatient student of democracy must not jump to the conclusion that, because this public talk cannot be captured by a tape recorder in any intelligible fashion, it is not meaningful. Nor must he assume that, because it is unlike orderly parliamentary debate and unlike a set of recorded instructions, it is thereby not a "behavioral" political activity. The public sends out messages in strange ways because it watches and listens from heterogeneous perspectives and because collectively it is an amorphous creature. This makes discussion of public reaction difficult but not less important. As has been implied before, difficulties in converting political activity into empirically recorded raw material is never a proof of the lack of importance of that activity.

CLIQUE, CAUCUS, AND PARTY

The Renaissance reached its full political expression in the great monarchies of western Europe, in the years of Henry VIII and Elizabeth in England, Philip II in Spain, Henry IV and Richelieu in France. Feudal baronies were, by that time, fully suppressed, and a new nation-state system had been built on autocratic centers of royal power. Around each of these magnets of power there gathered cliques made up of advisers, favorites, and mere hangers-on. But in England the process differed in at least one notable respect. The kings incorporated in their royal system the large medieval councils that made up a parliament. As a result, in England, the stage was set for a later shift from royal cliques to legislative factions, a change that took place too imperceptibly for current observers to notice. By the time of the Stuart Restoration, these groups became the predemocratic predecessors of what we now call political parties. By the time of George III, the king found it necessary to play the game of party politics in order to have a monarchy half as effective as that two centuries earlier. American statesmen in the same period, despite their opposition to factionalism, formed themselves into parties almost from the moment of the founding of the nation. In neither the colonies nor the mother country, it should be noted, were political parties invented in the way a tinkering mechanic assembled the first flying machine.

Perhaps the most intelligent way to understand the intrinsic meaning of political parties is to examine the elaborate history of their development out of early parliamentary practices. Such an intriguing enterprise would, unfortunately, demand hundreds of written pages rather than a mere handful. A more general approach will serve present purposes. Around a quarter of a century ago a useful theory was presented by E. E. Schattschneider in a book called *Party Government*.[1] He presented what could be called a caucus hypothesis, a visualization of political parties as dynamic products of competitive democratic politics. His germinal idea is worth new exploration because it may lead us to a clearer understanding of the peculiar features of political parties that make them a distinctive democratic kind of institution.

It would appear, following the logic of Schattschneider, that genuinely competitive, free elections will invariably bring forth some type of vote-mobilizing structures once those elections are established on a formalized, continuing basis. This will occur whether the voting is over policy issues or for the selection of leaders. A proviso, important to add, is that such caucuses are unlikely

1. (New York: Rinehart, 1942).

to develop unless the voting decisions are of sufficient significance to make the rewards of regularized organization worth the effort. There must be significant disagreement; there must be intensity of interest in the outcome of the vote; and there must be continuity among those voting—elements not always present in every voting situation but the normal rule when there is enough business to keep a large legislative assembly busy. Sometimes such mobilizing structures are barely visible. In smaller groups and communities caucuses may operate on a largely *ad hoc* basis with organization too informal to resemble a political party, assuming a form difficult for outsiders to detect.

The caucus process is near the heart of the democratic system. It is based, as Schattschneider put it, "on the discovery that a few members agreeing in advance can control a large body in which other members do not consult for this purpose." [2] But, as he was quick to see, one caucus quite frequently results in the development of a countercaucus. Once members of a group come to realize the power of organization as a device to win votes, two or even more caucuses will reach out for support sufficient to achieve the desired plurality or majority. The caucus theory is not, at least as seen here, a historical hypothesis. It merely provides a functional kind of explanation of parties. It seeks to illuminate the central purpose of parties by viewing them as one of a larger species, a species common in the smallest and in the largest democratic collectivities. The caucus provides a means of organizing electoral advocates for a particular viewpoint or candidate; it permits them to work together and to gather still more supporters, in opposition to similar tactics of opposing caucuses. The model caucus would operate like an ideal parliamentary cabinet; it would meet behind closed doors to fight out internal dissensions and to decide on objectives and strategies. Then, venturing forth into assembly or electorate, it would battle the common foe to collect as many votes as possible, masking from public eyes the existence of

2. *Ibid.*, p. 39.

disagreement among its own members. Needless to say, the ideal is rarely met.

The idea of a caucus is exclusively democratic, an American contribution to the language of politics, with no meaning in the language of autocracy. It is an implement in the competition for votes in a free and participating society. There need not always be a countercaucus. Unless a countercaucus is possible, however, there can, by definition, be no first caucus. Free competition and democracy are inherent in the concept itself. A community or assembly that has all of the requisites for democratic politics may sometimes lack substantial dissension. At other moments, disagreement may operate at so low a level of intensity that opposition does not bother to organize. On still other occasions, there may appear to be a single caucus when, in actuality, subgroups within that caucus provide the competing organizations. This is what happened in the American Solid South for many years. Confusion may also develop when post-democratic autocracies appropriate to themselves some of the language related to the caucus process as part of their general mimicry of democratic forms. They may refer to the organization that mobilizes support behind the regime as a political party and, less commonly, may borrow democratic terms to apply to the cliques that inevitably surround any autocratic center of power. True caucusing can take place, however, only when there is a genuinely competitive vote, which can only follow a bona fide process of free discourse.

Defined as an implement of democratic voting and discourse, the concept of caucus is a broad one. Nothing specifies the limits of its duration or the extensiveness of its organizational structure. A caucus may exist for one solitary vote, for one single issue, for one candidate alone. Leadership may be spontaneously generated among people who, for the moment, find themselves thinking alike. Such *ad hoc* caucuses are ubiquitous in democratic life. They may be observed in club meetings or in the midst of a national party convention, which is itself a more institutionalized kind of caucus. But there are obvious advantages in voting that takes place on a continuing basis; there is virtue in regularizing the process. Institutionalized caucuses concerned with the activity of governance become gradually more broadly oriented; they become less concerned with one set of issues or with a single group of men they wish to elect. They soon lose their identification with a particular era and with the names of specific leaders. They learn to attain sufficient flexibility of strategy and purpose to permit persistence over long periods of time, which allows them to gather the kind of strength that can come only from the possession of a historic tradition: they become political parties. As such, they eventually build up a collection of supporting workers who are as devoted to the vague, lasting goals of the party as they are to the particular men and programs of their time—men and programs that reflect the party philosophy but cannot speak for all of its generations.

The earliest parties were informal caucuses within a legislature. As the composition of an assembly became more and more dependent upon the support of voting citizens, however, nationwide parties emerged. They also developed numerous functions within the governing process so that no aspect of ruling a community could be immune from their influence. They reshaped the royal spoils system into a more equalitarian device. They contributed greatly to the civic education of men and women who were being given new communal responsibilities. They created the bosses and the politics of city machines. In general, they made democracy work. But, in all of this, their central function did not change. They remain caucuses, with their central point of attention still on the free and competitive process of voting.

POLITICAL PARTIES: VARIATIONS ON A THEME

Most modern democracies, with the British version the most notable exception, have specific birth dates. Even though they all have historic roots that antedate the moment of founding, they have required, at some particular point in time, the invention of formal governmental structures. Few have been able to rely, in their major formalized mechanisms, on the results of evolutionary processes. Political parties are the exception. They are generally less legalized, less the result of planning than other major structures in a governmental system. This difference makes matters confusing for political reformers. Since constitutional documents commonly require deliberate alteration to adjust them to the times or to eliminate errors in original construction, there is a natural tendency to attempt similarly formalized changes in the evolutionarily developed party system. Since all constitutional systems (of which political parties are an important part) contain both evolutionary and invented elements, it is difficult to know which parts should be left to gradual, unplanned alteration and which ones to purposeful reconstruction. This is particularly so when, as is so often the case, the formal and the informal elements are intricately interwoven.

There have been countless suggestions for structural change, which, one way or another, would alter the pattern of our party activity. The consequences of many of these might well have been disastrous. All such proposals are undoubtedly well intended; usually they are in the name of more democracy; and often they are at the expense of the political parties. A recent American example was agitation for a national presidential primary, something that might, at one blow, have shattered much of what remains of our national party system. Despite continued discourse about reforms, however, a considerable inertia regarding institutional change is also built into the American constitutional system. Parties are a natural subject of attack in a society that, although highly politicized, has long been suspicious of politics and politicians. This antipolitical bias persists despite the difficulty of picturing a kind of caucus-free, spontaneous democracy. Once the function of parties is known, it is as difficult to imagine a modern nation without them as it is to conceive of a city like New York very long without electricity. One cannot conceive of a nation of 200 million inhabitants nominating presidential candidates with no organized caucusing or of any complex nation choosing its leadership by the processes that a club of twenty members might follow. It is difficult enough to imagine the consequences of eliminating traditional national conventions for the party nomination of presidential candidates, to estimate how much wealth a private individual or group would need to be successful in a nationwide primary, or to guess how often a particularly flamboyant filmstar personality might arise to capture the nomination. But it is even more difficult to imagine a democracy having no parties at all.

The existence of political parties and caucusing is now generally, if somewhat grudgingly, accepted, even though there remains much ignorance concerning the fundamentals of party government. The caucus-party function is vaguely accepted, despite lack of agreement about proper patterns for this behavior. Although wide divergence in form is to be expected between communities, basic party functions are remarkably similar. Parties everywhere perform a leadership role; all act as mobilizers of publics; all have some concern with policy development. Everywhere they create channels for recruitment and development of democratic leadership, organizing it both for those in office and for those in opposition. They educate publics everywhere as to the character of competing leadership candidates; at the same time, they mobilize a general, community public out of the raw material of inactive citizens, focusing the attention of this public on officials and encouraging it to hiss or boo at appropriate intervals. Even the most nondoctrinaire parties, as those in the United States, can aid the development of broad creeds and ideologies, while calling attention to problems and policies currently the subject of debate. These caucus-related functions will be performed in a wide variety of ways, with widely different degrees of efficiency. The variables that combine in each community to make that pattern of party activity unique are called the party system, and those operational variations in the mode of conducting general party functions can be infinite.

It must be remembered that political parties are pragmatic instruments. They respond to specific needs of specific nations. Hence the first factor that explains the great diversity of party systems is the variety of constitutional forms and processes developed in modern communities. Although in the older democracies parties were not recognized as part of the structure of government, they became such as soon as they were born. Even now, wise constitution-makers leave as much of the party system to happenstance as they can; they may be aware of parties in drafting a constitution, but planning takes away the informal character of parties, making them less natural, possibly distorting the development of the kind of parties best suited to that particular environment. Although this is not the proper place for a comparative analysis of the relation of political parties to various constitutional schemes, it might be worth commenting on the increasing trend toward formalizing the party process. The custom of binding parties within an ever stricter legal framework is perhaps partly inevitable; yet it is also partly regrettable. In the United States and Great Britain—both leaders in party development—the parties were originally quite autonomous of governmental regulation. The unsurprising effect of increased regulation of the election process, however, is more control over political parties; it is recognized that such parties provide a major portion of the electoral machinery and that one cannot be controlled without the other. It would be difficult to imagine leaving such a crucial social activity as that performed by political parties strictly alone. Governments now regulate party expenditures and their sources of revenue. More importantly, they also create extensive controls over organizational matters and, inevitably, undertake various manipulations to favor one faction or party over another. The election laws of continental powers with complex multiparty systems are sometimes modified, regime by regime, in an effort to alter the balance of power. American legislatures long ago joined the trend, reorienting the whole party system through the invention of the famous direct primary.

The factor that usually receives the most attention in comparisons of party systems is the pattern of competition. This usually centers on the number of significant competing parties. Systems are commonly identified as two-party or multiparty, despite the numerous other characteristics that might define them. This is hardly surprising. If the basic function of any caucus is competition in a voting situation, it is reasonable to identify party systems by the divergent features of their competitive relations. Although there will be a few dissenters, it now seems almost established that dualism provides the more logical and practical competitive pattern. The logic comes from the argument that dualism is somehow natural to the voting process. Despite the present concern of parties with the election of candidates to office, they originated within legislatures, where their prime concern was with votes taking place on issues. They continue to have a major function in the legislative process where, according to the argument, the necessity of an aye or nay vote on each proposal tends to force them toward a natural dualism. The argument that dual parties are more practical arises from a related point. A two-party system can produce only a majority or a tie vote. This means that the larger of the caucuses can, all things being equal, act as effective government because it has majority support. Multiparty systems are forced to reshape their parties once they are elected to the legislative assembly, forming majorities through coalitions or blocs. These then become the patchwork equivalent of the parties found in the dual system, except that they lack internal stability—being inclined to fly apart on the slightest disagreement among leaders of the separate parties.

Despite the long list of advantages any textbook will present in favor of dualism of party competition and despite strong arguments that two parties are, in some sense, more natural, multipartyism is at least as common as dualism. Numerous communities have suffered with the instabilities resulting from multiparty politics. Their voters have faced the intriguing but unenviable task of trying to outguess the antics of leaders of parliamentary parties when, after the election, these parties need to gather with certain other parties into a coalition. But there are other kinds of hybrid party systems more familiar to Americans. One is that which we call a one-party system. Although it can be distinguished quite easily from totalitarian one-partyism through a democratic definition of parties as competitive instruments, it is still an idiosyncrasy requiring comment. Sometimes one-partyism arises from conditions of imbalance, which are often a result of some serious crisis or revolution in the political structure. In a postcolonial nation such as India, during its first decades after independence, the party of revolutionary leadership, the party largely responsible for independence, could retain unbalanced power, with only a number of splinter parties in opposition. The more familiar American examples occurred during the years following the decline of the Federalists early in the nineteenth century and during many decades in the Deep South after Civil War and Reconstruction. There was not so much an end to competition as a shift to a disordered type of conflict, one with shifting cliques, personality caucuses, and chaotic informal factions. All competitors flew the same party banner but without any sense of unity (except on the "settled" race issue) and with none of the orderliness that comes through institutionalized political parties. Competition under such confusing circumstances should be so unsatisfactory that party politics would soon revive—as it did on the national scene in the Jacksonian era. Sometimes, however, a series of factors, such as the race and sectional issues of the Civil War, will serve to stop any return to what might be called normality. If the single (Democratic) party had not proved a handy tool for the segregationists, it is doubtful that voters would have tolerated the lack of effective competition for so long. Rival politicians might otherwise have sought a more effective mode of political organization.

Within federal systems party competition may be expected to vary from area to area. Although many factors—economic, social, political, and legal—explain variations in party systems, the most easily diagnosed differences are still those rooted in constitutional systems. Parties are deeply affected by constitutional features and, in turn, have a very substantial effect on them. In fact, if a broad definition is used, political party systems can be looked upon as an integral part of the constitutional system of a community. The primary election system in the American South was a constitutional answer to the decline of effective party competition in the post-Civil War era, and, as its use spread it in turn affected party competition and structure. It works both ways. Legal forms are often responses to problems in the party system, and new patterns of party activity develop that help to alter formal constitutional patterns. There is a condition of mutual causation. In other nations, while the use of proportional representation was designed to ensure that the various parties in a multiparty system were represented in proportion to their support among the voters, it itself undoubtedly encouraged continued multipartyism. In the United States the large number of separated centers of power (resulting from federalism, from the separation of powers, and from the tendency at the state and local level to elect numerous executive officers) has helped to shatter party discipline, turning the parties into confederations as weak as the Holy Roman Empire or a league of nations. These divided centers of party power have brought even more pluralism to the already fragmented political system.

Party systems vary in numerous other respects. They differ, for example, in the meaning they put upon the concept of party membership. In a few situations there is a central body of formal members with duties and privileges such as might be found in a club or association. But the more common pattern is that in which a central core of activist workers is not sharply distinguished from the vague group of loyal partisans who may do little more for the party than support it in elections. Parties with the sharpest concept of membership are often those which are more doctrinal. The left-wing parties of the European continent have frequently included large bodies of supporters who are signed-up members. To doctrinal-minded outsiders as well as to radical elements within the society, American parties with their ambiguous labels (or British ones with misleadingly distinctive names) appear to be like two peas in the same pod. This is because they are remarkably nondoctrinaire, placing more stress on compromise than on sharply defined ideologies. This does not mean that they are entirely devoid of policy principles or that the average citizen has no choice. Rather, it indicates a great concern with the effective use of political power—power that can be based on compromise in a less doctrinal-minded society. Ideological purity is less than sacrosanct. There is a preference, on the part of both voters and leadership, for being half right, if this means being in a position to do something, rather than being altogether right but out of effective power. The citizen does have a choice, but that choice lies within a broad spectrum of centrist views and only rarely, as with the Goldwater nomination in 1964, does purity of principle override compromise. Differences in degree of doctrinalism, in membership affiliation, in internal organization, and in the pattern of competition are endless. They are also crucially important in comprehending a particular pattern of democratic experience.

THE INSTRUMENTS OF BATTLE

Political parties are strange kinds of war machines. They are forced to rely entirely on voluntary recruitment. They have no effective deterrent to desertion. Like no army ever known, the troops march only when they are happy with their officers, and, as they parade along, they argue endlessly about the proper road to take. Yet, like a marine battalion, they must sally forth united, shouting with patriotic fervor, attacking an enemy accused of horrendous atrocities. At the same time they curse the enemy with every acceptable profanity their command of language permits, they must attempt to woo away his foot soldiers. Parties try to halt their own continual bickering while taking full advantage of any dissension in enemy ranks, forever sharpening the conflict against the common foe. The caucus process results in paradoxical functions: it creates organs of combat which must also be instruments of integration. Whereas political parties are not, of course, the sole instruments of democratic conflict and compromise, they may well be the most institutionalized, the most "constitutional" of such instruments since they focus attention on the theme process of the democratic system—on the voting activity in assemblies and among electoral populations.

All combative groups find themselves deeply concerned with maintaining their own internal cohesion. Integrative processes become more important in a competitive situation. But political parties are inherently weak kinds of agglomerations, tending to fly apart on the slightest provocation. To grasp the peculiar nature of the combative-integrative function in political parties it may be as useful to observe a moment of failure as to examine the long, less dramatic periods of their relative success. The American Civil War presents a familiar and classic case. Unlike nineteenth-century revolutions in Europe, this was not a class conflict or one of autocracy against democracy. The virtue of democratic processes was accepted by both sides. It was, rather, a breakdown in the underlying basis of consensual competition, a collapse in that certain something that keeps the democratic battle peaceable. It was, in considerable part, a failure in the party system. From the perspective of parties, political breakdown occurred when doctrinal differences created an intraparty factionalism too intense for the continued functioning of the compromise that had glued the parties together. Party splits are a common phenomenon, but in this instance, the parties also happened to be the very last resort for compromise. The parties had been papering over a schism that had been cutting wide and deep through the community. The second of these parties, the Democratic, split in 1860. Its breakdown symbolized a more general failure in compromise, a collapse of the last hope for consensual solutions.

The story of the political breakdown we call the Civil War might have been quite different if the United States had based its democracy on a different kind of party system. In a dual pattern, the political parties function as creatures of the broadest possible kind of community-wide compromise. They become so nondoctrinal, so concerned with the prime function of electing men to office and controlling legislatures, that broad integration of divergent social and political forces becomes almost an instinctive way of acting. The histories of American and British parties describe a continuous patching together of factions. The diverse groups within each party bicker with each other between elections and then, when necessity dictates, unite to do battle against the other patchwork congregation. The long sweep of history shows remarkable cohesion in moments of battle, especially for collections of men combining such disparate elements. The marvelous speed the Democratic party displayed in bringing southern politicians back into national politics within a decade after one of the bitterest wars in history is a dramatic illustration of this patching process at work. The war began with the breakdown of that party, and its political settlement took place within that party. No one knows what would have happened to mid-nineteenth-century America under a multiparty system, but, if one is aware of the sharp contrast between French and Anglo-Saxon histories of democracy, it is obvious that the story would have been notably different. Perhaps there would not even have been a Civil War but merely a period of less stable coalitions. In any event, the configuration of party conflict in a democracy becomes crucially important. It may be a major element in the entire pattern of social integration or disintegration.

A dual party structure affords a particularly effective system of compromise. Each of the two conglomerates seeks a majority of voter support, and, unlike the situation in a multiparty community, the aim is well within reason. Each reaches toward the agglomeration sitting opposite, hoping to steal away partisans. Each tries to guard against such raids by reinforcing the widest possible base in sectional and interest-based factions. It is an unfortunate feature of this broad kind of dual conflict-compromise structure that its breakdown can, under certain circumstances, create a social crisis more serious than the perennial small crises created by the collapse of coalitions in the French Third and Fourth Republics or in postwar Italy. The dual system works, however, in large part because the particular social conditions are right for broad collections of factions. Unless the community has enough basic unity of purpose, the pastework creating each of two large parties would be so unstable that a crisis could easily tear it asunder, possibly wrecking the nation in the process. The Anglo-Saxon nations have generally maintained the kind of consensus that permits broad-based, dual parties. The existence of such a consensual foundation permits two-partyism to work; party dualism, in turn, helps to maintain the communal consensus.

The purpose of caucusing, whether there are two or many such caucuses, is to bring together the largest effective coalition of those who participate in the voting process in an election or assembly. This means that the caucus process is essentially expansionist. Each group reaches out until confronted with a rival congregation seeking the same electoral victory; each reaches into the territory claimed by opposing caucuses. If sectionalism or doctrinalism do not impose barriers that close off areas of recruitment, the caucus process gives each party the hopeful prospect of gathering a majority of legislators or voters into its ranks. Each will want to achieve a majority and, ideally, one with a margin of safety. Hence no sensible party sits back in contentment, happy with the support it has already gathered. Once a party has gathered a majority under its wing and has assumed the powers of government, it is sensible for those in opposition to unite as closely as possible into a second caucus, chipping away at the majority conglomeration. There will always be a potential second caucus if not, momentarily, an actual one. The affairs of men seldom result in total agreement, and there are almost inevitably some members of an assembly or community who will be attracted to any opposition faction that develops. Thus there will normally be undefinable, but no less real, limits to the expansibility of any single caucus. The existence of this expansionist drive of the caucuses provides the competitive force that makes democracy effective. The caucuses wish to maximize participation. In seeking supporters, they contribute to the democratic process, bringing men and women into active political involvement.

The expansionist goal of parties is not limited to a dual-caucus situation. However, when constitutional or historical circumstances create barriers to dualism, the ambitions of each party are reduced. Parties tend, under a multiple system, to reach out for additional support primarily in the area to their immediate left and right on the political spectrum. They generally find it hopeless to look all the way across the political community. Sophisticated doctrinal shifts are attempted in hopes of absorbing members from one nearby party without alienating those on the other side. Temporary alliances give some parties the partial taste of power and responsibility. These coalitions among parties take on a patchwork appearance similar in some ways to that which may be observed within the confines of a single party in a dual system, except of course, that what would be factions in a dual-party system maintain their organizational autonomy. The expansionist function is altered in a very different manner by the moribund kind of politics existing in what is called a one-party system. In the traditional Solid South, the opposition party made no effort to bring out the vote, and the various intraparty factions were more likely to play the game of palace politics, with the formation and manipulation of cliques, than to turn themselves into effective electoral machines.

Moderate politics, free from intense doctrinal and sectional antagonisms, arises from moderate social tensions. It cannot be created out of whole cloth by a system of dual caucusing. Such a system can do a great deal, however, to preserve it. It is clear that dualism helps to maintain a moderate level of conflict, partly because it focuses electoral combat on the center, emphasizing it as the battleground where the two forces join periodically in a dramatized duel. Each of two caucuses will fight for those middle-minded voters who do not much care, for those not deeply concerned with public affairs, for those with low intensity of interest in the party battle. Each party, when there are but two, reaches out for the men and women who inhabit the fog-ridden no-man's-land between enemy lines—those who have no objection to switching. One party (illustrated by the Democrats for several decades after 1932) may have a momentary grasp on this middle segment, but this very group of voters in the majority party provides a vulnerable target for the opposition.

The Republican tactic of appealing to the fringes on the political Right in 1964 shows what can transpire when, out of frustration, a party violates the norms of center-oriented politics. Nixon's 1968 campaign appeal to middle America, to "bringing us together," was a successful attempt to rectify the apparent tactical error of four years before even though it was somewhat offset by his "Southern strategy." The Goldwater episode served to underscore the centrist rule that it violated so disastrously. It convinced many previous skeptics (among the Republicans at least) that, in a conflict aimed at winning away the enemy's foot soldiers, common sense suggests aiming at the weakest, most convertible opposition squadrons. Fine doctrinal distinctions and class, economic, and sectional conflicts tend to be smothered by both parties in the process of making this convertible middle happy. It is important to realize, however, that there is, in dualism, a second cause of moderation in party position. The responsibilities of power—the awesome experience of meeting genuine problems with practical solutions—come to parties in a dual system often enough to reinforce this first factor, adding strength to the moderating effect of reaching toward the middle. A party like the Labour party in Britain, after starting out with a rather distinct doctrinal origin, begins to look as ambiguous and moderate as its opponent when it faces the realities of making difficult decisions and learns the hard lessons of gathering majority support.

The internal pattern of party organization is an essential element of the conflict-integration function of political parties. Some European observers, notably Roberto Michels, have commented on the autocratic internal organization of doctrinal parties in continental Europe, but the experience in a nonideological, dual-party system is different.[3] Even though British parties are better disciplined than the national parties of the United States, and although, within the

3. Roberto Michels, *Political Parties*, trans. Eden and Cedar Paul (Glencoe, Ill.: Free Press, 1949) (original edition, 1915).

United States, local parties have sometimes been quite autocratic in internal structure, the function of mobilizing a majority in a two-caucus situation makes tight cohesion difficult. The parties must depend upon a large body of partisans who are quite indifferent or even hostile to the leadership of the bosses. Parties must operate from a core of active workers, but the line between this core and the broader base of support is not always clear. It is seen at its sharpest in the Labour party in Britain and at its vaguest in the amorphous agglomerations that make up the national Republican and Democratic parties in the United States. There are a great variety of degrees of attachment to the creatures we call parties. This is because parties are strange congregations, anxious not to reject any prospective member, especially under conditions of dualism, when the attainment of a majority position is well within their reach.

Any instrument of battle, including a political party, needs cohesion to the extent that it is faced with effective opposition. It needs to integrate forces and to discipline them tightly to achieve maximum effectiveness. But the caucus function, particularly when aimed at a genuine majority vote, forces parties to offset this disciplinary objective with a countertendency, one that brings together as many dissident elements as can be gathered under one ambiguous roof. From one standpoint the party would like to be as tightly knit as a family or clan, closely united in common purpose against a feuding enemy who wants to obliterate it from the face of the earth. From the other standpoint it is as anxious to embrace the whole population as is the sales manager of the Ford Motor Company. Reformers first attacked American parties as tools of bosses and machines. Later, under the assumption that greater discipline meant greater responsibility, others attacked them on opposite grounds—for lack of discipline. Both attacks ignored the crucial fact that, under an effective dual system, the precise balance between cohesion and expansion is undefinable and is largely a matter of historical and environmental circumstance. It may be well to tinker as little as possible with that delicate balance.

THE SUPREMACY OF DISCOURSE

"Government by discussion," says Walter Bagehot, "breaks down the yoke of fixed custom." It eliminates the power of "sacred authority"—the idea that any one man or group has a monopoly of wisdom. "It gives a premium to intelligence."[4] Discourse is a civilizing process. It is basic to the democratic experience. One of the peculiarities of the discourse aspect of a free society, however, is that so little has been written about it. The other two phases of the central democratic process—the preparation of alternative choices and the succeeding act of voting on those options—have filled volumes of print. Those other phases of the scheme of democratic decision-making are relatively institutionalized. Voting is a highly formal process. It is among the most regulated and ritualized aspects in the democratic scheme of things. It must follow precise rules so that the voter may know what he is doing. Rules are needed to safeguard against cheating and to guarantee a noncontrovertible result in the arithmetical process of vote-counting. The other of the three elements, the preparation of alternative options, is also institutionalized, through the semiformalized activities of parties and the carefully defined committee systems and nomination procedures. But the heart of the process remains informal: it is the act of free communication. Unrestricted talk makes the whole democratic venture possible; yet, because it is so informal, fewer words are needed to describe the nature of that discourse.

It has already been pointed out that the discourse process differs materially between an election campaign and an assembly debate. Political parties are active in each, but in quite different ways. There is a risk, however, if one looks exclusively at the processes of electoral campaigning and assembly forensics, that the discourse process will assume the misleading appearance of continuous combat. It will, in fact, often take a polemic form; yet it is the role of elections

4. Walter Bagehot, *Physics and Politics* (New York: Knopf, 1948), pp. 166–68.

and of political parties to provide a focus for the process of political discussion—giving it an end product and organized channels of argumentation—rather than to provide the whole of that discourse. Democratic discourse is not merely a stage in the electoral process. Talk must go on before and after campaigns and separately from assembly processes. Elections do play a central role, and nations like Canada or England, in which elections can be called unexpectedly, will probably display, therefore, a somewhat more even flow of political talk. Parties under those systems must take responsibility for a continual campaign, since they might at any moment be given notice of an immediately impending election. But under any electoral system, the talk process goes on continually, democracies being societies in a constant state of conversation. Enjoying the full fruits of free communication and fully recognizing its values, democrats idealize uninhibited speech as a great boon to human civilization, as something that pushes mankind ahead faster than might otherwise be the case.

When broadly representative democracy was still a radical suggestion, in nineteenth-century England, those who advocated general suffrage discovered an effective rebuttal for their conservative critics. They advocated political education. If you do not wish to be governed by masses of ignoramuses, they suggested: "teach them," "educate your new masters." The political heritage of the Anglo-Saxon nations was, from the beginning, built upon government by discourse. The first legislative assembly was called the parliament, the speaking-place. But discourse traditionally took place among a relatively small educated class, the same class that made up the bulk of voters. As this class expanded, rather slowly in Britain and more abruptly in the United States, the quality of the discourse, not surprisingly, seemed to decline. In the United States, a nation noticeably lacking an aristocratic tradition, the discourse often embarrassed observers by its lack of gentility. Free speech, when it came to America, was not always well-mannered. But, as the people become used to their important place in the political process, they become more knowledgeable, if not more polite in their discourse.

To borrow a phrase: if the people must talk in order to govern, they must also govern in order to know how to talk.[5] Discourse improves with the experience of doing worthwhile things, such as that of participating in the governing process.

One man standing in the polling booth appears to act very much like any other man; the procedures for nomination seldom differ markedly between parties. But the discourse process is so informalized that no two men conduct it in the same fashion. It knows few rules beyond the traditions of polite manners. Because each political decision is largely a unique one, the talk that surrounds it will take a different form. Every man has, furthermore, a different stake in public policy. Although, in voting, his bodily motions are much like everyone else's, when he joins in discourse, he participates idiosyncratically—his manner of discourse is highly personal. Civic discourse roles, like civic capacities, are not regulable, or, at least, a democracy does not wish to regulate them. Each individual speaks from the perspective of a unique personal interest and from a slightly different social perspective. Every human creature is different, not merely in the mark left by his fingerprints, but in the words and thought he brings as a political animal to the public discourse. Democracy prides itself in this divergence. It also thrives on it.

There is no sufficient word, no language quite strong enough to emphasize the crucial importance of free discourse for the democratic process. There is little danger of overstating the fact that democracy is a talking process. Discourse is, quite possibly, the most important aspect of participation despite the formal significance of the central act of voting. The liberty most closely related to discourse—freedom of mind—is the most profound kind of liberty. Yet it must not be forgotten that the mind develops through listening, reading, and talking—through the elements of discourse. If democracy is a unique kind of society, one that maximizes freedom and works through participation, no aspect can be more crucial than

5. This paraphrases a remark by Susan Labin in *The Secret of Democracy*, trans. Otto E. Albrecht (New York: Vanguard, 1955), p. 218.

the talk element. But it is difficult to talk about talk, to discuss discussion. When generalized, discourse becomes an evasive topic. Beyond comparing formal discourse processes in varying societies and the educational machinery that determines its quality, there is not much to say about free speech except to praise it—a task best left to the poets, to the John Miltons among us. Other, less articulate souls, such as this author, are wise to make their simple point and then move along.

CHAPTER 6

The Policy Dynamics

A CAESAR may be starved for companionship, for the company of genuine friends, but he will never pine away for lack of colleagues to join him in the enterprise of power. The chairs of influence never lack for sitters. Nor do the risks of power drive people away. When political opportunity knocks, what man stands back out of fearsome contemplation of a lonely cell in the Tower of London or a bare cubicle in the Bastille? What leader hesitates out of fear of assassination? Neither Hitler nor Stalin lacked for colleagues despite the bureaucratic efficiency with which they liquidated former associates. Whenever there is power to make laws, to rule, to decree, to govern the lives of other men, there will be opportunity for favors. Government commands the resources of the community; what it can take can also be given away. When government acts, it commonly redistributes life's valued objects. Not all of these objects are material. It can take and give worldly goods, but it can likewise provide one man with high prestige and turn his brother into a nobody. It can make one man free and imprison his foes. It can provide the ambitious soul with the opportunity to manipulate others—apparently a much-enjoyed activity. Nor is the pleasure of power lessened when, as is true in a democracy, more men and women are permitted to seek it. Power does not lose its charm in a free society.

Democrats, once they recover from the discovery that the mass of men will not rule themselves, the fact that governing is done primarily by governors fewer in number than those governed, have other adjustments to make. They are forced to adapt themselves to the idea that special interests are not about to pass from the scene. Gradually these interests are conceived as less inherently devious; the terms "lobbyist" and "pressure group" slowly lose some of their negative connotation. Just as the king is discovered not to have been replaced as sovereign by the whole citizen body, the sycophant seems not to have disappeared; he has simply changed his stripes. Democracy did, nevertheless, bring about a major change. It both formalized and liberalized the process of influence. Formalization occurred through the practice of electing representatives of geographic interests and through elevating the privilege of petitioning into a fundamental constitutional right. At the same time, democracy brought pluralism. By dividing the structure of formal power, it opened most doors, permitting an almost unrestricted kind of competition in the process of seeking access. The new breed of influencer—the fixer, the lobbyist, the special pleader—is no longer haunted by visions of the Tower or the guillotine if he presses his case too far for the ruler's comfort. A new type of liberty of access, a new form of equality of opportunity for influence is created. Equality in the right of participation cannot be limited to the act of voting. It must be equally open to those with special petitions and causes—to those interested in specific policy actions. Freedom of access must be added to the freedom to seek office and to the right to choose between those seeking such positions for themselves.

The policy process in each of the democracies will vary even more than the voting processes. Because each constitution provides a unique structure and procedure, each will result in a different set of channels of access. Within a single governmental system, particularly one such as the United States, each area of policy—even each decision of policy—becomes a highly particularized matter. The ideal way to examine these processes—after having made the standard survey of over-all structure, after examining the list of stages a bill must take in going through the legislature—is to take a case-by-case approach. The more case studies one examines, the more intricate and intermeshed he will find the various parts and processes. He will also discover how fascinating the entire activity can be. But, having made this apologetic introduction, it is necessary to continue with generalities suited to a broad subject: the nature of the democratic experience. The difficulties of any general summary of the policy process do not lessen the value of the attempt.

THE PATHWAY TO ACTION

There was, immediately after the Civil War, a short burst of activity to help the new freedmen. Some of the accumulated anger of the war was put to good purpose, into an effort, not always well guided, to do something for the Negro. Unfortunately, for the South in general and for the Negro in particular, Americans soon became tired of both war and its aftermath. They found it preferable to forget about the Negro as they went about the business of nation-building. A new kind of oppression took over, one only partly rooted in a legal base; it was as much private as governmental in origin. Legal slavery had been abolished, but not much more had been accomplished. A few Negroes were given a minimal kind of education; but, more generally, in all of those areas in which the Negro's plight was particularly deplorable, government did little to help. When government finally did act, with court decisions and with the beginnings of effective legislation, it was after the Negro had already begun to make some headway due to urban migration, to the mixing process of two world wars, and to the painfully slow improvement of Negro education. Even after the Negroes themselves took dramatic action, in the early 1960s, government was slow to react. President Kennedy at first assumed that the time was not yet ripe for drastic action. He soon changed his mind; but not until after his assassination did a genuinely vigorous program of federal action come about, and then, notably, through the manipulations of a president who happened also to be unusually masterful in dealing with the legislature.

The story of the Negro's long, tragic history of suppression and ultimate revolt is filled with drama. Of particular interest here, however, is the cause of governmental action. It is a striking fact that government did not act on simple and obvious need. Had it done so, events like those that took place in the 1960s might have taken place in the 1890s, at the height of Jim Crow oppression—under Grover Cleveland rather than under Lyndon Johnson. Apparently, government action does not always begin with need, not even in a democracy. It was, interestingly enough, after the Negro's plight had improved somewhat, after he had acquired the courage and confidence to speak up, that government was propelled into a more active period of policy-making. It was not the social condition alone, objectively observable, that pushed government into action. Court decisions, statutes, decrees, and orders often come, not when the facts make them necessary, but when effective persons become aware of a need and act upon it. Policy arises, not out of need itself, but out of a feeling of need; even then, there will be no action until that feeling is effectively articulated. Years of ineffective talk preceded the burst of statutory law on racial issues that finally came in the mid 1960s. Not the real social setting but, as Walter Lippmann pointed out a half century ago, the perception men have of it in their heads, gained through education and the media of communication—this is what sets the foundation for policy.[1] All action, governmental and private, arises, quite unsurprisingly, out of response to environment, but it is the view men take of their cosmos, not the true condition of the external universe, that generates the reaction. As Lippmann saw, each of us perceives his world through stereotypes, through a set of tinted glasses, which predetermine what and how much we see. Among these never undistorted pictures, which provide the setting for policy-making, particular importance will, of course, be found in the stereotyped pictures in the minds of those who can be called opinion leaders.

It is reasonable to expect, if democracy is meaningfully unique, that its participatory processes will significantly alter the method of

1. Walter Lippmann, *Public Opinion* (New York: Macmillan, 1922), especially chapters 1 and 5 through 10.

policy-making. One important aspect of democracy's uniqueness has already been touched upon: democracy must, to a great extent, multiply the function of the discourse element in decision-making. "Government by discussion," as Bagehot stated, "broke the bond of ages and set free the originality of mankind." [2] Democracy starts the policy process by setting men free. It takes the lid off the bubbling pot of political expression. The generating force of democratic policy is the steam from that talking kettle. Free men do not necessarily perceive all of their own social problems—American democracy did not see the Negro's plight for decades—but when men do look, they talk about it. They respond, and the talk begins to move the wheels of action, oftentimes incredibly slowly. Sometimes the discourse is misdirected; like steam, it passes into thin air or turns a wheel that grinds no grain. Often the intensity of interest is too weak for action. Or rival forces may balance each other out. Pressure for gun legislation after the "great assassinations" of the 1960s evoked a strong, frightened reaction from gun buffs anl right-wing groups. Talk does not inevitably give birth to action. Much of the steam merely heats up the atmosphere, increasing the political humidity but producing little action. Despite the sometimes wasted effort, democracy encourages a kind of spontaneous political energy, a propelling force that stimulates public policy. The autocrat dislikes too much talk: discussion of public problems usually implies that something is wrong, and the all-powerful ruler quite properly takes such talk personally. The democratic governor, to paraphrase Harry Truman, is forced to stand near the fire; he must stand up and take it like a man, suffering the frustration of trying to make a community happy that chronically complains of its own and its leaders' imperfections. Such complaints are, after all, nothing other than the sometimes strident music of democracy, and the politician is never permitted to shut his ears to the noise. Sometimes the noise is disturbing to policy development as well as to the developer of that policy. President Nixon's plea for a moratorium on criticism

2. Quoted by Adlai Stevenson in "Party of the Second Part," *Harper's Magazine*, vol. 212 (February 1956), p. 33.

of his Vietnam policy in the fall of 1969 may have made sense from the standpoint of peace negotiations, but democracy does not allow the music to be stopped while the conductor reorganizes himself.

Even though early democrats were labeled radicals, and although there is a present tendency to consider liberalism and reformism as synonymous terms, these linguistic confusions disguise the fact that democracy is normally conservative. Sudden popular whims—changes in social mood strong enough to be felt at the centers of power—are relatively rare. Under normal circumstances, few segments of the population feel strongly about the need for social action. The masses are seldom revolutionary. Even when a general receptiveness to reform exists among large numbers of men and women, the sheer bulk of such a congregation cannot help but make it slow-moving. The agglomeration of the population is an unspecific social force, and it is less capable of action than its leaders; hence the winds of change from that quarter seldom reach hurricane force. The populace may sometimes delay facing acute problems for as long a time as Americans appear to have done with the racial issue, but there is no built-in reason for resisting change. Unlike the aristocratic hangers-on at Versailles before the French Revolution, they do not tremble in fear of change; the sin of the populace is more that of lethargy than of antipathy to progress. Many social difficulties may appear to drift along without governmental attention for decades for an ample reason—the lack of a genuinely adequate solution. In other situations, problems are often met through nongovernmental modes of collective action: through the efforts of business managers, labor unions, or other private groups. Many problems simply disappear as conditions change. Not all of the social worries that can afflict a commonwealth are suitable for governmental policy. Not all social action needs to be centralized. (The laissez-faire liberals were not all wrong.) Increasingly, however, the habit of looking to governments takes a firmer grip on the minds of men.

Granting that governmental policy has its origins in a feeling of need generated in a talking process in the broad society, nothing happens until all of this energy is focused, until the steam is directed into narrow channels that will propel the wheels of decision-making. Discourse takes place on all levels and at all moments in the democratic policy process. It is the most widespread form of participation and pervades the entire operation of democratic governing. But, as anyone with committee experience knows, someone must do his homework, someone must come to the meeting with a concrete plan of action, a draft proposal, before talk can be converted into policy. In American government, legislatures rely on committees, committees on their more effective leaders. In Britain, the super-committee that is the Government must bring something concrete to the House of Commons before action can begin. It was only when Parliament first found leaders of its own—men like Coke, Eliot, and Wentworth, during the Stuart era—that the legislature could become something more than a tool for monarchs. During the process of exploring the needs of society, participation must be at its widest, but at the moment that the formulation of precise programs of action begins, there is an inevitable narrowing, a focusing on a smaller handful of men.

When, as in Britain, there is a strong-party, cabinet-dominated system, policy begins with movement from an original narrow base to a broad discussion and then to the final vote. Sometimes in American policy process the executive or the bureaucracy dominates the process in a similar way, but, equally as often, policy takes a quite different path. Whatever the origins of a proposal, the independent responsibilities of individual legislators make legislative reconsideration very common. There is, then, within the legislature, a dual narrowing process: a simultaneous decrease in the number of persons at the center of action and in the diversity of remaining alternatives. As ideas are, one after another, discussed, modified, or rejected, the talk begins to center increasingly on a small handful of persons who are looked upon as leaders. The personnel may be different in each case. The process of narrowing may be quite spontaneous and informal, but it is nonetheless normal. Allow me to illustrate: When budget proposals are made for a state public school system, the first phase of action will normally be widespread discussion. Lobbyists, educators, bureaucrats, newspapermen, and all members of the legislature will talk among themselves, suggesting and rejecting, criticizing and proposing. If there happens not to be enough tax money to meet the request of the educators and if time is running out, the action will soon begin to narrow. Broad discussion will not necessarily cease, but, inevitably, a few persons will put their heads together, combining their talents to produce a single compromise plan. As the process of conflict and compromise progresses, it is quite likely that a handful of men—those who have arisen as leaders of the process—will join to bring the process to a conclusion. They may be imagined working late into the night, in an overheated hotel room near the legislative halls, searching for a key that will break the deadlock. When morning comes, when the central leaders have found a solution, many will be unhappy with the result. But, assuming that all are aware that definite action must emerge, that postponement is sometimes worse than compromise, there will be a general acceptance of the agreed-upon plan. After a little more haranguing on the floor of the legislature and perhaps another minor change or two, the proposal will become law. This is but one example. The narrowing will take place at different stages in the process, but the focusing aspect of decision-making appears to be universal.

Is it democratic for crucial decisions to be made in smoke-filled rooms? As long as the flow of discourse is not arbitrarily or prematurely stopped, there is little problem in answering this question in the affirmative. Yes, it is democratic, if—and it is an important "if" —the broader body of participants (legislators or voters) has the last voice in the decision. The answer can be yes, if the process returns somehow to a final action by the larger body. "Ratification" is a key word in the language of democracy. Most national party conventions are ratifications of decisions made by party activists prior to the beginning of the meeting and away from the convention floor. Most legislative decisions are ratifications of executive, committee, or caucus actions. Even elections commonly amount to a confirmation or rejection of the party in power, a kind of ratification or refusal to ratify. The mass-participation process provides for the acceptance or rejection of leadership itself or for the approval of work leadership has performed. The larger membership of an assembly can reject the policy of the leaders, while allowing them, if it wishes, to continue in their function of leadership; in an electorate, the more common decision is approval of the person himself, a cruder but more definitive kind of action. Democracy protects its principles by formalizing its processes. It requires ratification at regular stages in the proceedings. The system is seldom totally efficient. It sometimes collapses in such areas as military and foreign policy, where the plea of secrecy often prevents meaningful ratification. It is important, however, to realize that democratic participation, when it is not simply discourse, is more commonly one of policy ratification than policy decision.

In a constitutional regime, government cannot act without following certain preordained patterns. As will need to be noted in Chapter 7, no proposal is enforceable, under constitutionalism, until the formal elements of legitimacy have been fulfilled. But legitimacy is not identical with legalism, as will later become clear. Nor, it should be added, does all governmental action take the form of law. Many agencies of government act primarily by persuasion; sometimes merely through publicity, without issuing any commands. The Blue Eagle program during the New Deal was a device of economic recovery through voluntary action. Presidents Kennedy and Johnson were able to stop steel-price increases without issuing any decrees or relying directly upon any law. American legislative investigatory committees, like British royal commissions, achieve voluntary action by exposing what they see as the facts. Sometimes a mere statement of intent to investigate can bring action. But behind these voluntaristic tools lies a more general power of command. It is important that this kind of command, in a democracy, need not be obeyed unless it has been properly ratified through legally established rituals. When this is the case, the formal procedures of government, in all their diversity and intricacy, become an essential part of the democratic experience.

Each democratic jurisdiction will have a different process of formalized decision-making. But three overlapping and not always sequential steps are likely to be found in most instances: a developing feeling of need first becomes articulated and focuses on the governmental arena; specific programs of action are then produced by small groups of individuals; and those polices are finally legitimized in a formal process of ratification. The feeling of need seldom stops, even when action is allegedly completed, because the conclusion is normally a compromise unsatisfactory to many. The story seldom ends with the passage of a law; if it does, it is probably an action about which no one much cares. Each political element usually retires to try another day. Often the contending forces simply aim at another target in some other part of the structure—by appealing to the courts, for example, or by trying to shape the method of administration. In 1965, after having been an issue of contention since the end of World War II, a major school-aid bill was passed. One reason given for the willingness of contending interest groups to compromise on the bill was the fact that, under the strong hand of the Johnson administration, some school bill was certain to pass, and the interested groups wanted to be sure that they would be in the good graces of those who were to administer the act.[3] Some issues, such as the farm problem or labor-management relations, clog the machinery of government policy-making for decades; they may be momentarily settled on the surface, but they are not at all settled in the minds of active group interests. The unfinished nature of governmental business is notorious in a democracy, since no autocrat can decree that "the problem is hereby solved." Policy rooted in open discourse may, in many important

3. See Eugene Eidenberg and Roy D. Morey, *An Act of Congress* (New York: Norton, 1969), for the story of the 1965 act. For the full story of postwar school bills up to the fateful 1964 election, see Robert Bendiner, *Obstacle Course on Capitol Hill* (New York: McGraw-Hill, 1964).

ways, be more socially efficient and may satisfy more people, but it is often frustratingly open ended. Frequently the historian is the only one who can mark the end of the story.

THE STRUCTURING OF POWER

The big-city boss, according to one of his admirers, George Washington Plunkitt of Tammany Hall, made "the machinery move so noiseless that you wouldn't think there was any."[4] The urban political machine, at its heyday in the early twentieth century, made others less happy, particularly those who footed the bill for "honest" as well as dishonest graft. But the heritage of the city boss has significant democratic aspects. It indicates the general principle that a free society cannot forbid its citizens (one or few or many) informal access to power. A democracy can, and it usually has, put a stop to specific abuses of informal power, but influence cannot itself be forbidden. The city boss may be looked upon as the product of a distorted kind of democracy, but his coming into existence was no accident. A democracy is forced to provide a complex set of formal structures and procedures to ensure that its decisions are legitimate. It must also give its citizens the kind of liberty that encourages them to supplement this formal machinery with informal processes and relations. Democratic nations, said Tocqueville, "stand more in need of forms than other nations, and respect them less."[5]

A social system whose ultimate aim is liberty must structure itself with special care. Freedom for civilized man is unlikely to come by accident. He has to plan for it, and in particular, he must design or inherit a careful pattern of government. Yet, regardless of the meticulousness of planning, there will remain an intricate, informal framework of communal relations. With liberty, there always exists

4. William L. Riordan, *Plunkitt of Tammany Hall* (New York: Knopf, 1948), p. 110.

5. Alexis de Tocqueville, *Democracy in America,* trans. Henry Reeve (New York: Oxford University Press, 1946), p. 498.

an ability to work around the structure of power as well as through it. An autocracy could, at least in principle, be ruled by a man or clique of men on the basis of arbitrary whim, suiting the structure to the mood of the moment or to the necessities of each circumstance. There was a considerable degree of such informality in Adolph Hitler's Third Reich. Most systems of governance include both formal and informal structures. If, however, a community is to preserve certain areas of freedom, it must be especially careful to define governmental power and prescribe its form. It may be stated again that, if a government is to be based on popular participation and consent, there must be sufficient order in the governmental processes for the members of the wide community to be able to discover how to participate. Whereas an autocracy could, in theory, be operated in total informality, without ritualized procedures, modern democracy, unless it is not much larger than a family, must rely upon established forms. The existence of formalized activity implies the inevitable development of informal supplements. The observer of governmental process must usually suffer with the difficult task of keeping his eye on two intertwined rings of the same political circus.

Only in our imagination is it possible to construct a democracy with totally centered government, a perfectly hierarchical structure with control exercised by the people from the top down. There might, as has already been implied, be more effective control, in abstract theory, if a single elected king or a city manager sat at the apex of government. He could be imagined reigning with a firm hand over all subordinates in response to a mandate from the voters —a perfected kind of majority rule, a totally responsible kind of government. But we do not deal with simple mandates. There is no cohesive, singular kind of populace with a will of its own. Nor is there a creature called the majority. Instead, within a complex population, there is a vast plurality of varied interests demanding the kind of government that offers numerous responses, not always totally consistent one with another, to intricate and subtle variations in the opinions of plural publics. This is a fact about a free society that bears repeating at each stage in the discussion of the democratic experience.

The traditional American attitude has been more sympathetic to the separation of, than to the centralization of, power. But the tripartite scheme no longer seems so sacrosanct; there is, instead, more concern with the general virtues of political fragmentation. Pluralism is more valued than it was a century ago. Democracy tries to encourage widespread discourse rooted in a pluralistic, competitive political community. The democratic process of expressing rival ideas, the talk aspect of the system, must arise not only in the public spheres but in leadership segments and within government itself. A democratic government must be so organized as to mirror the diversity of views existing among the various publics. It must create such diversity out of rival centers of leadership within government. To be truly effective, pluralism must be represented within the formal governmental system; that system must both reflect pluralism existing in society at large and encourage it by creating numerous channels of access to formal government. This does not require, however, that members of the executive be prohibited from serving as members of the legislative assembly, providing there remain distinctive forces within that body such as back-benchers and a critical, well-organized, opposition leadership. Nor does it require that the judiciary be a distinct third branch, assuming that the courts remain free from the kind of pressures that threaten to destroy aloof justice. There can be three branches, five branches, or a dozen. The forms are, of course, important, so important that they will again need our attention at a later point. No specific structure is required, however, as long as political diversity and competition are reflected within government as much as they are in outside groups and publics. In smaller communities, formal structure will be simpler, and fewer divisions will be needed. Large democratic nation-states have had to develop a wide variety of constitutional formulas that provide a multiple division of function and power; in a village pluralism may perhaps often be achieved through the presence of diverse personalities within a simple and intimate *conference* kind of government.

In communities covering wide geographic expanses, there are arguments for local autonomy founded upon the virtues of efficiency of administration. Even the Soviets have discovered that effectiveness is lost by an overcentralization of power and function. For democrats, however, these advantages are supplemented by others that are more compelling. If, for example, it is a purpose of democracy to maximize communal participation, it is mere common sense to add opportunities for such action. It is not that local governments provide an ideal school for democracy. Since regional and neighborhood governments often deal with different kinds of problems, it is not to be expected that experience at one level of government will lead to knowledge in dealing with different kinds of problems at another level. But it is reasonable to assert that men and women will become better democrats, more firmly tied to the ideas of freedom and participation, if they enjoy a chance to practice what they preach through enjoying the privileges of the democratic experience close to home. A democratic nation makes a mistake if it allows its provincial government to lapse into ineffectiveness or concentrates too much power in a centralized bureaucracy. None of this, however, argues for a precise federal structure. Each community must base its pattern of participation, its competitive power structure, on its own historical experience.

Traditional discussion of governmental forms might prove more interesting if, instead of speaking in organization-chart language and drawing outlines of various governmental branches and subbranches, we could speak in terms of points of public access. The American system might then be described not only as a federal or separated-powers scheme but, more meaningfully, as an *unfocused system*—one in which lines of access do not converge at a single point but travel parallel or at odd angles from each other. The British system, by contrast, although it, too, has numerous lines of influence, tends to have a more central focus, concentrating channels of influence on Parliament, which contains leaders of administration as well as of policy development. To chart all lines of access in a large national community like the United States would, however, prove an impossibility. The diagram would need to take the form of an Einsteinian kind of universe, one with no sharply determined boundary, with space somewhat curved. Government itself, at the core, would appear vague in its limits, as well as infinitely complex internally. Some interest groups and all political parties are half private and half governmental; they are partly in government and partly on the outside looking in. Other groups would occupy more remote locations on this cosmic chart. Toward the periphery of this multidimensional diagram would be seen certain cloudy substances called publics. The lines of influence, direct and indirect, formal and informal, would be almost too complex to untangle. The whole scene would be more intricate than the wiring in a modern computer. Attempting to conceive of such a diagrammatic picture of government based upon actual lines of power and communication will help to explain why traditional textbooks prefer the traditional, neat-looking squares on their charts. Nonetheless, contemplation of what a realistic chart showing lines of access and influence might look like makes one more aware of the immense complexity of power relations in modern government.

From the standpoint of patterns of influence, or channels of participation, the access system of a democracy is compounded beyond generalized description. In addition to access through election (running for office or selecting among those who are candidates), there are literally thousands of pathways of influence leading to those already in power. These unmapped roads lead not only toward the many elective offices but also toward the infinitely larger number of hired hands who staff the various bureaucracies. Each variation in the mode of selecting an official, in the nature of his constituency, in the term of his office, and in his relations with other officials will change the pattern of access. One becomes dizzy contemplating its complexities. But, fortunately for the man or woman who wishes to influence governmental policy, he or she need not deal with this entire pattern. Like a neurosurgeon, he can pick out one particular spot for his target and follow a few, thin nerve lines to reach that point. No sensible man attempts to achieve access to an entire network of power of the size of the United States government. This would be purposeless. Even the president cannot claim control over the entire cluster of bureaucracies. No one brain center acts as master of the whole whirling mechanism. Influence is an individual matter, dealt with case by case. Democracy tries to keep the lines open and access to them competitive. In so doing it adds to the complexity of the total system: it is more open but harder to comprehend. When, as in this book, we desire an overview of the whole apparatus, it is best to use several overlapping approaches: first to see the process as one of representation; then as a matter of access factors; and, finally, in terms of the accountability of governors to governed.

REPRESENTATION IN A DEMOCRACY

In England as early as 1213, King John, having his trouble with an unruly kingdom, commanded that "four discreet men" be sent from each county "to speak with us about the affairs of our kingdom." Fifty years later, Henry III asked that two "lawful, upright, and discreet knights" be elected from each county and two burgesses from each of the boroughs, "setting aside every excuse and leaving all other business." [6] The men who made the long trip from remote counties to the king's council for a kind of "talking shop" were, as Henry's summons implies, frequently reluctant to do so. They had more important chores at home. The excursion to the royal court would be costly in out-of-pocket expenses, and the knights and burgesses knew that the king wanted their help as much as their advice. They would be forced to return home to wheedle such cooperation and cash as they could from friends and neighbors. They did not picture themselves as agents of the people to the king

6. Quoted in Goldwin Smith, *Constitutional and Legal History of England* (New York: Scribner's, 1955), pp. 153–54.

but as agents of the monarch, giving him aid and advice—in the words of the summons, out of "faith and love." Theirs was actually a dual function, however: they expressed the needs of the central governmental authority to the people back home and transmitted the worries and problems of local constituents to those in power at the top. Representation under a medieval monarch and in a modern democracy differ greatly in particulars but less than one might suspect in fundamental roles.

The existence of what is now meant by representation is at least as old as the thirteenth century, when the first parliaments were being summoned. But the notion of representative government is modern. Like the related agency function of government mentioned earlier, the representative relation—one person acting or speaking for others—is, in no sense, necessarily democratic. Nothing is implied about participation, about free expression, or about other operating principles of democracy. Additional elements are required. *Acting for* must be conjoined with *acting under the direction of.* Any governor can be called an agent: he acts as spokesman for the community in the performance of its basic functions. He may even, without a touch of democratic procedure, quite accurately reflect the viewpoints of his people. Democratic governors must be more than merely spokesmen, more than mirrors of the popular will. Sometimes the democratic idea of representation is distinguished by the addition of one key word, that of "consent." But this word, without careful qualification, does not define the difference. Consent may be engineered. By whatever means at its disposal, a government may obtain substantial support. Hitler succeeded by combining an effective propaganda ministry, a strict system of censorship, and a secret police that removed dissident elements from the body politic. Furthermore, consent may be a strictly passive act. Mere consent is not enough. Democracy requires an active and voluntary kind of participation from its community, one based on effective, free expression.

For a free society a crucial issue is the nature of the practical process relating actor with consentor, agent with principal. No one word can describe that relationship. Even the notion of access, much used in this chapter, does not quite summarize the process of democratic representation. The serf had access to his master when he made servile prayer for redress of grievances. There were prayers and petitions in Parliament long before these were converted into legislation and ages before legislation became the product of democratic government. One of the problems with the ideas of representation and consent is that even in the most effective democracy, the elected leader is not the recipient of any magically transmitted people's will. Matters are by no means that simple. Specific wishes of segments of the constituency are difficult to uncover. As for the single, traceable community desire—it seldom appears to exist in fact. It was once popular, when men thought in terms of a popular will, to debate whether or not the elected legislator should follow this will of his constituents or whether he could better serve them by following his own "wise conscience." Edmund Burke is famous for an eloquent pronouncement of the latter argument.[7] Now that so many people have faith in the accuracy of opinion-polling, the issue may revive. But, even for those who consider the issue to be a bit academic, its discussion can lead to a clearer understanding of the complexities of representation. If observers of democracy are fully aware of the rich historical background of the concept of representation, they will have a better understanding of the operational nature of the process; they will be able to convert the idea of a popular will into a complex set of political relationships among representatives and various constituencies that influence them—relationships difficult to generalize sufficiently to include all legislators, at all times, on all issues. To recognize that the response created by the democratic processes of election and political influence is one of infinite variability is to arrive at the beginning of wisdom when it comes to understanding representation.

Perhaps the most important single feature of the democratic

7. See his address on "The Representative and His Constituents," in Ross J. S. Hoffman and Paul Levack, eds., *Burke's Politics* (New York: Knopf, 1949), pp. 114–17.

representative is that he is a politician—a name Burke might not have liked. Although no two living politicians conceive of their roles as identical, the typical politician plays a role that requires continual compromise: he grapples with his own conscience; he makes compromising kinds of choices between competing elements among his various constituencies. He deals with matters of principle because, like all of us, he is a moral-minded man. He deals with matters of politics because that is the purpose of the democratic electoral system; unless he does so, he will be out of office and unable to act at all. This archetypal politician operates from a foundation of moral ideals while playing the down-to-earth game that keeps him in power. Rarely does he make a distinction between principle and politics; instead, he merely acts as sensibly as he can. He operates under the pervading influences of broad ethical ideas emanating from the whole community and from his own background; he acts in awareness of the subtle intricacies of winning elections and of the complex ways of getting things done in the governmental process. Representation ensures that this model of a man who has discovered politics to be his vocation will listen, but the voices will come from all directions, including the internal voice of conscience. This ambiguity, it must again be said, is inherent in the democratic experience.

Representation is itself a compromise. It is an imperfect solution, aimed at bringing the benefits of democracy, in a somewhat diluted fashion, to large and complex communities. Rousseau did not like the idea.[8] He saw its imperfection. Representation is not, as he could see, a complete substitute for an informal, fully cooperative group such as the democratic family. The line between actors and non-actors in such a small group will often be so informal and so constantly shifting that the assignment of special roles does not appear to make one member less influential than any other. But a complex society must create a more formalized division of labor. Representation is, after all, simply an aspect of specialization of function.

8. Jean Jacques Rousseau, *Social Contract,* ed. G. D. H. Cole (London: Dent, 1913), particularly chapter 15 of book III, pp. 77–80.

The particular kind of representation called democratic differs by providing significant roles to both the governors and the non-governors. It modifies the specialization and division of labor, creating a new function—that of influence or access. Those who do not fall within the specialized category of rulers have an active role of their own—the exertion of effective influence over those performing the governing function.

Our comprehension of the process of democratic representation is aided if we make a distinction between its formal and informal aspects. Although these are not as distinct in practice as they might appear to be, the ritualized, preplanned, official processes are capable of separation, for purposes of discussion, from the flexible, personalized activities that support, surround, and sometimes contradict them. The most convenient base for formal representation is geographic: the British have ridings, and the Americans have a maze of electoral districts. With each locality represented in an assembly, a diversity of political viewpoints is virtually guaranteed. Because no geographic area has a single point of view on every question, the assemblyman cannot speak equally well for every member of his constituency. He will, furthermore, be less than human if he does not think in terms broader than the needs of his own district. He can hardly avoid being concerned with community-wide problems. He lives, works, and has friends and colleagues in the capital; he is a member of a national party; he would indeed be a strange creature if ideas and interests from outside his own constituency did not influence his actions. The existence of a system of geopraphic representation as the near-universal form of all democracies does not mean that each agent responds only to influences from within the boundaries of his district. Geography is a formal way of electing and affects the total system of representation deeply. Despite its near universality, it has disadvantages. At best, the formation of district boundaries is rather arbitrary, it is relatively inflexible in reflecting shifting interests, and it stresses quantitative elements rather than such intangibles as intensity of interest. At worst, it can be the device of party manipulation (gerrymandering) or a refuge (through malapportionment) for political forces that are declining in social and economic importance. But geographic representation is not and can hardly be the total system, nor does it necessarily even dominate the process. Informal representation exists as an all-important means to offset it.

If there are those who demand such perfection in the representative process that each tiny interest is fully represented through the formal processes, they should be aware of the consequences of their desires. What they ask for, whether or not they are aware of the fact, is ever larger assemblies and ever smaller legislative districts. The end result—the ultimate logic of such a demand—is no representation at all, or at least a one-to-one relation of agent and principal, each spokesman acting for one man's interests. We would be returning, in effect, to the idea of a direct kind of democracy such as was idealized by Rousseau. If, on the other hand, it is impractical for every particular will to have its spokesman, it is equally unlikely that the higher interests of the unified community, Rousseau's general will, can be represented in any clear-cut fashion. It may be, however, that a combination of informal and formal representation will come closer to meeting both of these ideals than any arbitrarily designed formal structure. Unfortunately, however, one trouble with admitting informal processes into our scheme is that the apparatus immediately becomes cloudy and ambiguous: we can no longer be precisely certain what the process of representation looks like. Although informal access increases vagueness, it does permit the formally elected representative to speak for larger interests. Furthermore, although they may obscure our view of what we idealize as being a clear-cut governmental structure, informal channels of influence have the virtue of permitting the smallest interest groups to bring pressure to bear at the most effective point.

Sometimes the suggested solution to the problems of representation has been a change of the rules, a formalization of what is presently informal. But any formal system, by definition, contains an element of arbitrariness. No amount of tinkering with the formal system can ensure that all viewpoints and interests will be presented with exact justice. No one has succeeded in formulating a precise scheme for counting the overlapping numbers in each area of economic interest, to say nothing of finding ways of formalizing less material-oriented categories such as religious, reform, or racial groups. Nor, despite decades of application of arithmetical methods in the social sciences, has anyone yet invented a foolproof way to measure the intensity of group interest, an important element in the present combination of formal and informal representation. Pure interests, as distinguished from the present formalized representation by population and geography, are important to a functioning democracy, but it is probable that there are no means of formalizing them without making matters worse, creating graver injustices than those under the present system.

Explaining the impossibility of formalizing all aspects of the representation process does not require an assertion that there are no injustices in the present scheme of things. The very concept of informal processes implies a distortion of the constitutional plan. There are inherent dangers in any twisting of legal schemes. The inevitability of informal distortions does not eliminate all evil consequences. The most serious charge is that of inequity. The educated may be expected to be more effective than the ignorant. The rich are more familiar with instruments of influence and more likely to take full advantage of them than are the poor. The meek will not inherit the earth under a representative system; they are more likely to fail by not heeding its first command, which is to speak up. Knowledge of social problems and their solutions, political skills, understanding of governmental processes, the ability to hire experts—these are not assets by any means equally shared. But it is important, when focusing on the informal, not to forget that the formal processes do not thereby cease to operate. The system is, after all, a dual one. Every single voice still counts with equal weight in the formal electoral process. Elections do not cease to provide an ultimate, ratifying factor. The existence of formal constitutional and statutory rules helps to eliminate the crudest of abuses, keeping the system more or less honest. Formal rules and processes will not eradicate all injustices. If, however, they are designed in full awareness of the functioning of informal processes, they can surely go part way toward providing both a just and a balanced total system, which is suited to the wide diversity of interests in a modern society.

THE ACHIEVEMENT OF INFLUENCE

Few generations of men can boast many trail-blazing books in any field of academic endeavor. Nor do such books often receive much fame until later generations have had the opportunity to take a second look. Then, the temptation is to convert them into something like biblical texts. One such late-discovered book was Arthur Bentley's *Process of Government.*[9] First published shortly after the turn of the century, it was not generally discovered until after World War II. Bentley attacked and attempted to replace much of the conventional wisdom of his time concerning the methods by which democratic policy is achieved. In common with many other innovators, he tended to overstress his theme, but once he began to be widely read, the study of government was never to be the same. His pluralistic approach, sometimes called group theory, was quite unlike other perspectives that had dominated the thought of political science. Some writers in the early decades of this century were formalistic, concerning themselves with the complexity of constitutional structure and the intricacies of law. Those concerned with informal aspects often became muckrakers; they assumed that newly discovered realities could be swept away through proper reforms. Some were, consciously or unconsciously, influenced by Karl Marx. A peculiarly American kind of economic determinism built around special interests, the machinations of big business, and the political boss brought a look of realism to governmental studies. But again, these political entities were seen as foreign bodies attack-

9. Arthur F. Bentley, *The Process of Government* (Bloomington, Ind.: Principia Press, 1935) (original edition, 1908).

ing the body politic from the outside, distorting it rather than making up its flesh and blood.

Bentley undoubtedly overstated his point; he was a bit too anxious to counteract current beliefs. Government became, in his thinking, almost nothing but the product of group pressures. He saw no reason to contemplate a larger community or to talk about other less tangible factors. He wanted to deal only with concretely observable facts. He and some of his later followers began to look upon the political process in a mechanistic fashion, as a balancing of power factors, as a machinelike activity with an input of pressures and an output of policy. Sometimes this group of empirically oriented pluralists appeared merely to have substituted power determinism for Marx's economic determinism. They looked for a kind of equilibrium process at work in politics not unlike the equilibrium model of classical economics so familiar to Marx. Government became an agency for the ratification of settlements made among rival outside groups. The individualized personality and such ambiguous elements as the public tended to be ignored or understated. Less attention was given to environmental background and historical setting as influences on the policy process than would now seem proper.

The one sin the group theorists would least like to have been accused of was a failure to see the complexity of the political process. They realized that access was not a simple matter; they assumed an intricate pluralism of forces. They were overly anxious, however, to be called realists. They wanted almost too desperately to see the hard facts. They particularly avoided what they considered to be myths and amorphous intangibles. In attempting to concretize the phenomenon of the governmental process, they tended to underemphasize the broader situational context of policy activity. They leaned so far over backward in stressing informal factors that they forgot how deeply such elements are sculpted by the formal, constitutional, and structural rules of the game. They sought concreteness, and, to a lesser extent, they desired symmetry. Both of these goals would have been less attainable if they had stressed the importance of a social environment that stretches out toward the infinite horizon and of a historical background that drifts off endlessly into historical time. But both elements are, in fact, unavoidable. If a governmental act affects the broad social environment, it must also be affected by it. If each policy development shapes the course of history, it is also true that history has had its role in shaping that particular political event. It is, perhaps unfortunately, impossible to remove a segment of it to create a model equilibrium of semimeasurable power elements; it is impossible to do so without a partial distortion of the reality. Too much concern with concrete forces may, in fact, be less realistic than broader and more historically oriented approaches. The discovery of group analysis pushed political studies far ahead but not without costs in the form of new confusions.

It is highly unlikely that any scholar will produce a grand theory of policy development or any single formula that can be followed in each instance of governmental action. But, if such a formula could be imagined, it might well include a magical factor called fortune. This element of luck could, supposedly, be reduced to a combination of intricate factors of social behavior; but the intricacy is so overwhelming, when one examines only a few of the hundreds of case studies of political action published, that generalization is extremely difficult. From the standpoint of the actor (as opposed to the historian viewing the situation with hindsight knowledge), the word "luck" seems highly suitable. In the matter of timing alone, a political leader needs almost an extrasensory kind of perception to know when to act and when to wait. There are moments for dramatic action and moments for cautious patience. Hubert Humphrey's idea for a Peace Corps came into effect after a few short years, whereas Harry Truman's proposals for federal medical care and aid to education experienced nearly two decades of frustration before action occurred. As repeatedly mentioned, the plight of the Negro was of little political concern until, almost overnight, it became a central matter of governmental action; suddenly the time became, almost magically, ripe. A true behaviorist cannot avoid being aware that mystery exists in all political activity, even though he may reasonably claim that all such unknowns could eventually be subjected to empirical analysis.

Part, but only part, of the policy process is a matter of the balance of group power. The manipulator, if he deserves that appellation, must be ready to deal with political accidents such as the assassination of a president or the unexpected nomination by the minority party of a candidate so unpopular as to destroy that party's normal legislative strength. His tools are not simple. The technique of propaganda, for example, is complicated because 90 percent of its success depends upon public predispositions beyond the propagandist's control. The variety of tools of political access never quite equals the variety of ways in which situations change. History is seldom guided by the action of one man or group of men. Men might be able to steer it a bit, but it is unlikely that they can turn it in reverse or even in a right-angle direction. It is not only the outer environment that makes policy development complex; government has a life of its own; it is no blank tablet to be writ upon. The shifting balance of party strengths, the realignment of inner-party factions, changes in leadership personalities—all of these elements and more are needed to explain why Congress frustrates certain attempts at action, while, at other times, such as 1933 and 1965, it moves so fast that it almost trips over itself.

It is important not to assume that government is merely a recording machine that ratifies bargains reached entirely among outside forces. Each branch of government, each agency, each committee, each faction and clique has ideas of its own—its own tradition, its own loyalties, and, above all, its own easily offended leadership personalities. Complex ethical codes, varying ideas of professionalism, group *esprit de corps*, personal idiosyncrasies, and old-fashioned stubbornness—all of these are factors to be included in explaining what makes the governmental leviathan move. The peculiar behavior of "Judge" Howard W. Smith and his private principality in the House Rules Committee was as essential in explaining the lack of extensive progressive legislation in the 1950s as the role of any bloc of interest groups. The leadership capacities of Sam Rayburn and Lyndon Johnson, on the other hand, were crucial in explaining how some significant legislation managed to get by his veto. As proposed policies shift around within the government from official to official, from agency to agency, a different set of circumstances will be encountered at each stage. The same multiplicity and diversity is descriptive of outside groups. They, too, have their biases and peculiarities. And, it is important to recall, that these outsiders are as often the subject of manipulation by governmental officers and politicians as vice versa. There is no effective way to summarize the intricacies of such an involved, personalized process, particularly when one is fully aware of the plurality of forces that are active in it.

Government, as was stated earlier in this book, has a mediation function. But this mediation activity is not always apparent on the surface. The clearest example of it occurs when conflict appears to be dual, as in the case of labor-management issues. Multisided conflict may be just as common, but it is less normal to consider government's role in such instances as mediation. In any situation with competing forces, the object of government is supposedly clear: it must give as much as it can to each group in the conflict and deprive each of as little as possible. It must distribute benefits and burdens, happiness and unhappiness, as best it can, with the threat of future elections at least vaguely in mind. In some circumstances, there appears to be only one side to an issue. In other cases, the elements seeking favorable decisions are parts of the government itself or, as with the powerful Corps of Engineers, they are government agencies in alliance with outside interest groups. In the realm of foreign affairs the interest groups might even be foreign powers or ancestral categories within the United States who hold psychological ties to "the old country." The balance-of-power concept is inclined to take as its model those governmental policies in which government in some way or another is involved in a distribution of shares, in an economic regulation, or in some related activity. But quite different approaches are needed to examine foreign policy in Southeast Asia, legislative reapportionment, foreign aid, marriage laws, rules for presidential succession, or aid to dependent children.

There are not many indisputable axioms that can be used to describe the policy process of an intricate governmental system. One relatively safe principle, however, is that complex procedures and divisions of powers, typical in the United States, tend to favor the negative side, unless, that is, some new leadership element or a dramatic environmental event sweeps aside all restraint. Economic interests with clear-cut geographic bases, such as silver and cotton, have advantages that are the envy of other interests possessing no precise home base—a logical consequence of our formal system of representation. There is a diminishing-point-of-returns principle in the spending of money in the "influence game." There is also a diminishing point in lobbying and propaganda, when added pressure begins to hurt more than it helps; officials take pride in their profession and deeply resent the suggestion of being manipulated by anyone. Another rule of thumb is that influencers should never forget a mysterious element known as the moral factor—the feeling and appearance of purity being sacred to the heart of a politician. An entire interest-group campaign, carefully planned in every other respect, can fail if there is the slightest hint of bribery. This happened, for example, with an attempt to reduce regulations of natural gas during the Eisenhower period, when one man offered an alleged bribe to a prominent senator.[10] An otherwise easy passage was thwarted by a single act of supposed venality. While politicians are seldom totally devoid of sin, most of them try to be honest, and the others are aware of the poisoning effect of appearing dishonest. To add further confusion to any analysis of the moral factor, it happens to be difficult to define a concept like bribery; there are numerous kinds of *quid pro quo* circumstances within the political process. Political sin is defined differently by different people. No matter how erratic the definition, however, it is safe to assert that the ef-

10. Edith T. Carper, *Lobbying and the Natural Gas Bill* (University, Ala.: Alabama University Press, 1962), Inter-University Case Study No. 72 (now available through Bobbs-Merrill, Indianapolis).

fective politician develops a keen sense for detecting its odor; he needs to know when to run the other way.

To these various rules of thumb, each with its vagaries, can be added a complex picture of what seem to be power factors: elements of political support helping or hindering each of the parties-in-interest. Some of these factors are roughly quantifiable, unlike the element of political morality just mentioned. Wealth is the most obvious of these. Money, it has been said more than once, cannot buy everything. If judiciously used, however, it can be made to "talk." It is often a prerequisite to being heard, even though a listener may not always, or even most of the time, provide the desired response. Material wealth does not convert directly into influence—it is not possible to "buy power" in the straightforward manner of buying a piece of land—but wealth can be helpful in making an entry into the political process. To the recipe for success in democratic policy-making can next be added another relatively quantifiable factor: the size of a constituency or, more concretely, the number of direct members of an interest group. But the formula is still incomplete. It would be necessary, if one wishes to think in mathematical terms, also to discount or multiply the effective power of any group by a factor based upon the degree of cohesion with which the membership supports its leadership. It is obvious, for example, that the legislative spokesman for the American Legion does not have the fullest backing of those who join the organization for the sole purpose of using its bars and dance floors. It would also be necessary to recall, in preparing our recipe, the almost universal habit of special pleaders to overestimate their constituencies. The spokesmen for the AFL-CIO, unsurprisingly, will claim to speak for all labor even when they have neither all of the unionized workers nor all salaried employees within their specific constituency.

From these relatively measurable elements of wealth and numbers, the list of factors contributing to influence on the policy process moves toward more intangible elements and then disappears into total obscurity. One such factor, already mentioned in other connections, is that of intensity: the depth of feeling with which a group or individual attacks will surely affect its success in combat. If the group does not descend too far into fanaticism, intensity of interest will generally add to the effectiveness of its attempted influence. Negatively, the lack of such intensity may help explain why the category called consumers is ineffectual. All of us are members of that category, yet few of us consider the purchasing-agent role the most important element in our lives. The quality of the influencer's effort, the degree of cohesiveness of an association in its attempt at access, its knowledge of processes and policies—all of these and related items help to tell the story of factors in group power. When considerations such as the extent to which the group activities appear as morally justified are added to the analysis, it becomes obviously necessary to combine measurables and immeasurables. Even among the measurables there is no common denominator. Money does not divide or multiply with numbers of constituents. Public reputation cannot be added arithmetically to a measure of intensity of interest. Political knowhow is a different kind of factor from leadership skills. Intangibles, immeasurables, and the lack of a common denominator spoil the arithmetic in the balance-of-power image. Politics of influence is like a strange sort of poker game, with all cards wild. The process of democratic access is open to all, but it is an extremely complex game, requiring the best skills human ingenuity can invent.

THE POLITICS OF ACCOUNTABILITY

Greek political thinkers made considerable use of a tripartite classification of governments into the one, the few, and the many. Although this is, perhaps, a set of categories not notably inferior to some invented since, it is unlikely that any governing system has ever fallen neatly into one of the three categories. In actual governments, including democratic ones, there is quite frequently a central figure dominating the scene. But there is also a small group, "the influential establishment," which either surrounds the top man in an outwardly monocratic structure or acts as the leadership element in a supposedly polycratic one. The many will, furthermore, be an element of political influence in most regimes, listened to even if not worshipfully followed. Any system of governmental power is likely to be so complicated that it will be an error, or at least an oversimplification, to point to any man, group, or mass of men and say, "there goes the ruler." When the subject of investigation is a democracy, it must be remembered that this splintering of power is no mere accident—it is a guiding principle. Democracy makes multiplicity a virtue. It aims, quite purposefully, to achieve a pluralization of political power. Sovereignty is broken into so many bits and pieces that the concept either loses its entire meaning or needs badly to be redefined. Both representation and the methods of influence are made intriguingly complicated by this pluralization, and accountability is made difficult because knowledge of all the complex organs of government is not easily achieved.

The use of three different perspectives—representation, access (or influence), and accountability—in approaching the policy processes should bring clearer meaning to the relation between democratic governors and governed. It is important to remain aware, however, that these different concepts do not describe separated processes. The intricate policy function is being circled about in an attempt to see it from front, back, and side—in each case being concerned with its responsiveness to forces in the community. When our perspective is through the concept of representation, stress is on the governmental actor as spokesman for interests other than his own. When the focus is on access, our concern is not merely with the governmental actor as recipient of outside influences but also with the behavior of the man who acts as influencer. When our conceptual view turns toward the idea of accountability, we are more apt to be concerned with after-the-fact kinds of activities. We want to know how and through whom the actor-in-government reports to the sector of the community most concerned with his actions as well as to the community at large. How do we keep track of his activities? How do we ensure that he is doing what is expected by those (communities, groups, or individuals) for whom he is supposedly acting as a kind of subordinate agent. Such a perspective is a convenient one for observing the operations of our vast multiplicity of bureaucracies. No one who exercises power in a free society should, according to the principle of accountability, be free of a relationship of obligation and response to some entity outside himself and, ultimately, to broad elements in the general community. The policeman on the beat has much discretion, but in a democracy he should ideally be accountable to his superior officers, to the mayor and the city council, to a citizen's review board, or, more informally, to the citizens he protects. If he is a fair-minded person, he even holds himself accountable for justice to the suspected lawbreaker, who is his most direct client.

The processes of accountability are embarrassingly dwarfed when seen in relation to the giant they attempt to control. With so much activity scattered through numerous bureaucracies, it is impossible for anyone to know what is going on everywhere or to make certain that all of that activity stays within prescribed rules and limitations. Although big government appears in popular parlance as a worn-out cliché invented for propaganda purposes by out-of-power politicians, there is still good reason to be concerned about the sheer bulk and multiplicity of governmental activity. The rapidly inflating size and number of bureaucracies creates a greater demand for expertise, because the new tasks are usually technically complex. Modern government brings into being a vast body of civil servants whose power is based on alleged knowledge and whose function it is to serve and to regulate community life, but who, it must never be forgotten, need regulation themselves. To compound matters further, a number of these bureaucratic agencies are staffed with military and intelligence personnel who admittedly hide much of their activity from public view under the rationale of national security. The growth of various bureaucracies has resulted in a sometimes rather meager-looking expansion in accountability mechanisms. The presidency now has special agencies, like the Office of Management and Budget, which address themselves to problems of accountability. The courts spend an increasing amount of time on cases of administrative review. Congress makes more and more use of its committees to investigate apparent trouble spots among the bureaucracies. Yet one wonders if existing devices come anywhere near meeting the problem.

There is—because there must be—an endless search for more effective methods of holding governing officials accountable to someone outside their own organizational unit. The French Conseil d'Etat, British Treasury control, the Scandinavian ombudsman, the Parliamentary Question, the Congressional Investigatory Committee—all of these are, at least in part, efforts to ensure accountability. The judiciary remains important in the over-all system since it is able to retain an aloofness and a kind of amateur standing. The judges are experts not so much in subject matter of governmental functions as in the procedures of law. But their value is limited by their role. They hear only cases and controversies; they do not attempt to provide a full system of accountability. The study of any system of accountability requires an examination of the entire structure, of all the relationships: who commands whom; how and when reports are made; when, where, and in what manner a client can appeal a decision. Accountability is a matter of organization. It is also a matter of knowledge. In a leviathan-sized government it is difficult for anyone to possess enough information to control its intricacies. It is a major function of elective officials, however, to be certain that the effort to achieve comprehension is made. If the whole community cannot know how each part of its government works, who does what and how; and if the legislators cannot know a great deal more, then they must hire others to work directly for them or at least to work in independence of the various bureaucracies, to attain this knowledge.

It was, for a long time, the assumption of American students of government that the way to achieve accountability was through concentration of power. This was part of the reasoning behind the advocacy of responsible party government, behind the demand for a more centralized party system. It was the logic supporting many discussions of administrative reform in the early part of the twentieth century. By putting more power at the center, with stronger parties pulling legislators into cohesive blocs and stronger executive regulation of the bureaucracies, it was assumed that the general public could exercise more control. It was argued that fewer channels of accountability would be more manageable. The apparently more centralized power in the British system was again the model. The goal at that time was to "put all of our eggs in one basket," relying on a few men to control the whole system for the community. It is probably beyond reason, however, to expect any leadership group to possess the immense and intricate knowledge required for control over an overwhelming multiplicity of governmental organs. There seems to have been both an understatement of the existing plurality of the system and an underestimation of the values of control through multiple channels. More coordinated accountability may be useful, but it must be accompanied by methods that recognize the plurality of activities. A multiple government demands multiple means of accountability.

One major error in discussing accountability of the bureaucracy can be discovered in the words themselves. We deal not with the bureaucracy but with numerous bureaucracies. There is—and should be—coordination. But coordination does not, however, change many into one; rather, it attempts to ensure a general overview. Such an overview is important because there may be contrary forces at work within the total system of accountability. For example, the relation of an agency to its own clientele, to professional groups, to separate interest groups is a valuable—even the most valuable—kind of accountability; yet it may be in conflict with the program of a chief executive or with policies pronounced by the legislature. The United States is a fragmented society with an infinity of specialized activities. Each man knows his speciality well enough to resent the outside amateur. The modern in group is the specialist. The out group is the rest, who pay his expenses and gain from his services and who are commonly asked not to interfere. Those who lack knowledge are told to be seen, not heard. If rule by the amateur is by now too utopian, democracy demands at least the chance of overruling the expert.

Each man who is expert-in-part is also an amateur-in-part; there is, however, a scarcity of generalists, of modern Renaissance men, and this makes it all the more imperative that each democratic citizen encourage the development of that part of him which is generalist, that he retain something of his amateur standing. It is also important to place high value on the politician—a man who remains amateurish in the particulars of government but becomes a capable general student of most aspects of governing. A kind of specialist among amateurs or amateur among specialists, the politician must keep a broad perspective from his seat at the center of governmental power. The expert will then need to communicate with at least one generalist in order to have matters his way in the execution of governmental functions. Some of the functions of accountability can be delegated—to ombudsmen, presidential aides, assistants in legislative committees, judges, and budget officers—but the prime responsibility must be in the hands of the man elected to office. He must not neglect the control function of a democracy. Despite the preference the politician may reasonably have for the more enjoyable task of converting fresh ideas into exciting new policies, he must learn to delegate enough of that innovative *idea function* to permit him to perform adequately in his more routine *control function*.

CHAPTER 7

Constitutionalism and the Age of Crisis

IT is one of the functions of storm and stress to bring out the character of the men and societies that suffer through them. Can the democratic pattern survive moments of extremity—times of war, cold war, and domestic emergency—leaving its principles intact? If not, it hardly deserves the high praise men have heaped upon it. Times of crisis no longer seem so rare, and it has become obvious that democracy must be more hardy than a hothouse plant. The American record in facing crises has not always been ideal. Even such a fully committed democrat as Abraham Lincoln was forced to take autocratic shortcuts during the Civil War. Fortunately, however, the Supreme Court was not obliged to sanction the worst of those abuses. It did approve Lincoln's unauthorized blockading of southern ports, but by 1866, when the crisis was becoming a matter of history, the court had the courage to disapprove the application of military justice to civilians in nonwar zones. It then had the boldness to say that constitutional principles must apply "equally in war and peace." [1]

The task of sanctioning war-based deprivations of fundamental rights was left as an embarrassing task for later judicial generations. Paradoxically, it was Justice Black, one of the court's great lib-

1. *The Prize Cases,* 2 Black 635 (1863) and *Ex Parte Milligan,* 4 Wallace 218 (1866).

ertarians, who undertook the unenviable task of justifying, on the slender grounds of military expediency, the imprisonment of over a hundred thousand Japanese-Americans in what the court's dissenters called concentration camps. The vigor of the dissenting opinions made them historical landmarks. It does not, however, erase the deep stain that case left on the fabric of American democracy. Justice Jackson, in an intriguing dissent that raised as many questions as it answered, labored unsuccessfully to convince his colleagues of the long-run dangers of judicial approval of such a crude and cruel deprivation of liberty. Even when military judgment cannot safely be questioned, he said, there should never be a bending of constitutional principles to fit such demands: "A civil court cannot be made to enforce an order which violates constitutional limitations even if it is a reasonable exercise of military authority." Once a judicial opinion rationalizes such an expediency, he said, it weakens the whole constitutional structure.[2]

It is probably inevitable that a democratic community will, on rare occasions, violate its own principles. The effort to see the democratic pattern of social behavior in a pragmatic light implies a certain flexibility in application of principles. There may be occasions during a crisis when civilian statesmen must take the advice of military men, even when the action violates basic rules of the game. But, if, with Justice Jackson, we admit that exceptions are sometimes justifiable, they must be undertaken in full awareness that they *are* exceptions and that all such exceptions are dangerous. The rules themselves must not be altered to fit emergency circumstances. This is what worries him most. Rationalizing some apparently necessary violation of rights rationalizes the Constitution itself, bending it out of shape. It cannot sustain too much twisting without losing its ability to bend back into shape, its ability to keep a tight rein on autocratic practices through the application of legally enforced principles. Democracy implies certain rules of conduct. Constitutionalism makes sure that such rules are followed. It con-

2. *Korematsu* v. *United States,* 323 U.S. 214 (1944); see especially Justice Jackson at pp. 244–48.

verts the democratic ethic—the social imperative underlying the whole behavior pattern of a free community—into effective legal concepts. Both the nature of that social imperative and its implementation through constitutionalism need briefly to be examined. This, plus a quick excursion into the overwhelmingly complex crisis of our time, is the purpose of this chapter.

LAW AND PURPOSE IN A FREE SOCIETY

A society in which man fears his fellow men, a community infected with social paranoia, a nation on the verge of civil war—these are not the most likely places to expect democracy to flourish. Everything said up to this point implies that democratic collectivities will rest upon some degree of social agreement. There must be something of a consensus even if that something is merely a vague spirit of voluntary cooperativeness. There must be a general belief that social cooperation will not damage individual freedom and personal integrity. There needs to be not only consensual accord on the value of social participation but also a general willingness to allow men and women to enter community activities in their own individual way or, if they wish, to stay out altogether. The essential democratic idea must have a degree of general acceptance: the community must place a high value on creative, individual diversity as well as on socially productive participation. But a consensus of this kind will be too vague to uncover with normal empirical tools; even polling techniques are not well adapted to discovering the existence of such amorphous values. Observation is made doubly difficult by the varying modes by which the consensus can be expressed and by the lack of total unanimity of any articulated view. The democratic consensus does not need the express agreement of everyone, but it must be the inarticulate premise of most opinion leaders. Failing this, it is unlikely that democracy will survive.

This general acceptance of the virtues of freedom and cooperativeness constitutes a social imperative guiding a democracy in its day-to-day affairs. It provides a moral substructure for the successful operation of democratic practices. This kind of talk—of morality and social imperatives—has, however, an old-fashioned quality. One is reminded of antique concepts of moral-philosophy or of natural-law theories that declared certain ethical elements to be essential for communal living. It is unfortunate that the slightest hint of these medieval-sounding phrases tends to repel modern men and women. There are undoubtedly aspects of those archaic concepts worth preserving. The natural-law idea was valuable because it assumed a kind of human nature that might be viewed as driving men to cooperate and to seek freedom. It placed high among potential human traits a capacity for moral judgment of the mature kind, distinguishing free men from slaves. Had it stopped at that point—asserting no more than that men have the capacity for cooperation, for liberty, and for judging the virtue of individual and community actions—there would be no problem of a clash with modern psychology or with the rationalist mode of scientific thinking.

One virtue of the old idea of natural law is that it is relatively easy to relate it to down-to-earth laws of men in political communities. But nevertheless, it is probably best to avoid its use in contemporary discussion of social behavior. Its ancient lineage has so deeply encrusted it with religious, sometimes sectarian, stains that modernists, quite reasonably, cringe at any effort at its revival. The word "law" has, by now, narrowed in popular meaning after having too long been associated in the public mind either with legislation or with scientific principles. The word "nature" has taken on a more materialist meaning than it had in its original connection with natural law. But abandonment of old concepts does not free us from concern with general moral imperatives for communal living. It does not eliminate the necessity for an approximate synonym to replace natural law. For a community to continue working toward a maximization of individual liberty and social participation, large numbers of members of the collectivity will need to be affected by what might be called a social imperative—a set of ethical beliefs compatible with communal goals. Life in a community that has some meaningful direction will have imperative aspects—a widely spread concern with ambiguous ethical goals. Most importantly for discussion at this point, such a social imperative, despite the difficulties of its articulation, will provide a value base for the more specific set of laws and customs governing the conduct of men in society. In this respect it is not unlike Walter Lippmann's idea of a public philosophy.[3]

It has always been easier to accept the idea of a general moral imperative in the abstract than to agree to any specific rules providing for the governance of men or to decide who should interpret its meaning. Its specificity was shattered by the demise of the concept of a heavenly authorized clergy. With the growth of modern skepticism, universal agreement about specific implications of the social imperative became unlikely. The best that modern man can do is to examine his role in society and to make certain hesitant assumptions concerning the obligations it requires. As already implied, there appears, for example, to be an imperative connected with freedom. The potentiality for creative autonomy seems inherent in man's nature. Man, as described earlier, is not entirely himself, not a fulfilled creature, until he has tasted liberty and the burden of its responsibilities. In a democratic community this imperative toward freedom is converted into a social obligation, which demands that the whole community work toward maximizing self-directed personal creativity.

These remarks about the social imperative are generally consistent with earlier discussions concerning the meaning of democratic goals. But the latter parts of this book have been dealing with more concrete kinds of democratic phenomena, with processes and practices rather than with abstract ideas and ideals. It is time to ask what relevance this discussion of broad democratic obligations has to the operation of a democracy. The answer would seem to lie partly in the legal system. It is assumed that law, although

3. Walter Lippmann, *The Public Philosophy* (Boston: Little, Brown, 1955); for other contemporary revivals of natural-law ideas, see the Bibliographic Notes below.

not always perfectly matched with the ideals of a community, should in some way reflect accepted ethical values. The translation of exceedingly ambiguous concepts, such as have been mentioned in these past paragraphs, into concrete rules of behavior, leaves room for much leeway and disagreement in application. But, no matter how crudely it is done, lawmakers normally try to fit detailed policies to broad ethical foundations. As the community meets specific problems of the day, it will attempt to find solutions consistent with a general value system. Unfortunately, it must do this without being able to define that value system with perfect clarity. It is possible that a community can have a consensus so broad and fundamental that it settles few specific arguments concerning day-to-day policies. This does not negate the value of tying the social imperative into the governmental system through constitutionalism, but it does give that process an almost mystic quality.

Although all law reflects moral values of the society and may be expected to incorporate the existing inconsistencies of a community's ethical system, it is of particular importance that the more lasting kind of law we call the constitution should be closely compatible with deeply felt and permanent values. The laws and customs establishing the basic structure of power, the method of selecting key personnel, limitations on governing power, and the rights and duties of the citizenry, because they incorporate more fundamental kinds of legal principles, must attempt to demonstrate maximum consistency with the ambiguous moral imperatives held by the larger part of the community. By this time, it should be obvious that the constitution for a democracy will need to provide an enduring set of legal principles that will ensure the protection of personal freedoms as well as guaranteeing effective popular participation. Compatibility with the social ethos is somewhat easier to achieve when the constitution is an evolutionary product, as with the British type, since there will be a gradual inculcation of values as the whole pattern evolves. With a consciously drafted constitution of the American type (and that of most modern nations) the challenge presented to those founding fathers who must draft the core document is overwhelming. They must possess a profound understanding of lasting community values and be prepared to sort these out from transient fads in political thinking. Since those basic values are so undefinable and current political talk is so much in men's minds, the challenge is more difficult than any mere statement of its general nature can possibly imply. Good constitutions, even those of the "written" sort, are made in heaven.

CONSTITUTIONS AND CONSTITUTIONALISM

The history of constitution-making in the modern French nation provides object lessons in the relationship of constitutions and constitutionalism. There has been a continuous redrafting of the basic constitutional charter. The first French attempt to create a democratic constitution was approximately contemporaneous with the writing of the present American constitutional document. Yet the basic scheme, the written Constitution of the United States, has, with a few important amendments, managed to survive intact, whereas each succeeding French generation appears to have demanded at least one opportunity to create its own basic plan of governance. Between bouts of constitution-writing, furthermore, it has sometimes been the practice to reshape basic electoral systems periodically in order to help maintain the bloc of parties then in power. The instability of the French system has been both the cause and the effect of frequent constitution-making. But the most important result was to deny the nation the advantages of a deeply rooted sense of constitutionalism. Frenchmen learned to design constitutions but not to respect them. A constitution is, as already noted, a plan of government including all of the fundamental elements in terms of relationships, the roads to power, and rights and obligations. It may be a consciously adopted scheme, as are most modern instruments of government; it may be something handed down by a semimythical figure like Solon for the Athenians; or it may be a collection of historical documents, statutes, and customs, as in the British case. But constitutionalism is a different matter: it constitutes the attitude of high respect for constitutional traditions, a reverence that frequently develops only after the particular constitution has aged sufficiently to gain the kind of veneration men enjoy devoting to historical traditions of their community. Constitutions can be created in a few days or weeks by a handful of men, as Charles De Gaulle's friends and subordinates did when they created the Fifth Republic. Constitutionalism, on the other hand, is most likely to arise gradually, through years of general community deference to a constitutional plan.

It becomes clear that constitution-creating, when repeated periodically for each generation of men, is a handicap to constitutionalism. Awesome regard for a constitutional plan does not come easily. It will surely not arise if men feel that constitutions are ephemeral plans, easily altered to conform with current political fads, designed to meet transient, short-term political demands. But what is so great about constitutionalism? What are the alleged virtues of an attitude of respect for a traditional constitutional scheme? What makes constitutionalism so crucial an element in the achievement of a well-functioning democracy? The first part of an answer takes us back to the discussion of the social imperative that motivates a community and to earlier talk of the liberal tradition as a particularly important factor in the democratic experience. It has already become obvious that no democracy should be expected to produce a sharply defined credo, stating in precise language its interpretation of the liberal tradition that guides it, or to give a neat definition of the social imperative its citizens feel obliged to follow. But the community can reasonably be expected to institutionalize the ideals and ethical imperatives guiding it, to display the effects of its ideology and value system in practical social mechanisms and rules of governance suitable to that particular culture.

The transmission of democratic-liberal ideas and moral commands of a community into popular beliefs, of rules of social conduct, and of operating political processes is achieved in all of the numerous ways in which cultures can be developed. Formal education is important; so are mass communication, the arts, religion, and the family. But it is particularly important to be aware of the self-generating character of political institutions themselves as instruments for inculcating the constitutional tradition. The institutions of a democracy are the best single expression of its purposes. They help to transmit the value scheme of a free, participating society from generation to generation. The constitution of a community, whether it is centered in a core document or is of the historic British type, expresses more than law and precedent; it also proclaims a set of political and social beliefs. Constitutionalism, then, provides a kind of bridge between political processes and political ideas. It infuses the governing system with a communal attitude that both supports the basic plan and imbues it with ideological, ethical coloration.

To obtain a clearer notion of the function of constitutionalism, it is important to recall that democracy does not eliminate political realities. The power of men over men remains. Relations of dominance and submission, leadership and influence are not abolished. Democracy attempts to increase individual freedom and general participation without destroying the kind of orderly society that builds around the power of leadership. It is the contribution of constitutionalism to instill the general goals of democracy so deeply in the political habits of both rulers and ruled that behavior inconsistent with democratic ideals can never tempt them. Effective constitutionalism provides each set of political processes with a protective coating consisting of ideas about political conduct, about governing and being governed, which are so profoundly rooted in tradition that to violate them would be unthinkable. A perfected constitutionalism need not bar the way to innovations in policy or governmental forms. It can, however, provide a protective safety device that will ensure maintenance of broader, more permanent community goals. Constitutionalism may thus correctly be called a conserving force, discouraging impetuous change but not necessarily impeding cautious reforms.

It is important to announce, at an early stage in the discussion, that constitutionalism, while essential to a successful, stable democracy, may also support other kinds of regimes. Constitutionalism can provide an attitude of supportive legitimacy for any traditional pattern of government. It can make an autocracy more legitimate, ensuring that kings and princes will act in a nonarbitrary fashion, just as it protects and legitimizes democratic processes. In England, constitutionalism predates democracy by several centuries. When democracy finally came to that nation, it built on a strong foundation; respect for constitutional tradition had already been firmly established under aristocratic rulership. But even though an autocracy can, in theory, stay within traditional constitutional limits, and although monarchies have sometimes been constitutional, there is an inherent temptation in a regime with highly concentrated power to act arbitrarily, ignoring the constitutional custom. An autocracy can, with no immediate difficulty, operate on the transient whims of a ruler like Hitler or a Communist party clique such as that found in Eastern European nations. But a democracy, because it must guarantee certain freedoms and must provide effective channels of popular participation, is compelled to act in a predetermined manner, through processes exhibiting respect for traditional, orderly modes of action. If either those who rise to power in a democracy or those who elect them to high positions do not believe in the traditional rules supporting the democratic system, only the goddess of fortune can be relied upon to permit a democracy to continue for very long. Any kind of regime may become legitimized if it has sufficient stability to build a tradition. But democracies have special problems. They require a more firmly established pattern of legitimacy. The history of democracies, as pointed out by ancient Greek thinkers, demonstrates that they have often been on the verge of deteriorating into demagogic tyranny, against which the only sure safeguard is a firmly established constitutional tradition. A democracy asks a wide body of citizenry, with varying degrees of political sophistication, to become political activists—to take a small but important part in the decisional process. Since it places reliance upon the participation of large numbers of people, it becomes especially crucial that nearly all men—as potential participants—be guided by traditional concepts compatible with the underlying purposes of the system.

Constitutionalism supports the constitution. In so doing it relieves some of the sting of political power, removing much of its arbitrariness without devitalizing the governing and leadership functions. It does not, as has been said, eliminate power. It is clear by now that any such dream is utopian in the extreme. It unites power with authority, legitimizing it, ensuring that it will follow predetermined paths, paths approved as "proper" by a legal document or by long-established custom. Constitutionalism is not simply a set of ethical imperatives. It attempts to guarantee, not that men in power will always do what is good, but merely what is proper. It does not try to ensure that governors will always be ethical, but it attempts to make certain that they operate within legally oriented concepts of propriety. The traditions incorporated in law are not always precisely just, even when they have the support of ancient custom. Law normally attempts to follow moral imperatives, but since it must have generalized application and a quality of permanence, it does not always do what is best or fairest under every specific circumstance. While constitutions, with the support of constitutionalism, attempt to socialize power, to make it follow rules of the game, they do not guarantee perfect justice. As a result of such imperfections, the governors of a constitutional regime may argue about the precise nature of those rules of the game and disagree about the particular meaning of constitutional edicts, but they can never argue that no such limits exist.

It will be recalled that during earlier discussions, stress was laid upon the general virtues of governmental orderliness and its relation to freedom as well as to practical access to those with governing power. It should be obvious that constitutionalism provides a major role in that ordering function. Constitutions formalize the governing system, and constitutionalism ensures that the formal scheme of government is normally followed. Formalization, in dictionary meaning, refers to a "strict adherence to prescribed forms." By increasing the formality of a process or institution, we contribute to its certainty, ensuring that well-known, predetermined patterns of behavior are followed. Formalized constitutional guide lines make the location of responsibility easier and help to determine when men are overstepping the bounds of rightful authority. The edicts of rulers, under constitutionalism, can be freely ignored if such commands are not properly formalized. But, most importantly, formalization makes knowledge easier. As implied earlier, those who desire access to government or who wish to enter official positions themselves, discover that it is important to have thorough knowledge of the channels that exist. Formal constitutional rules make this immeasurably easier. The existence of formal rules does not, as has already been stated, eliminate informal supplements to the system. Formal constitutional institutions never tell the entire story, but their existence is essential to knowable government.

In contributing to the orderliness of a constitutional regime, constitutionalism also provides an element of efficiency. It contributes to efficiency by ensuring that some or most elements in the system remain relatively stable and hence knowable. It is important to be able to count on certain fundamental rules when attempting to develop policy out of a governmental system. An individual man desires an element of routine and ritual in his daily life so that he need not spend his time deciding how to tie his shoelaces or whether or not to wash the dishes. Orderliness in daily living permits him to concentrate on matters contributing to a richer life, allowing him to concentrate most of his resources and talents on being creative, on solving his most perplexing problems. In the same fashion, a respect for constitutional traditions gives a government time to make crucial new decisions because it has established predetermined patterns of behavior, telling it how to go about its daily affairs and how to approach the decision-making process. Orderliness in the processes of personal living and in public policy-making is, then, partly a matter of efficiency. Constitutionalism, even though conservative in giving reverence to an established order of things, can, by making the processes clear, also help to encourage innovation when new circumstances and new problems face the governors. A constitutional approach to processes of government, an established pattern of basic relationships, if not overly rigid, can help to provide defined channels for progressive creativeness in meeting unexpected crises and in dealing with great social upheavals or with novel foreign-policy complications. To accomplish the kind of creative direction any community needs, it is well for it to have sufficient stability in its regular behavior to permit it to concentrate its rarer skills where they will count most at a given moment.

Before further elaborating upon the functions of constitutionalism, it may be well to take parenthetical notice of the fact that the form of a constitution will affect the nature of popular reaction to it. Reference has repeatedly been made to the peculiar advantages of the evolutionary kind of constitution exemplified in the British system. Most other nations have what are confusingly called written constitutions. (A large part of the British constitutional structure can, in fact, be found in bits and pieces of writing—in the form of charters, laws, and historical documents.) Most other nations differ in that they possess core documents around which a constitutional plan is built. It is vitally important, however, not to assume that this central core must constitute the sole element in written constitutions. The relatively brief Constitution of the United States makes up only a portion of a complex system of fundamental law and custom. The core document presents a starting point, but it is worth little until it has been encrusted with a heavy overlay of precedent and interpretation handed down over the years by legislatures, courts, political parties, chief executives, and popular beliefs. When the core document tries to do too much, when it is too long and too specific—as with most American state constitutions—the effect is to inhibit effective action so frequently that constitutions are circumvented and disrespected. The founding fathers who draft constitutional documents need the kind of wisdom that ensures humility. If they arrogantly assume that they know best how governments should be operated for centuries to come and they then proceed to lay out plans in great detail, they are almost certain to be proven wrong. The result of their arrogant efforts will either be an endless series of amendments cheapening the original documents or even a series of new constitutions. In either case, the consequence will be a lack of deep-seated reverence for the constitutional tradition. Too much constitution-writing, as has been stated, can destroy constitutionalism.

THE INHIBITION OF TYRANNY

Whenever democrats have looked over their shoulders, they have seen the frightful specter of the tyrant, ready to rule through demagogic appeal to the masses. The military hero home from the wars, the man of facile tongue who promises to lead the populace out of troubled times into a promised land, the right-wing demagogue, the left-wing fanatic—all of these have, with reason, put fear into the hearts of those who hope for a community built upon freedom and participation. For the Greeks, the word for such a governor was "tyrant," the leader who dominated a community by illegitimate, one-man rule—the natural result of deterioration in a democracy. Continental European experience provides an ample number of modern examples, and no democrat can safely dismiss the threat of tyranny as a mere historical curiosity. Although part of the antidote for tyranny lies in constitutionalism, there remains danger of confusing the issue. Constitutionalism is not a rigid barricade. It provides no sturdy wall of stone, no barbed-wire fence, not even a thin bamboo screen to stand between free government and tyranny. It is not a physical impediment but an attitude of mind, which creates a situation in which governors are indoctrinated with the desire not to act arbitrarily, not to go beyond normal and proper patterns of authority.

Although the general usefulness of constitutionalism as a curb on tyranny is found in its establishment of taboos, some regimes, most notably that in the United States, have established explicit devices to guard against the abuse of power. It may be that newly established regimes, those with consciously created constitutions, unlike the evolutionary kind of government which has now become a rarity in the world, have a particular need to devise distinct kinds of sentries to guard against political abuse until a firm constitutional tradition has had time to develop more informal constraints. Two such formal devices are now commonplace. One is the device of sharing power through a division of governing functions. The other is the development of a collection of particularized interdictions, "thou-shalt-not" rules, formulated in order to prevent the abuse of power. The first is designed to inhibit tyranny through the very method by which power is granted: it allocates functions of governance in a way that will supposedly permit action but frustrate its abuse. The second device spells out constraints designed to curb those who govern and to protect those who are governed. Despite the sometimes bewildering complexities of government that have resulted, a major contribution to the art of constitution-making occurred when the American Founding Fathers made use of both kinds of specific checks.

The American application of the theory of separation of powers has been mentioned in Chapter 6. The idea was originally based on an assumption that the British system had made a crude start toward the creation of a set of distinctive powers through the then competing influence of Parliament and crown and through the existence of an independent judiciary. The idea of balancing rival centers of power through a division of functions was given deliberate emphasis in the United States. It was incorporated permanently, almost rigidly, into the system. Division of labor and specialization of function is, of course, a feature of all but the most primitive governments. The idea of divide and rule, aimed at keeping power closer to the people in the United States, can, however, have an opposite effect. Joseph Stalin, a political genius in his own right, made use of this ancient device of divide and conquer to sustain his autocratic power. By setting the party against the bureaucracy, the secret police against the army, and by creating other kinds of rivalries, it is possible for the autocrat to increase his arbitrary base of power. This would seem to indicate that, by itself, the division-of-power idea is not inherently democratic. In a fully developed modern democracy, the key to the success of a check-and-balance system lies more in the source of power behind each separated branch than in the mere separation of functions itself. In the American system the separate elections of the president and of members of the House of Representatives and the Senate provides three distinctive power centers. The life terms given to federal judges help to preserve autonomy of the courts as a fourth branch. The complex set of competing controls exercised by both president and Congress over the bureaucracy makes it into a fifth branch. The number of such divisions might increase as one looks further into the system. The basic point, however, is that the officers in the different branches have a degree of autonomy because each is selected in a different manner and because each receives his basic power through the particular system that selects him.

The Constitution of the United States lists governmental functions in three separate articles. This is the formal base of the idea of a tripartite separation of powers. More importantly, it also provides divergent methods of selection, a variety of kinds of constituencies, unsimilar terms of office, and different patterns of accountability—all serving to provide the roots for a genuinely significant division of power. Power follows function, and in the United States the different functions assigned to each branch are expected to result in different kinds of power. It bears remembering, however, that in Britain there are similar divisions in the assignment of function and also that there are variations in method of selection. The British judiciary has distinctive functions resulting in a firmly established independence. The bureaucracy operates under permanent secretaries who head each civil service department in a manner that possibly provides even more autonomy than that of American administrative agencies, despite the fact that British bureaucrats operate under the top command of ministers who are also members of Parliament. The monarch is no longer the independent source of power he appears to have been at the time of Locke and Montesquieu, but he still can, on rare occasions, conceivably exercise influence in his own right. The loyal opposition is a more organized and distinctive force than that in the United States; it acts under a government-paid leader and is a formalized source of competition against the party in power. Within the majority party the distinction between leaders and back-benchers can occasionally become a source of important friction. The prime minister and his cabinet, although chosen from among members of Parliament, are selected in a special way for their executive positions and, because of their distinctive functions, their powers are quite different from those of ordinary members of that body. Even the anachronistic House of Lords sometimes influences policy. The British system, unlike the American, is, as has been indicated earlier, a *focused* one, but it, too, displays some of the features of separated power that may help prevent the occurrence of arbitrary power.

The shared-power aspect of the British constitution is less obvious because so much of it is found in custom rather than in documentary form. The same can be said for those rules of conduct which act as impediments to the arbitrary use of power. Common-law precedents, ancient manifestos, and the even more ambiguous idea that certain things "are simply not done" provide none of the explicitness found in the list of constitutional prohibitions in the American constitutional document. But the point is the same. In the constitutional schemes of all free societies, there are stop signs for protecting democratic freedoms and preserving democratic participation from arbitrary uses of power. Ideally, however, a bill of rights should concern itself primarily with the more fundamental freedoms. As has already been stated, there is a dangerous tendency to write too much detail into any bill of rights or to use it to express transient ideas of political and social philosophy. Fashionable but unenforceable rights, such as that of full employment, are best omitted from constitutional documents. Even the United States Constitution, generally better than most, includes a few archaic items, such as the right to indictment by grand jury and the right to bear arms in an old-fashioned militia.

There is still merit in the concept of inalienable rights expressed in the Declaration of Independence. It is not so much that rights cannot be alienated—in fact, they frequently have been—but that underlying rights such as freedom of expression have a deep, fundamental importance, which places them on a higher plane than a more specific matter such as the right to trial by a jury of "twelve good men and true." This inalienability concept is part of the argument supporting the absoluteness and preferred position of the First Amendment right of free expression. (It is essential to qualify the inalienable-absolutist free-speech position. Although there should, ideally, be no socially imposed limits upon what a man thinks, says, or publishes, this does not mean that there need be no curbs on the consequences of such expressions. The man who has yelled "fire" in the crowded theater—in that cliché example of free expression—could not be punished for his utterance, but he could have been punished for the results, if there had been damage to life, limb, or property in an ensuing panic.) If any rights are to be absolute—if in First Amendment language, "no law" is to be enacted limiting them—then these rights must be peculiarly fundamental in importance and few in number. If any rights are to be called inalienable, in the hope that they will never, under any circumstance, be violated, they need to be quite carefully selected. When a constitution is less formalized, having an evolutionary rather than core-document form, it is possible to conceive of a hierarchy of rights, some of which are more important than others. The necessity of drafting them in legal language, however, makes this more difficult. Codified rights either exist or they do not. Halfway rights, to be used when not inexpedient, when no one objects to their enforcement, are not worth talking about. But some rights do seem more basic. The resulting quandary reappears frequently in the extremely difficult task of interpretation of liberties undertaken by the United States Supreme Court. It has been the heart of much debate on and off the Court concerning the flood of rights cases in the past several decades.

A codified bill of rights does have definite virtues. Beyond the obvious function of making specific rights part of the legal system, it also educates the citizenry about the basic meaning of constitutionalism. The average person might not grasp all the niceties of constitutionalism; yet he begins to grasp its essence when he hears discussion of proposals such as the District of Columbia Crime Act passed under the Nixon Administration. The worrisome "no knock" and "preventive detention" provisions of that measure are provided with some minimal safeguards and the citizen realizes that no such law will become fully effective until tested in the courts for constitutionality. Even during epidemics of crime and of repression of alleged criminals, the citizen of a constitutional democracy is aware that men have quotable rights that can be used as a personal weapon against the arbitrary power of government officials. The man who says "I have my rights" may not grasp all that is significant about constitutionalism. He does come, however, to see law as his protector as well as his controller. The stop signs found in a bill of rights are but one aspect of constitutionalism; yet they give concrete expression to the fact that law and legal traditions are a boon to human freedom.

One of the contrasting advantages of the unwritten British kind of constitution, despite some ambiguities caused by the lack of a codified set of civil rights, is that it emphasizes another useful aspect of constitutionalism. Although it is true of any constitutional scheme, a constitution built primarily upon custom especially emphasizes the incorporation of history into the processes of governance. This is true not only in Britain, where the constitution is itself history, but in any regime that is truly constitutional. Constitutionalism gives the governing processes of the community a time sense, adding a historical perspective to the political pattern. It becomes important not to violate tradition. This protective attitude is a valuable shield against arbitrariness. A constitutional regime, whether or not it possesses a core document, is one that worries about precedent. This is not a mere matter of following established court decisions. More importantly, it establishes the viewpoint that past customs of governing must not be uprooted without pausing consciously to decide whether it is desirable to change the system. A consciousness of history can, if the tradition of freedom and participation has been a real part of that history, be a substantial defense against violations of the rights of man. Expedient innovations that might trespass upon established traditions of freedom and general participation become less available as an answer. Constitutionalism, with its great respect for tradition, is admittedly a conservative force. It impedes the process of developing new ways of governing. But such caution is normally valuable as long as it does not deteriorate into blind negativism toward social change. These is nothing about the concept of constitutionalism that makes it inherently opposed to all progress.

It is characteristic of a constitutional regime that debates over policy issues will often take on the color of constitutional argumentation. This can sometimes be merely a shabby trick by conservatives to hide more substantial issues or to disguise stubborn resistance to change. It can often obscure the real issues in an argument. At the same time, the very existence of that habit may be an indicator of the strength of constitutionalism. The existence of sometimes sterile legalism in political debates is a reminder of the all-important fact that incremental changes in governmental policy and processes can, quite conceivably, destroy the constitutional fabric. Gradual erosion is no less a threat than the coup d'état of a would-be tyrant. A negative Supreme Court decision, a presidential veto, a congressional committee chairman pigeonholing a bill are actions sometimes intended as resistance to potential encroachments on the basic constitutional scheme. Such actions have a place in safeguarding the system, even though they may sometimes be misguided. A constitutional regime must be equally effective in turning back minor invasions destructive of the basic fabric of the system as it is in forestalling dramatic revolutions of radicals of the right or the left. If the constitutional tradition is sufficiently imbued in the society, people will often see that the more patently false uses of constitutional language are a device of reactionary resistance. The more effective enforcement of Fourteenth and Fifteenth Amendment freedoms for Negroes in the

1950s and 1960s was, for example, not effectively halted by those segregationists who raised the cry of constitutional states' rights.

It is time to return to the original issue of this section. Can a constitution impede tyranny? Do well-defined structures of checks and balances and carefully outlined statements of rights and liberties provide the protection a regime needs against the rise of a Hitler or a Mussolini? The answer to the question put in that manner must be no. But let us change the question. If we ask whether constitutionalism can make such constitutional provisions effective, the answer will be more affirmative. Effective constitutionalism implies that, throughout the community, there will be a sufficiently widespread attitude of respect for traditions, for fundamental laws, and for the rights of men to ensure that the chief elements of the constitutional scheme can be maintained. Constitutionalism may collapse under stress. There exists no totally convincing evidence that the United States or even Britain might not someday break with their own constitutional traditions. But the important point is that the preservation of the attitude of constitutionalism is the chief bulwark against arbitrary power. This suggests that a new nation would be wise to design the simplest and best kind of constitution it can, with prime emphasis on flexibility and permanence, and then bend every effort toward making it work long enough to build a firm tradition supporting it. This is a task more difficult than it might seem to Americans, who have had a fair share of historical good luck, with only one civil war (so far) disrupting the foundation of law and tradition protecting the whole complex constitutional scheme.

Constitutionalism offers a democracy an opportunity to be self-generating. Although nothing can make a regime totally self-perpetuating, the democratic purpose, when firmly imbedded in a constitutional tradition, can help to maintain the processes of a free society relatively intact. The longer such a tradition remains effective, the stronger it will become. The age-old story of successes and failures of the democratic idea makes it clear that democratic constitutionalism is much more difficult to create than is a democratic constitution. Constitutional documents may be copied and adapted to differing environments, but democratic constitutionalism requires the dissemination of a unique spirit of freedom throughout the population. This cannot be done by any single action or by any single generation of men. The liberal tradition, discussed in the first chapter of this book, must gradually become incorporated into a concept of legitimacy. That tradition must determine the proper ordering of governmental institutions and processes. Liberalism, as defined earlier, must be integrated, in short, into the constitutional scheme of things. Constitutionalism brings the tradition of freedom directly into government itself, making it firmly part of the pattern of politics, converting it into a direct influence on the way things are done. As we have been observing, democratic constitutionalism is not easily manufactured. Once achieved, however, its advantages show that it is well worth having waited for.

HIGHER LAW AND THE POWER OF JUDGES

Law is "something more than mere will exerted as an act of power," or, at least, this is the viewpoint of one justice of the United States Supreme Court.[4] Having accepted the idea that there must be limitations upon the arbitrary power of governors, the question arises as to the virtues of having, in the American style, a special agent hired to enforce those limitations. There then arises a second question: who should that agent be? In the American republic, the courts, most notably the Supreme Court of the United States, have taken this review function upon themselves, finding it their function, in the words of Justice Field, a notable judicial activist, to ensure the citizenry that the community is not dependent merely upon "the mercy of a majority of its legislature."[5] Chief Justice Marshall set the tone from the beginning. Perhaps his most crucial words were those stating that "It is *a constitution* we are expounding."[6]

4. Justice Matthews in *Hurtado* v. *California,* 110 U.S. 516 (1884), 28 L.Ed. at p. 238.
5. Dissenting in *Munn* v. *Illinois,* 94 U.S. 113 (1877), 24 L.Ed. at p. 89.
6. *McCulloch* v. *Maryland,* 4 Wheaton 316 (1819) at p. 407.

The sentence is simple, but the italics give a generous hint as to its later importance. He is asserting that the American constitution is not a set of ordinary laws. It is something special, a higher kind of law, a peculiarly fundamental set of rules. A constitution is a set of supreme principles, and the Constitution of the United States, as he sees it, is in a class with all other such superior laws.

Not even in the United States, the homeland of judicial review, are the courts the only interpreters of the constitutionality of acts of government. The other branches have joined in that function. Furthermore, as the idea of some kind of constitutional review has spread, with the advent of hundreds of written constitutions, the ordinary courts do not always get the job. Nor is the necessity for any formalized system of review a settled question among political theorists. Britain is frequently used as the classic case of a nation without such review. However, one must be careful not to use the British example too freely. The unique lack of a constitutional core document in that nation makes it less than likely that the judges would have developed such a function although, in the time of the Stuarts, Chief Justice Coke did try valiantly to provide a kind of judicial review based upon the common law. Rejection of constitutional review through the courts or through any formalized review council by the British does not indicate a lack of concern for issues of constitutionality. Such questions commonly arise in Parliament when novel process or policy changes are advocated. The concept of a higher law does not require a system of judicial review. The practice of judicial review, however, seems to demand a belief in a more fundamental status for constitutional law. No modern democracy is without constitutional law; it may not, however, follow the American practice of enforcing it partly through judicial review.

The concept of a higher law does not need a constitutional core document to make practical sense. Law has generally included both particular rules for specific conduct, subject to frequent change, and more fundamental kinds of regulation less in need of periodic revision. It does not seem essential, furthermore, to provide this higher law with an elaborate metaphysical base in the manner of Saint Thomas Aquinas. It is not necessary to believe in a direct or an indirect relation between the law of God and the laws of man to accept the notion that some laws seem almost to be rooted in the nature of man as a social animal. It is safest merely to argue that each community is inclined to have a particular ideology, a concept of the social imperative, based on a fundamental viewpoint about the nature of man. That viewpoint is reflected in broad legal notions that appear more basic than specific, day-to-day kinds of legal regulations. It is reasonable to suppose that men can create laws at several levels of significance. The more fundamental ideas of propriety then become a basis for critical evaluations of current efforts to legislate details of human life. If men accept the idea that there are degrees of importance in laws, it is not surprising that they argue the merits and validity of proposals for lesser laws in terms of notions of what constitutes the higher law.

If men believe there are underlying rules of legitimacy providing a lasting foundation for all acts of governance, why do they argue that this higher law must be subject to the particular process of judicial review? In a nation with a core document around which constitutional rules are built, what gives the judges a special competence? The answer given by John Marshall in 1803 still serves as an outline for response.[7] The argument begins by stating that when, in normal practice, a new law is promulgated, it supersedes previous laws with which it is in conflict. But, it is argued, how can this be true if the two rules are not on an equal plane in the hierarchy of law? If there exists a more fundamental, superior kind of law, upon which is founded the authority for legislating particular, ordinary laws, then such lesser legislation must always be compatible with the higher. The ordinary new regulation cannot supersede the higher law even if it is later in date of promulgation. Day-to-day legislation must be based on the authority of the constitutional document in its mode of enactment and must be consisent with constitutional content. If not, the legislators have acted beyond their authority. No

7. *Marbury* v. *Madison,* 1 Cranch 137 (1803).

such unauthorized acts have any proper existence. There can be no law inconsistent with the Constitution. Unconstitutional acts are but nullities.

But Marshall has not completed his argument. He must next take note of the existence in all governments of a certain kind of officer who has the function of applying generalized rules to particular cases, deciding when the law fits and when it does not. The core constitutional document is a type of law, differing from other types primarily in its superior, more lasting character. Judges in the common law tradition of Anglo-Saxon nations are officers particularly familiar with the chore of applying the more ambiguous kind of law to concrete, new situations. The judge must finally decide which rule to apply to any case when the contending parties disagree about what law is binding. If there are conflicts in the rules, the court must decide which law is controlling. If one of these rules turns out to be located in the written constitutional document, it is obvious, at least to Marshall, that the judge must apply the superior rule, automatically invalidating the ordinary one that contradicts it. Marshall made judicial review appear to be quite natural, totally inevitable. It is, of course, by no means that simple. But although judicial review presents manifold complications and difficulties, it is obvious that ordinary statutes and constitutional pronouncements are seldom clearly in conflict. The real problem arises when there is doubt, as there quite frequently is, about the meaning of each kind of rule. It is seldom possible, as Justice Roberts tried to argue in an attack on Franklin D. Roosevelt's farm program, simply to place a statute alongside the constitutional clause and observe, on the face of it, that one is inconsistent with the other.[8] The whole history of judicial review is made up of difficult, arguable cases. The easy cases do not usually reach the higher courts. Constitutionalism is itself enough to stop legislators and executives from attempting quite flagrant violations of the clear-cut rules written down in the Constitution, and lawyers do not often argue cases they are certain to lose.

8. *United States* v. *Butler,* 297 U.S. 1 (1936) at p. 62.

After admitting that Marshall's argument is somewhat simplistic, after accepting the fact that some regimes do perfectly well without judicial review, after agreeing that the judicial review task is both extremely complex and politically risky, there are still arguments for letting the judges continue in the function Marshall encouraged them to adopt. The conservative bias of the Anglo-Saxon legal profession—the habit of looking backward to ancient precedents and age-old codes—is compatible with the idea that constitutionalism amounts to an incorporation of history into contemporary governing activity. Lawyers and judges are historically oriented both in training and in their daily efforts to deal with the application of old rules to new situations. The judicial subgroup within this larger legal guild takes particular pride in its attempt to achieve an aloofness from the sort of strife bringing cases before it. This tradition of seeking an objective, equitable handling of cases, plus the concern for tradition itself, should, under normal circumstances, help to provide the essential public support for otherwise unpopular invalidations of actions of elective bodies. In the common American practice, furthermore, no court will provide an advisory opinion. It will deal only with cases of genuine legal controversy, and this has the virtue of limiting the area of constitutional review, allowing the courts to avoid certain of the more intensely political issues that might otherwise come before a reviewing body.

Despite all of the advantages judges possess as performers of the constitutional-review function, that activity presents them with a crucial role in policy-making, thus subjecting them, with good reason, to the charge of being political. Judicial activism is praised by some at the very moment that it frightens others. Judicial action is inevitably controversial when it breaks a logjam such as that which had, for generations, frustrated effective action on racial discrimination. The Negro revolution of the 1960s was not caused by the Supreme Court's 1954 decision, but because it was more dramatic than the long line of cases leading to it, it may have helped to provide a final spark which, after a few years, burst into flames of action on numerous fronts. It is not surprising that sparks of radical change partly ignited by court cases can leave political scars and create bitter enemies for the courts. Unless the judges abdicate the constitutional-review function, repudiating Marshall, there will be occasions when the image of olympian aloofness of the judges will be tarnished temporarily. This would seem to suggest, not the frightened withdrawal apparently advocated by followers of Justice Frankfurter, but a sharpened judicial awareness of political realities. The courts need not surrender to the demands of segregationists or to the more general cry for order regardless of law. There is, however, enough discretion available to the judges in handling their cases to permit them to bend slightly in the wind—just enough to maintain their constitutional function, just enough to avoid creating a dangerous anticonstitutional frame of mind in a large sector of the public. Court decisions need not be bland or cowardly. On the other hand, they need not be so provocative as to recklessly stir potential fanatics into overt opposition. The difficulties are obviously overwhelming, but with political discretion, there is no reason that decisions could not be designed in such a manner as to move the Constitution ahead with changing times on the stable base of ancient traditions, as advocated by Justice Holmes.

At times there have been efforts to turn the American Supreme Court justices into nine infallible high priests, reigning in lordly and lonely magnificence from their tomblike marble palace. This was the dream of the conservatives of the 1930s who thought that judicial activism had saved the nation from the horrors of New Deal legislation. It has been the hope of recent liberals who have praised the boldly libertarian rulings of the court since World War II. It was, also, somewhat paradoxically, the hope of Justice Frankfurter and other advocates of judicial restraint, but it appears doubtful that a mildly restraintist role can keep the court out of the much-dreaded political thicket. Only abdication could do that. The practice of constitutionalism is by no means apolitical. If constitutionalism incorporates a historical tradition such as liberalism into the governing process, it must have practical application in day-to-day political controversies. Only in a uselessly abstract sense are concepts of freedom and popular participation immune from political considerations of a mundane nature. Unless we stubbornly refuse to apply basic constitutional principles to issues of the day, hence giving up the idea of constitutionalism altogether, there will be arguments about their meaning—with the usual political repercussions. The interpretation of the constitutional tradition is a political act. If not, constitutionalism would become meaningless; it could not affect what governments do as a practical matter. The American courts are formally involved in this interpretive process in a striking manner. Hence, their interpretations are more constitutionally conspicuous than those of the other branches. Other interpreters of the Constitution—congressmen, presidents, and bureaucrats—think quite frankly about political repercussions as well as about constitutional significance when they act. The courts need to do likewise. At the same time, they must do so without losing their unique aloofness from everyday political manipulations—an exceedingly challenging assignment.

DEMOCRACY AND THE CRISIS OF ABUNDANCE

By the early 1970s, as the words of this book are falling into place, Americans seem to have reached a state in which crisis is something perpetual, almost, by now, a bore. After decades in which emergencies have seemed endemic, dull anger has replaced excitement as the reaction to everlasting tension. Reaction, whether or not the word "crisis" still applies, is peculiarly acrimonious at the moment of this writing. A few are excited; almost everyone else is angry. Despite the comforts of high prosperity, the public mood is one of slow-burning wrath. Constitutionalism must be prepared to survive such bad-tempered moments. Democratic electoral and access processes must somehow satisfy the frustrations of an irate element of the public when that segment is as large as it now appears to be. Frustration over the long, bloody, and momentarily unresolvable conflict in Vietnam is compounded by a new awakening to urban and racial problems and to the damage commerical exploitation has created in our once natural environment. More fundamentally disturbing, however, is the fact that affluence gives the appearance of raising as many problems as it solves. How, in the face of all of this, can this book take the optimistic note that it has? Is it reasonable to assume that democracy is still feasible for modern man, in the midst of all the fury and gloom of this day? How can an essay written at such a time be anything but pessimistic? A total answer would require a different, much longer book, one containing a full diagnosis of the numerous present ailments as well as a search for more hopeful prospects. Such has not been this author's intention. Regardless of the risks of addressing the subject in a few paragraphs, however, there is an obligation to end this book with a few words about democracy and the crisis of our time. Neither this author nor any other can provide a satisfactory prognosis of the future of democracy at this perplexing moment. We are all too deeply confused. But the present environment can never be totally ignored in any essay that proposes to speak about democracy. Democracy is always of the here and now. Present problems and future fears cannot be overlooked.

Why is this essay so lacking in pessimism? Part of the explanation is that it has attempted to root itself firmly in history. But history is partly a personal matter; it is built on the perspective of a particular age. A man born in 1916, as was this author, can expand his perspective by reading broad histories of his own and other civilizations. But that history which he has lived through will still affect his perspective most deeply. The World War I baby began to take contemporary history seriously in the 1930s and to live it, fighting its battles, in the 1940s. These were years when there were depressions to be conquered and wars to be won. Democracy was under frontal attack, first from economic forces and then from quite definite enemies like Hitler and Stalin. The era of Churchill and Roosevelt was an era of faith in democracy—faith supported by WPA battalions, by men in tanks, planes, and ships of war. But the product of that generation also had reason for frustration. It was forced to sit impatiently through the leaderless 1950s, that dismal and apathetic decade, notable chiefly for its complacency and for the ugliness of the tail fins on its cars. The man who is in his middle years in the 1970s will have developed some tolerance for the protestations of youth, even when, in good conscience, he cannot join their demonstrations or approve their destructiveness. But his view of history is inevitably different. As Philip Toynbee put it in the London *Observer,* it is true that the condition of the world can reasonably be called "intolerable," as it has been by the rebellious new generation.[9] The middle-aged man, however, must instinctively qualify any support for his younger friends. His past concern has been with finding solutions and with fighting specific enemies. His experience in trying to do things warns him of the complexities of all social action. He is forced to say, "Yes, but . . . ," instead of joining youth on the barricades. He may understand, but he is unlikely to participate in the rebellion.

Even a middle-aged optimist cannot overlook the current spasms in this continuing time of troubles. A first, superficial look at society is enough to give him pause. The world does, indeed, look different —unlike anything in man's historical experience. In the first place, no previous period of social confusion had its roots in an excess of abundance. No crisis ever before arose out of what our forefathers liked to call progress—a word that now frightens contemporary men. But America of the 1960s and 1970s has also told another story. American democracy in this disturbed era has seemed to demand an unusually emotional kind of eloquence from its leaders. Yet the madmen that society produced and then supplied with arms and ammunition were unable to tolerate men of eloquence. Much of the key to the need for this oratory lay in the Negro revolution. When that movement burst forth, it was bound to be inflammatory. It demanded a special brand of eloquence because there was no full solution readily at hand. Too much injustice, too much guilt, was stored up to be safely released so suddenly. Martin Luther King was typical of the leadership of that revolution. He seemed spontaneously propelled into it, and there seems little indication that

9. *Observer,* June 23, 1968, p. 21.

he had any control over its direction. He possessed what was demanded—a remarkable kind of compassionate articulateness that appealed to both white and black alike, thus frightening paranoiacs and racists. The Kennedy brothers seemed involuntarily propelled into eloquence in the same fashion, although their efficient headquarters and smooth political craftsmanship gave that oratory a more manufactured quality. Fine phrases were badly needed. Yet they were also dangerous. The era of emotive eloquence was also the era of assassination.

The anger that produced political killings was different from, but not unrelated to, that other fierce hatred of the period—the anger of a substantial segment of the community toward Lyndon Johnson and anyone associated with him (an anger later transferred to Richard Nixon). In sharp contrast with the Kennedys and Kings, Johnson was a man devoid of suavity, whose language was of a now antique variety, more suited to the age of Jackson than to a generation trained to listen to the smooth, subtle voice of the television commentator. Paradoxically, this newfound "enemy of the people" had already displayed a phenomenal ability to extract positive action out of the stubbornly resistant American legislative machinery. Previous performance did not matter. The surface cause of this intensely bitter reaction was the Vietnam policy, which President Johnson, with his typical compulsiveness for seeing things through, accepted from his predecessors and drove to dreadful, but probably logical consequences. Johnson finally did for American foreign policy what the cold-war concept demanded: he took the last step to push a nation that had not yet lost all isolationist tendencies into a situation in which victory was unattainable and in which "staying there" was outrageously costly in lives and wealth. But the anger of the times was not entirely tied to the policies of President Johnson. It did not die with his withdrawal from the presidential race in 1968, with the beginnings of protracted Vietnam negotiations in Paris, or with the coming of a new President with different modes of appealing to the public. The episodes in the spring of 1970—the reactions to the Cambodian invasion, the killings at Kent State and Jackson State, the hard hat brutality in New York—were, for example, but surface manifestations of a deeper kind of anger arising from the whole nature of the times and not solely from the words or actions of a Nixon or a Johnson. It was an anger related to urban tensions, to racial revolutions and counter-revolutions, to bureaucratized universities, and not merely to an interventionist foreign policy.

This is not, as has been said, the proper place to diagnose the ills of an era. It is doubtful that the author could succeed if he tried. But the troubles of the times are relevant to the broader issue of the future viability of democratic traditions and processes. One of the several apparent roots of the contemporary crisis is the comfortable society. The first reaction to the new postwar abundance was to simply sit back, in smug contentment, and enjoy it. The new generation of the 1950s felt slightly bored, a bit intimidated by anti-Communist crusades, and still a little chastened by the recent depression and by new threats of an atomic war. It was annoyed with Harry Truman's persistence in trying to revive the New Deal and with the Supreme Court's disturbance of America's long tradition of apparent racial peace. With a retired hero as its reigning chief of state, there was superficial contentment. But such apathetic, half-fearful smugness could not last. Rich kids are soon spoiled. Material comfort ceased to satisfy the generation that followed. They refused to be contented with their overstuffed environment. Instead of keeping themselves properly occupied, consuming more and more of the world's goods, they began to demand a richer life in a quite different, nonmaterial sense. The underprivileged young people, centered in the Negro subculture, suffered from this same spoiling. It was not that they had much comfort or an overabundance of material goods, but rather that they, too, became captured by the revolution of rising expectations sweeping their world. The gains the Negro had made in the 1960s awakened him to potentialities for significant change. But he still found himself an outcast, lacking individual identity in the wider community. He shared only peripherally in the new richness of the country at large. He had excellent justification for being angry. Both blacks and youthful nonblacks were caught up in the same unhappiness despite the gulf that otherwise separated them. The crisis of abundance found its first confused expression in the younger generation and among Negroes.

With all of the foregoing in mind, it must be asked: can democracy withstand abundance? This is quite the opposite of the conventional question, which asked whether the poorer nations could become democratic before they had reached our own high state of economic advancement. It is historically obvious that western democracies were developed during an era of great economic progress, at least in the English-speaking world. A forward-moving kind of economic situation seems peculiarly compatible with the development of a democracy. But just as one can question the viability of democracy in a community sitting statically in poverty, an issue can be raised about those countries which seem to have "made it," wallowing in economic abundance rather than working for its achievement. Can democracy survive the very economic goal its community has been long working for? The question is so new that there is no place to go for a ready answer. This author remains tentatively optimistic, even though there are, in this day and age, numerous reasons to despair. On the basis of existing knowledge of history, our only real source of insight, there is still no conclusive evidence of impending doom. The existence of crisis is nothing new. If, however, there is truly a crisis created by the fact of abundance, it will clearly be an emergency of a new kind, with new tools needed to combat it.

Unfortunately, neither the concept of an abundant society, stressed in these pages, nor any other single analysis of contemporary problems will suffice. But whatever the fundamental causes of these problems (and they are bound to be multiple), the political consequences are often a bit frightening. Will a society that seems both spoiled and frustrated be sufficiently patient to tolerate the old-fashioned kind of democratic politics based on long-winded discourse and on the assumption that most differences can be compromised sufficiently for practical action? Signs of trouble are all around. Politics seems to have taken a turn toward the wild side. The unique campaigns of Barry Goldwater in 1964 and Eugene McCarthy in 1968, for example, brought fresh vigor to the political scene, but although both campaigns made spasmodically effective use of existing political mechanisms, there was also a strange naïveté concerning such processes. There was a bitter kind of anger when it was discovered that democratic mechanisms may not always lead to the triumph of a just cause. In these two instances, Americans were presented with candidates less propelled by ambition than by strength of conviction. Both were moderate men supported by followers more intense than themselves. Both sometimes showed a disdain for usual political tactics. Was this disdain itself a major element in their attractivenes? If political discourse, confrontation, and eventual compromise are at the heart of the democratic process, does the appearance of these (and other) movements imply a fundamental rebellion against basic democratic customs? It almost seems so, particularly when, as the 1970s arrived, there occurred a wave of political violence, which was countered by an increasing inclination toward suppressing unconventional means of protest. Democratic values such as free expression and other civil liberties can hardly survive when much of the community is so frustrated that compromise becomes something of a naughty word. Nor is such a mood of frustration, anger, and fear one from which constructive reform is likely to emerge. At the moment of this writing there is reason for those who are not themselves militantly angry to make every effort to protect their constitutional traditions, to preserve them for further times of stress ahead.

There have been, throughout the history of democracy, ever present reasons to fear for its future. But they have so far provided no convincing argument for relinquishing the conservative hope that the liberal tradition will see democracy through. Nor is there yet any convincing reason to reject all belief in progress—to reject a view of history that shows mankind as having advanced over a rough but eventually ascending path. Looking back, the tradition of western democracies seems to demonstrate that liberalism is a workable philosophy. The success of that tradition, as has been implied earlier, makes the democrat a conservative; he wants to hang on to what has already been achieved. The democratic view of history shows a trend toward freedom and toward increasing popular participation in communal decision-making. In wanting to continue that trend, the democrat becomes a moderate progressive. Optimism seems to be a crucial democratic attitude. It is the natural enemy of fanaticism. The fiercely moral soul, the angry man, young or old, who sees the world with no touch of humor, wanting to tear it all apart and reconstruct it on a model of perfected justice, is a threat to freedom even when he claims more perfect liberty as his objective. The democrat fears such revolutionary moralism as much as he fears the dictator who would be needed to execute it. He knows that revolution normally concludes its process by postponing liberty for the sake of an ultimate, great cause. The democrat is a gradualist because he is an optimist and because human freedom is his highest moral value.

If the democrat is an optimist, a man of faith, it is because he trusts his fellow men. He assumes his colleagues to be fair and honest until there is specific evidence of evil, rather than the other way around. Democracy relies on trust. There is no substitute for it. General fear of one's fellow creatures is inherently antidemocratic. Democracy must assume a general human capacity for fair dealing; it must operate through a process of compromise; it must base its procedures on trust, even though it takes a few precautions to guard itself against the occasional bad apple. Without this optimistic trust, the democrat could not want other men to be free. He could not want them to participate in decisions that will deeply affect his own life. The democrat assumes that free communication among individuals and their organized groupings is essential for reaching communal agreement, and he assumes that such communication can only rest on a substantial degree of respect for one's fellow man.

The democrat may find comfort in history and solace in personal experience of dealings with his fellow men, but part of his belief must rest upon an intuitive kind of optimism. Experience may help to convince him that democracy is workable, but there are times when empirical evidence is insufficient. It is crucial, at such vital moments, that the democrat also be a man of faith.

Bibliographical Notes

CHAPTER 1

The proper study of man begins with history. So, too, with democracy. There can be no understanding of the purposes and processes of a free and participatory society without knowledge of the evolution of concepts of freedom and knowledge of the practices of parliamentary, constitutional government. No student of democracy can ignore the political and legal history of Great Britain, nor can he properly escape concern with the American branch of that development. It would also be downright foolishness not to be well informed regarding the particular historical difficulties created by the French Revolution for continental democracy. Historical study of as many democracies as possible should be followed by a country-by-country examination of present-day forms and practices or, perhaps, by a reading of a cross-national survey of democratic processes such as that by Dell G. Hitchner and William H. Harbold, *Modern Government* (New York: Dodd, Mead, rev. ed., 1965) or Leslie Lipson, *The Democratic Civilization* (New York: Oxford, 1964).

Moving from such beginnings in history and in comparative analysis, the reader might direct his aim toward more general political theory, sources for which are almost endless. A particularly valuable source of theory is the recent, rather monumental, effort of a scholar who has devoted a lifetime to the analysis of political behavior, Carl J. Friedrich's *Man and His Government* (New York: McGraw-Hill, 1963). The very breadth of Friedrich's view, his concern with value questions, and the length of his experience in political analysis, make his book atypical of the latest fashion in academic writing. There is, however, no safe way to designate the typical contemporary theorist since fashions now change so rapidly. One of the most accepted of this generation of writers, a modernist who is deeply concerned with the nature of democracy, is Robert A. Dahl. The reader might wish to supplement a reading of Friedrich with Dahl's short book on *Modern Political Analysis* (Englewood Cliffs, N.J.: Prentice-Hall, rev. ed., 1970).

Critics of democracy have made a special contribution to democratic analysis by poking vast holes in the more simplistic notions of democracy. One clear statement of the weakness of what Joseph Schumpeter calls "the classical" view is in chapters 20 to 30 of his *Capitalism, Socialism, and Democracy* (New York: Harper, rev. ed., 1947). A recent, elitist view of American politics that helps to shatter ancient myths is that by Thomas R. Dye and L. Harmon Zeigler, *The Irony of Democracy* (Belmont, Calif.: Wadsworth, 1970). For a survey of some American antidemocrats out of our older tradition, read David Spitz, *Patterns of Anti-Democratic Thought* (New York: Macmillan, 1949). The flamboyant James Burnham has written a lively review of European critiques of populistic notions of democracy in *The Machiavellians* (New York: John Day, 1943). For the sake of wit and perversity, the reader might also enjoy the curmudgeonly grumbles of Henry L. Mencken in *Notes on Democracy* (New York: Knopf, 1926).

Views of democracy that provide a contrast with those of the author are of obvious value for any reader who begins his reading with this book. An economist-oriented perspective is provided by Anthony Downs, *An Economic Theory of Democracy* (New York: Harper, 1957). A writer who sees democracy as an effort "to associate concrete data with reckonable numbers and to treat them by quantitative methods," is Marie Swabey in *Theory of the Democratic State* (Cambridge: Harvard University Press, 1937). The concept of the majority as a concrete entity that must somehow rule is still alive, or at least it was in 1967 when Willmoore Kendall wrote an article, with George W. Carey as coauthor, entitled, "The Intensity Problem and Democratic Theory" in *The American Political Science Review* (hereafter cited as *APSR*) (vol. 62, March 1968). More typical of his argument is the book he earlier wrote with Austin Ranney, *Democracy and the American Party System* (New York: Harcourt, Brace, 1956). In some ways, Henry B. Mayo's *Introduction to Democratic Theory* (New York: Oxford University Press, 1960) follows this same view of democratic processes.

Moving to general works on democracy that supplement this author's views more than they contrast with it, the foremost names that come to mind are Giovanni Sartori and Robert Dahl. Although Sartori's work is definitional in approach, it is much broader than its original title, *Democrazia e Definizione,* might imply. The American edition, translated by the author, is called *Democratic Theory* (Detroit: Wayne State University Press, 1962). Equally sophisticated but close to the contemporary tradition in American analysis is the book Professor Dahl wrote with Charles Lindblom, *Politics, Economics, and Welfare* (New York: Harper, 1953) and Dahl's *Preface to Democratic Theory* (Chicago: University of Chicago Press, 1956). J. Roland Pennock has valuable ideas concerning democratic processes. They are best explored through some of his short articles, such as "Responsiveness, Responsibility, and Majority Rule," *APSR* (vol. 46, September 1952) and his "Democracy and Leadership," in William Chambers and Robert Salisbury, eds., *Democracy in the Mid-Twentieth Century* (Saint Louis: Washington University Press, 1960). Highly useful analyses by non-specialists, that is, by men who do not call themselves political scientists, are Charles Frankel's *Democratic Prospect* (New York: Harper, 1962) and an article by John Cogley, "Notes Toward a Definition of Democracy," in *Center Diary* (No. 16, January–February 1967). A cultural and psychological orientation to democratic theory is provided in Zevedei Barbu's *Democracy and Dictatorship* (New York: Grove Press, 1956). Professor C. W. Cassinelli presents a set of propositions that are valuable because of their boldness, creating the beginning point for healthy discussion, in his *Politics of Freedom* (Seattle: University of Washington Press, 1961). It is also useful to turn back to a somewhat older generation, to the continuingly useful ideas of Robert M. MacIver and John Dewey. Both MacIver's *Web of Government* (New York: Macmillan, 1947) and Dewey's *Public and Its Problems* (New York: Holt, 1927) are still available.

Turning now to some of the specific topics included in the first chapter, the idea of liberty overwhelms the bibliographer. This is why Mortimer Adler performed a useful function when he provided us with *The Idea of Freedom* (Garden City, N.Y.: Doubleday, 2 vols., 1958, 1961), a good catalogue for beginning the exploration of the concept. For a recent symposium on freedom and on equality, the reader will gain from examining two volumes in the excellent Nomos Series (both published in New York by Atherton Press). Carl Friedrich edited the 1962 volume on *Liberty* and Roland Pennock and John Chapman the 1967 volume on *Equality.* Since Hannah Arendt is so significant as a contemporary social thinker, it would be well to read her chapter on "What Is Freedom?" in *Between Past and Future* (New York: Viking, 1961). If there is interest in further discussion of the relation between freedom as self-fulfillment and concepts of maturity, one might begin by examining Marie Jahoda's survey of *Current Concepts of Positive Mental Health* (New York: Basic Books, 1958).

Histories of political thought will provide surveys of the development of liberal ideas. The text of this book mentions Frederick Watkins in particular because his *Political Tradition of the West* (Cambridge: Harvard University Press, 1948) has this as a specific goal. It helps to reduce the provincialism of the American concept of liberalism to understand the European view as outlined in Guido de Ruggiero's *History of European Liberalism* (New York: Oxford University Press, 1927), translated by R. G. Collingwood. A convenient source on American liberalism is Louis Hartz, *Liberal Tradition in America* (New York: Harcourt, Brace, 1955). Examples of commentaries on contemporary liberalism include Theodore J. Lowi, *The End of Liberalism* (New York: Norton, 1969) and Robert A. Goldwin, ed., *Left, Right and Center* (Chicago: Rand McNally, 1967).

The issue of the practicality and feasibility of democracy under varying environmental conditions and particularly in the new nations might begin with history of well-established democracies. Having done that, one can turn to a number of works which relate free societies to their environments. The first that comes to mind is David M. Potter's *People of Plenty* (Chicago: University of Chicago Press, 1954). Seymour Lipset has an article on this issue in the *APSR* for March 1959 (vol. 53), entitled "Some Social Requisites of Democracy" and has written a book entitled *The First New Nation* (New York: Basic Books, 1963), although some of the latter book is less relevant to this question than its title might imply. Professors Ernest Griffith, Roland Pennock, and John Plamenatz joined in a symposium on cultural requisites of democracy in the *APSR* for March 1956 (vol. 50). A flood of materials has, quite naturally, arisen out of concern with those new nations formed since World War II. To mention but a few, shorter, general sources, there is Rupert Emerson, *From Empire to Nation* (Cambridge: Harvard University Press, 1950); William McCord, *Springtime of Freedom* (New York: Oxford University Press, 1965); and Gabriel Almond and Bingham Powell, *Comparative Politics: A Developmental Approach* (Boston: Little, Brown, 1966).

CHAPTER 2

On the general topic of the nature and functions of government there is no substitute for the classics. The issues raised by Hobbes, Locke, and Rousseau in particular are by no means antique, despite their use of the social-contract idiom. On the matter of the leadership function, it may be well to begin not with works directly aimed at that subject but at books concerned with public reactions to leadership, on the assumption that leadership is tested by such reactions. This being the case, a particularly useful source is the work of V. O. Key, Jr., *Public Opinion and American Democracy* (New York: Knopf, 1961), a book highly conscious of the leadership factor, despite its title. A productive approach, but one that requires some sophistication on the part of the reader, is through the use of biographical-historical writings concerning supposedly great leaders. It is obvious that an admiring author can, despite his love for the hero of his story, provide insight into the nature of leadership. For example, an author such as Arthur Schlesinger, Jr., can, with proper reading, be helpful in such a book as *The Age of Jackson* (Boston: Little, Brown, 1945) or even in a more recent period such as with *The Age of Roosevelt* (Boston: Houghton Mifflin, 3 vols., 1957, 1959, 1960); but much more critical reading is required when he speaks as an alleged insider in his review of the Kennedy administration entitled *A Thousand Days* (Boston: Houghton Mifflin, 1965). All such works require considerable sophistication on the part of the reader, but this is somewhat less a problem with case studies unless, as in the instance of Robert Kennedy's *Thirteen Days* (New York: Norton, 1969), they are authored by a member of "the team." Case studies by outsiders are concerned with all aspects of the event, not directly or solely with leadership abilities of the actors; hence there is less chance of built-in bias. One good example is Louis Koenig's "Kennedy and Steel," in Alan F. Westin, ed., *Centers of Power* (New York: Harcourt, Brace, 1963). A happy compromise among recent works is that by Richard Neustadt. Although near the center of power during much of the postwar period, he retains his aloofness and yet makes full use of the case method in the original version of *Presidential Power* (New York:Wiley, 1960). He has more difficulty, however, when he adds an addendum on the puzzling Kennedy era in the 1968 paperback version.

Moving to works that attempt to deal directly with the general subject of leadership, the quantity of useful sources seems relatively small. It might be well to begin by repeating an earlier reference to Roland Pennock's article on "Democracy and Leadership" in *Democracy in the Mid-Twentieth Century* (Saint Louis: Washington University Press, 1960). Other useful essays are found in Alvin Gouldner, ed., *Studies in Leadership* (New York: Harper, 1950), as well as in complete issues devoted to the subject by *The Annals* for September 1959 (vol. 325) and by *Daedelus* (vol. 90, autumn 1961). Chester I. Barnard's *Functions of the Executive* (Cambridge: Harvard University Press, 1937) remains a source of productive ideas, as do some other works on administration and organization. For example, see Victor Thompson, *Modern Organization* (New York: Knopf, 1961). The phenomenon of leadership may be approached through books on political power. Recent examples include one book by a leading sociologist, Arnold Rose, *The Power Structure* (New York: Oxford University Press, 1967), and a somewhat uneven work by a political practitioner who is also a student of economic power, Adolph A. Berle, *Power* (New York: Harcourt, Brace, 1969). Several decades ago there were more such works on power, among whose authors Harold Lasswell gained a notable reputation. Another tangential perspective, an approach from a direction opposite of that in the case study, is through community studies. Robert A. Dahl's *Who Governs?* (New Haven: Yale University Press, 1964) or Robert Presthus' *Men at the Top* (New York: Oxford University Press, 1964) are good examples because both are much concerned with the theory of leadership. A dialogue in which Dahl defends his concern with leadership elements in democracy against an attack by Professor Jack L. Walker may, incidentally, be read in the *APSR* for June 1966 (vol. 60). And, finally, it is essential to mention the classic study by Max Weber on types of authority, from which has come the much-confused idea of charisma. A. M. Henderson and Talcott Parsons have compiled (and translated) many of his ideas in *The Theory of Social and Economic Organization* (New York: Oxford University Press, 1947).

CHAPTER 3

If one wishes to begin the examination of the participatory aspects of democracy with two sharply contrasting viewpoints, he could examine the works of Jose Ortega y Gassett and Carl Friedrich. Ortega views the public as a vast conglomerate in *Revolt of the Masses* (New York: Norton, 1932), whereas Friedrich tried to revive a lost faith in the democratic everyman in an early work entitled *New Belief in the Common Man* (published by the author at Brattleboro, Vermont, 1942). As with so many topics of this essay, most of the major thinkers from Plato to the contemporary period have addressed themselves to the problems of the community and the individual's role in it. Among recent works, one might examine Robert A. Nisbet's *Community and Power* (first entitled *Quest for Community*) (New York: Oxford University Press, 1953) or two relevant volumes in the valuable Nomos

Series, both edited by its founder, Professor Friedrich: the 1959 volume on *Community* (New York: Liberal Arts Press) and the 1962 volume on *The Public Interest* (New York, Atherton).

It is wise to make use of the work of the pollsters in uncovering a few clues as to attitudes and behavior of the broad community. Again the reader can find long bibliographies of published reports assessing public competence, activism, and attitudes. A major producer of such survey materials is the Michigan Survey group, working under Angus Campbell and others. A recent example of one of their compilations is entitled *Elections and the Political Order* (New York: Wiley, 1966). A book that combines the reports of such survey work with a helpful general analysis of implications for democracy in its final chapter is entitled simply, *Voting;* it is the work of Bernard Berleson, Paul Lazarsfeld, and William McPhee (Chicago: University of Chicago Press, 1954). A comparative survey of public attitudes in various free societies is especially useful for the student of democracy; one such work is *The Civic Culture* (Princeton: Princeton University Press, 1963), compiled by Gabriel Almond and Sidney Verba. V. O. Key's previously mentioned work on *Public Opinion and American Democracy* is an example of political analysis that utilizes the results of pollster efforts, sometimes a bit too uncritically but generally with excellent results. Also valuable is Key's short, posthumous work, *The Responsible Electorate* (Cambridge: Harvard University Press, 1966). Other books concerned with what goes on in the minds of the public participants of the American democracy include Robert E. Lane's *Political Life* (Glencoe, Ill.: Free Press, 1959) and his *Political Ideology* (New York: Free Press, 1962). Also see Seymour M. Lipset, *Political Man* (Garden City, N.Y.: Doubleday, 1960); Murray B. Levin, *The Alienated Voter* (New York: Holt, 1961); and a now almost antique book by David Reisman, Nathan Glazer, and Reuel Denny, *The Lonely Crowd* (New Haven: Yale University Press, 1950).

Few authors have written concerning the nature of humor and even fewer in regard to its social and political significance. It is a slippery concept. Zevedei Barbu is an exception; see his *Democracy and Dictatorship* (New York: Grove Press, 1956). Other writings are seldom society-minded. For example, see Norman Brown's neo-Freudian *Life Against Death* (Middletown, Conn.: Wesleyan University Press, 1959); Stephen Leacock's insightful but lighthearted *Humor and Humanity* (New York: Holt, 1938); and Johan Huizinga's concern with the related concept of play in *Homo Ludens* (Boston: Beacon Press, 1955).

More has been written about rationality than about humor, perhaps because it has been of inevitable concern to self-examining intellectuals and of more obvious concern for democratic decision-making. Again the Nomos Series presents a symposium on the subject in its 1964 edition under the editorship of Carl Friedrich, *Rational Decision* (New York: Atherton, 1964). Herbert Simon was concerned with rationality in his *Administrative Behavior* (New York: Macmillan, 1945), and Charles Lindblom has written extensively on the subject. See his recent paperback on *The Policy-Making Process* (Englewood Cliffs, N.J.: Prentice-Hall, 1968) as well as two earlier works: *Intelligence of Democracy* (New York: Free Press, 1965) and (with Robert Dahl) *Politics, Economics and Welfare* (New York: Harper, 1953).

CHAPTER 4

References made above with regard to voting behavior in connection with democracy as participation in Chapter 3 are, of course, relevant in connection with Chapter 4 as well. But a few other works, concerned with voting as a logical or not-so-logical process need to be added. For example, see James M. Buchanan and Gordon Tullock, *The Calculus of Consent* (Ann Arbor, Mich.: University of Michigan Press, 1962) and Anthony Downs, *An Economic Theory of Democracy* (New York: Harper, 1957). The views of sociologists differ somewhat from those of an economist. A distinguished member of that clan, Talcott Parsons, has contributed to the discussion of voter behavior in a chapter of a generally useful book by Eugene Burdick and Arthur Brodbeck, eds., *American Voting Behavior* (Glencoe, Ill.: Free Press, 1959). More traditional concerns in regard to electoral systems are discussed in W. J. M. Mackenzie in *Free Elections* (London: Allen & Unwin, 1958) and Gerald Pomper, *Elections in America* (New York: Dodd, Mead, 1968).

Concern with the use of elections as a mandate for policy-making has close relation to the issue of disciplined party government, a question also discussed in Chapter 5. Hence, some of the relevant publications will be listed in that section of the bibliography. For sources that center almost entirely on the mandate or responsible-party issue, one might begin with the now famous (or infamous) supplement to the *APSR* of September 1950 (vol. 44), written by a committee under E. E. Schattschneider, and to articles in succeeding issues that attack or defend that report. A few years later Austin Ranney produced a monograph entitled *The Doctrine of Responsible Party Government* (Urbana, Ill.: University of Illinois Press, 1954). A strong defense of the existing weak

American party system is found in Pendleton Herring's *Politics of Democracy* (New York: Rinehart, 1940) and in a more recent article by Edward Banfield in the symposium edited by Robert Goldwin as *Political Parties, U.S.A.* (Chicago: Rand McNally, 1964). Ivor Jennings deals with the British history of mandates in parliamentary elections in *Cabinet Government* (Cambridge: At the University Press, 2nd ed., 1951). On the closely related concept of consent see C. W. Cassinelli's article in *The Western Political Quarterly* (vol. 12, June 1959) and Hannah Pitkin on the consent theory of obligation in two issues of the *APSR* (vols. 59 and 60, December 1965 and March 1966). Analyses of the idea of representation are sometimes also relevant to this issue, and a few such references are found below in connection with Chapter 6.

Several political analysts focus considerably more on the equalitarian aspects of democracy than does this author. For contrast, therefore, the reader might wish at least to examine Harold Laski's article on "Democracy" in the *Encyclopedia of the Social Sciences* (New York: Macmillan, 1947). More recent discussions of equality occur in Sanford A. Lakoff's *Equality in Political Philosophy* (Cambridge: Harvard University Press, 1964) and in the 1967 edition of Nomos, edited by Pennock and Chapman and entitled *Equality* (New York: Atherton, 1967).

On the issue of popular sovereignty and majority rule, a number of academic as well as popular writings refer to the majority as a specific political force that can make policy or tyrannize the minority. Among the earlier modern writers who used the concept in this manner was J. Allen Smith, who spoke of "the will of the majority" in *The Spirit of American Government* (New York: Macmillan, 1911). The "domination of the majority" is spoken of in Hans Kelsen's long article, "Foundations of Democracy," in a special supplement to the October 1955 edition of the journal, *Ethics* (vol. 46). The leading majoritarian among recent academicians was, however, the late Willmoore Kendall. Reference has already been made to his final journal article entitled, "The Intensity Problem and Democratic Theory," in the March 1968 *APSR* and to the textbook he composed with Austin Ranney on *Democracy and the American Party System* (New York: Harcourt, Brace, 1956). He also wrote a monograph on *John Locke and the Doctrine of Majority Rule* (Urbana, Ill.: University of Illinois Press, 1941) and an article entitled "Prolegomena to Any Future Work on Majority Rule," *Journal of Politics* (vol. 12, November 1950). This last work was in rebuttal to an earlier article by Herbert McClosky in the same journal (vol. 11, November 1949) on "The Fallacy of Absolute Majority Rule."

CHAPTER 5

Few contemporary works on public opinion are anything like a match for V. O. Key's *Public Opinion and American Democracy* (New York: Knopf, 1961), but Walter Lippmann's early effort on the subject, *Public Opinion* (New York: Macmillan, 1922), is still worth reading, and there is a short paperback by the same title by Robert Lane and David Sears (Englewood Cliffs, N.J.: Prentice-Hall, 1964). An earlier student of democracy who stressed the discourse aspect was Walter Bagehot; see his *Physics and Politics,* published in 1869 but reissued in 1948 (New York, Knopf). There has been a steady flow of reading materials on the media of communication, which has flowed even more heavily since the growth of television. The issue is both lively and current and in need of much more analysis by those concerned primarily with the implications for modern democracy. See R. Fagen, *Politics and Communication* (Boston: Little, Brown, 1966) and also several articles reprinted in recent issues of *Current* magazine: one by Charles Reich in the issue of June 1965, and others by A. M. Rosenthal and Areyh Neier in the issue of February 1969.

The problem of free expression takes on a valuable concreteness when actual cases provide the focus of discussion. The members of the United States Supreme Court, have, since World War I, been forced to address themselves to both practical and theoretical aspects of the subject. The views of Justices Frankfurter and Stone provide a good example of the nature of the restrictionist versus libertarian positions in *Minersville School District* v. *Gobitis* (310 U.S. 586 [1940]). The most famous contemporary libertarian is Justice Hugo Black, whose views have proven more sophisticated than some of his admirers once thought. In *Barenblatt* v. *U.S.* (360 U.S. 109 [1959]) he argues that the First Amendment protects the interest of the whole community, not simply the persecuted party. *Cox* v. *Louisiana* (379 U.S. 536 [1965]) exemplifies his distinction between speech and conduct. His so-called absolutist view of free expression is clarified in an interview with Edmund Cahn, published in the *New York University Law Review* (vol. 37, June 1962). It should, of course, be added that the pioneer judicial exponents of free expression were Justices Holmes and Brandeis, whose ideas are well expressed in *Gitlow* v. *New York* (268 U.S. 652 [1925]).

Most American writers on political parties have been aware that they were dealing with an institution that is particularly central to the democratic process and hence, even when not discussing democracy directly, college texts are valuable references for the student of a working democracy. Major textbooks such as those by Hugh Bone, V. O. Key, and Frank Sorauf are all useful in this respect. The latest edition of these three authors' works are respectively entitled: *American Politics and the Party System* (New York: McGraw-Hill, 3rd ed., 1965); *Politics, Parties, and Pressure Groups* (New York: Crowell, 5th ed., 1964); and *Party Politics in America* (Boston: Little, Brown, 1968). A more lighthearted but thoroughly analytical bit of writing on the subject is Clinton Rossiter's *Parties and Politics in America* (Ithaca, N.Y.: Cornell University Press, 1960). As the pages of this essay note, E. E. Schattschneider was something of a pioneer in the development of a theory of parties in his *Party Government* (New York: Rinehart, 1942). For comparative analyses, see Maurice Duverger, *Political Parties,* translated by Barbara and Robert North (New York: Wiley, 1954), and Leon Epstein, *Political Parties in Western Democracies* (New York: Praeger, 1967). Richard Rose writes a comparative analysis of politics and politicians in the United States and Great Britain in *People in Politics* (New York: Basic Books, 1970).

CHAPTER 6

It is, somehow, more difficult to abstract and theorize concerning the democratic policy process; at least, efforts so far seem particularly remote and esoteric. A few attempts are listed above as sources of reference for Chapter 3. Possibly the best approach is still through the examination of case studies that report particular policy developments. Such cases are the source of theories the reader can develop on his own. Many cases are published as separate books, but the reader may prefer to start with collections such as the two books edited by Alan F. Westin: *Uses of Power* and *Centers of Power* (New York: Harcourt, Brace, 1962 and 1964). Also useful are Rocco J. Tresolini and Richard T. Frost, eds., *Cases in American National Government and Politics* (Englewood Cliffs, N.J.: Prentice-Hall, 1966); James Christoph, ed., *Cases in Comparative Politics* (Boston: Little, Brown, 1965); and Gwendolyn Carter and Alan Westin, eds., *Politics in Europe* (New York: Harcourt, Brace, 1965). A long list of separately published cases is available through the Inter-University Case Program, published by Bobbs-Merrill in Indianapolis.

The present author contends that governmental structure is a significant element in the success of democratic ideas, but books aimed at the general subject are rarer than one might have suspected. Much is written on federalism, an important aspect of division of powers but less on the general topic. Examples of such general analyses include two

British publications: Douglas Verney, *The Analysis of Political Systems* (London: Routledge & Kegan Paul, 1959) and M. J. C. Vile, *Constitutionalism and the Separation of Powers* (London: Oxford University Press, 1967). The primary source continues to be standard textbooks on the governments of various democracies and such comparative analyses as Carl Friedrich's *Constitutional Government and Democracy* (Waltham, Mass.: Blaisdell, 1968). Among more recent nontextbook discussions by American writers are Morton Grodzins, *The American System* (Chicago: Rand McNally, 1966); Arthur N. Holcombe, *The Constitutional System* (Chicago: Scott Foreman, 1964); and an article by Martin Diamond in *The Public Interest* for autumn 1965 called "Conservatives, Liberals and the Constitution." On federalism, see K. C. Wheare, *Federal Government* (New York: Oxford University Press, 4th ed., 1963); Daniel Elazar, *American Federalism* (New York: Crowell, 1966); and Robert Goldwin, ed., *A Nation of States* (Chicago: Rand McNally, 1963).

The 1962 and 1964 Supreme Court decisions on reapportionment opened a flooodgate for writings on representation. A few works need mention here. Directly related to reapportionment but including some general concern with theories of representation are: Gordon Baker, *Reapportionment Revolution* (New York: Ramdon House, 1966); Robert McKay, *Reapportionment* (New York: Twentieth Century Fund, 1965); and Robert G. Dixon, *Democratic Representation* (New York: Oxford University Press, 1968). An author with a long-term interest in the nature of democratic representation and provocative ideas concerning apportionment is Alfred de Grazia. His early book on the general subject is entitled *Public and Republic* (New York: Knopf, 1951), and his reaction to the reapportionment cases is presented in *Apportionment and Representative Government* (New York: Praeger, 1963). Professor Robert Goldwin presents a Kenyon College symposium on this topic of the same high quality as other books edited by him and mentioned heretofore. This one is called *Representation and Misrepresentation* (Chicago: Rand McNally, 1968). Recent discussions less tied to apportionment are Joseph Tussman, *Obligation and the Body Politic* (New York: Oxford University Press, 1960) and Hannah Pitkin, *The Concept of Representation* (Berkeley: University of California Press, 1967). See also her two articles on "Obligation and Consent" in the *APSR* (vols. 59 and 60, December 1965 and March 1966). The Nomos Series has again collected articles on this subject in its 1968 edition edited by Professors Pennock and Chapman: *Representation* (New York: Atherton, 1968).

On the whole question of access to the policy process and the group theory, one must start with Arthur Bentley, whose *Process of Government* was first published in 1908. (My edition is printed at the Principia Press, Bloomington, Indiana, 1935.) David Truman's more recent and less doctrinaire version is entitled *The Governmental Process* (New York: Knopf, 1958). Other group-oriented writings include Earl Latham, *The Group Basis of Politics* (Ithaca, N.Y.: Cornell University Press, 1952) and Bertram Gross, *The Legislative Struggle* (New York: McGraw-Hill, 1953). If one wishes to note the parallels between the group theory and the balance-of-power concept he might examine Hans Morgenthau for analysis of the latter in *Politics Among Nations* (New York: Knopf, rev. ed., 1967). Among commentaries on the group theory is an article by David G. Smith, "Pragmatism and the Group Theory," in the *APSR* (vol. 58, September 1964); a symposium edited by R. E. Dowling, Myron Q. Hale, and Robert T. Golembiewski in the same journal for December 1960 (vol. 54); and articles by Oliver Garceau and Alfred de Grazia in *The Annals* for September 1959 (vol. 319). Contrasting critiques of the theory are found in David Easton's *The Political System* (New York: Knopf, 1953) and in Louis Hartz's *The Liberal Tradition in America* (New York: Harcourt, Brace, 1955). Theodore Lowi's provocative *End of Liberalism* (New York: Norton, 1969) is highly critical of an ideology he believes to have resulted from this group theory, something he calls "interest-group liberalism." Other recent discussions of the pluralist approach include George D. Beam, *Usual Politics* (New York: Holt, Rinehart, & Winston, 1970) and an article by Darryl Baskin on "American Pluralism" in *The Journal of Politics* (vol. 32, February 1970). Recent among books dealing with American power groups is that by R. Joseph Monsen and Mark Cannon, *Makers of Public Policy* (New York: McGraw-Hill, 1965). The role of interest groups in other nations is discussed in Samuel H. Beer, "Representation of Interests in British Government," *APSR* (vol. 41, September 1957) and in a collection edited by Henry W. Ehrmann under the title of *Interest Groups on Four Continents* (Pittsburgh: University of Pittsburgh Press, 1958). The intensity factor is discussed by Robert Dahl in his *Preface to Democratic Theory* (Chicago: University of Chicago Press, 1956).

On the issue of accountability and control there is another volume, edited by Professor Friedrich, in the Nomos Series, this one entitled *Responsibility* and published in 1960 (New York, Liberal Arts Press). Chester Barnard's critique of a book by Charles S. Hyneman and the ideas in that book itself present a useful dialogue on the problems of responsibility; see *APSR* (vol. 44, December 1950) and *Bureaucracy in a Democracy* (New York: Harper, 1950). The problem of expertise in a democracy has been the source of much discussion. One might start with an unusually lively government document that provides a compendium of comments on the subject; see *Specialists and Generalists* (90th Congress, 2nd Session, Washington: G.P.O., 1968). Virtually all texts on public administration deal with problems of accountability. Particularly notable is the book on *Public Administration* by Herbert Simon, Donald Smithburg, and Victor Thompson (New York: Knopf, 1950). Robert Merton and others have collected useful writings on bureaucracy in a *Reader on Bureaucracy* (Glencoe, Ill.: Free Press, 1952), including writings from Max Weber up to the recent past. More contemporary works include: Robert Presthus, *The Organizational Society* (New York: Knopf, 1962); Victor Thompson, *Modern Organization* (New York: Knopf, 1961); Anthony Downs, *Inside Bureaucracy* (Boston: Little, Brown, 1967); and Peter Blau, *Bureaucracy in Modern Society* (New York: Random House, 1956).

CHAPTER 7

It now appears that the idea of natural law, much refurbished, is less dead than sometimes presumed. Recent discussions of the virtue of a revival include an article by Raghavan N. Iyer in *Center Diary* (No. 16, January–February 1967) as well as a pamphlet by Robert Hutchins *et al.*, from the same Center for the Study of Democratic Institutions, entitled *Two Faces of Federalism* (Santa Barbara, Calif., 1961). Walter Lippmann takes a similar position, in effect, when he speaks of the values of "traditions of civility" in his *Public Philosophy* (Boston: Little, Brown, 1955). Speaking in relation to consensus, the liberal Catholic theologian, John Courtney Murray, appears to be making a closely related argument in *We Hold These Truths* (New York: Sheed & Ward, 1960). But consensus has a different, more directly operational meaning for most contemporary political scientists. Useful discussions of that concept are found in V. O. Key's *Public Opinion and American Democracy* (New York: Knopf, 1961); Carl Friedrich's *Man and His Government* (New York: McGraw-Hill, 1963); and Professors James Prothro and Charles Grigg in "Fundamental Principles of Democracy," *APSR* (vol. 22, May 1960).

Although concern with the virtues of ancient ideas such as natural law and contemporary concepts such as consensus is not shared by all writers who delve into purposes and processes of democracy, there is a widespread assumption that underlying values have an important role in the democratic system. Gunnar Myrdal made a practical exposition of the risks of inconsistencies in such values in his famous *American Dilemma* (New York: Harper, 1944). John Hallowell stresses the necessity of a *Moral Foundation of Democracy* in his book by that title (Chicago: University of Chicago Press, 1954). All books that place great value on the liberal tradition, such as those already mentioned by Frederick Watkins and Louis Hartz, are, in effect, emphasizing the crucial importance of deeply imbedded value concepts to democratic processes.

Although all too many writers concerned with processes tend to ignore the behavioral significance of legal concepts for the political animal, there remains a substantial body of literature of recent vintage relevant to constitutionalism. For short studies on the subject, see Edward S. Corwin, *Higher Law Background of American Constitutional Law* (Ithaca, N.Y.: Cornell University Press, 1955) and Charles S. McIlwain, *Constitutionalism: Ancient and Modern* (Ithaca, N.Y.: Cornell University Press, 1947). And, once again, it is essential to list some of Carl Friedrich's relevant writings: his older book, *Constitutional Government and Democracy* (Waltham, Mass.: Blaisdell, 1968); the more recent *Man and His Government* (New York: McGraw-Hill, 1963); and, in a related vein, his *Philosophy of Law in Historical Perspective* (Chicago: University of Chicago Press, 2nd ed., 1963). The reader should probably also be reminded of the recent writing of another senior political analyst, Arthur N. Holcombe, whose *Constitutional System* (Chicago: Scott Foresman, 1964) emphasizes the importance of law for American democracy.

One of the major sources of confusion concerning the democratic process and the proper relation of legal elements to operational political processes is a result of failure to keep in mind the intricate relationships of formal and informal elements and the major significance of each. The distinction is well defined by writers concerned with administration and organization, such as F. J. Roethlisberger in an article entitled "The Foreman" in the *Harvard Business Review* (vol. 23, spring 1945); by Chester Barnard in *Functions of the Executive* (Cambridge: Harvard University Press, 1937); and by Simon, Smithburg, and Thompson in *Public Administration* (New York: Knopf, 1950).

The problem of meeting crisis and emergency conditions and at the same time preventing the governors who are responsible for solving such problems from being converted into tyrants is discussed in a historical perspective by Clinton Rossiter in his *Constitutional Dictatorship* (Princeton: Princeton University Press, 1948). But the best source for understanding the problems is again found in the words of Supreme Court justices forced to deal with concrete cases according to constitutional rules. *Korematsu* v. *U.S.* (323 U.S. 214 [1944]) on World War II

Japanese relocation camps is a good modern example. But long ago the Court was forced to discuss the fundamentals of limited government in *Calder* v. *Bull* (3 Dall 386 [1789]). The nature and problems of emergency power are also analyzed in such cases as *Home Building and Loan* v. *Blaisdell* (290 U.S. 398 [1934]) and the *Steel Seizure* case (343 U.S. 579 [1952]).

When discussing the problems of judicial review, it is eminently sensible to obtain the court's own views, starting traditionally with *Marbury* v. *Madison* (1 Cranch 137 [1803]). To offset the expansionist view of the judicial function expressed therein by Chief Justice Marshall, one might read the restrictionist views of Justice Frankfurter in, for example, *Dennis* v. *U.S.* (341 U.S. 494 [1951]) or *Rochin* v. *California* (343 U.S. 165 [1952]). A restatement in modern language of the traditional Marshall argument for judicial review is found in Charles L. Black's *The People and the Court* (New York: Macmillan, 1960). The list of books on judicial review is almost endless, but one recent, short work might also be mentioned: Howard E. Dean's *Judicial Review and Democracy* (New York: Random House, 1966).

Students of democracy have often concerned themselves with the proper environment for establishment and development of a free society but have dealt less often with new environmental trends to which established democracies must adapt. The specialized and esoteric nature of much social science writing makes the search of professional journals for insight into contemporary problems somewhat of a disappointment. One journal that brings professional opinion to bear on contemporary issues is *The Public Interest*. Also useful for its reprinting of scattered articles on contemporary issues is *Current* magazine. Publications of the Center for the Study of Democratic Institutions in Santa Barbara, California, are sometimes a provocative source of ideas on current democratic problems. Three Center pamphlets closely relevant to the subject of democracy and the affluent, technological society are Walter Weisskopf and Raghavan Iyer, *Looking Forward: The Abundant Society* (1966); John Wilkinson *et al.*, *Technology and Human Values* (1966); and Wilkinson's *The Quantitative Society* (1964). Similar essays inspired by the Santa Barbara Center are found in a book edited by Edward Reed, *Challenges to Democracy* (New York: Praeger, 1963).

Among available books that have relevance to the issues of democracy and the environment of affluence and technology is a historical study by David M. Potter, *People of Plenty* (Chicago: University of Chicago Press, 1954). Lewis Mumford has had a lifelong concern with the effects of technology and a long list of books to his credit. Perhaps the most useful approach, however, is his historical survey in *The City in History* (New York: Harcourt, Brace, 1961). Older writers concerned with effects of affluence are Thorstein Veblen and R. H. Tawney. *The Portable Veblen,* edited by Max Lerner (New York: Viking, 1958), will give the reader a sample of the thinking of that author, and some of Tawney's ideas may be read in *The Acquisitive Society* (London: Bell, 1921). Among contemporary critics of the comfortable society, a quite dismal view is presented by Andrew Hacker in *The End of the American Era* (New York: Atheneum, 1970). What might be called a humanist-radical position is taken by Eric Fromm in *The Sane Society* (New York: Rinehart, 1955). Harvey Wheeler relates the problems of democracy to the general one of achieving a world order in *Democracy in a Revolutionary Era* (Santa Barbara, Calif.: Center for the Study of Democratic Institutions [Center Occasional Paper], vol. III, no. 3, April 1970). A more radical and, I suspect, basically antidemocratic view, is presented by Herbert Marcuse in *One-Dimensional Man* (Boston: Beacon Press, 1964). A less doctrinal critic of present democratic dilemmas is Michael Harrington in, for example, his *Accidental Century* (New York: Macmillan, 1965).

When one enters the realm of contemporary problems there is a danger that any bibliographical notes will seem antique within a matter of months. For example, at the moment of this writing vast numbers of pages are being devoted to the youth problem, a matter that certainly has relevance to any discussion on democracy. But much of the writing is too timely and too crisis oriented for bibliographic listing. Undoubtedly, writers such as Kenneth Keniston have much to say about the costs of affluence and, by implication, threats to democracy in such affluence, but it is too early to settle on a permanent list of publications.

INDEX